The Last Tiger

But the tiger cannot be preserved in isolation. It is at the apex of a large and complex biotope. Its habitat, threatened by human intrusion, commercial forestry, and cattle grazing must first be made inviolate. Forestry practices, designed to squeeze the last rupee out of our jungles, must be radically reoriented at least within our National Parks and Sanctuaries, and pre-eminently in the Tiger Reserves.

Indira Gandhi, Prime Minister of India, in 1973
at the launch of Project Tiger

Perhaps it would not be an exaggeration to say that since the launching of Project Tiger, the current situation presents the biggest crisis in the management of our wildlife.

Shri Manmohan Singh, Prime Minister of India
1 March 2005
(in a letter to the Chief Minister of Rajasthan)

The Last Tiger
Struggling for Survival

Valmik Thapar

OXFORD
UNIVERSITY PRESS

OXFORD
UNIVERSITY PRESS

YMCA Library Building, Jai Singh Road, New Delhi 110 001

Oxford University Press is a department of the University of Oxford.
It furthers the University's objective of excellence in research, scholarship,
and education by publishing worldwide in

Oxford   New York
Auckland   Cape Town   Dar es Salaam   Hong Kong   Karachi
Kuala Lumpur   Madrid   Melbourne   Mexico City   Nairobi
New Delhi   Shanghai   Taipei   Toronto

With offices in
Argentina   Austria   Brazil   Chile   Czech Republic   France   Greece
Guatemala   Hungary   Italy   Japan   Poland   Portugal   Singapore
South Korea   Switzerland   Thailand   Turkey   Ukraine   Vietnam

Oxford is a registered trademark of Oxford University Press
in the UK and in certain other countries.

Published in India
by Oxford University Press, New Delhi

ISBN-13: 978-0-19-568000-3
ISBN-10: 0-19-568000-6

Typeset in AGaramond 12/15
by Eleven Arts, Keshav Puram, Delhi 110 035
Printed in India by Thomson Press, New Delhi 110 020
Published by Oxford University Press
YMCA Library Building, Jai Singh Road, New Delhi 110 001

This book
is
dedicated to the memory of
INDIRA GANDHI
and her remarkable ability
to take decisions
in the interest of the
tiger and India's forests and wildlife.

Contents

Annexures

Preface and Acknowledgements

I would never have believed that I would live through a year like 2005. It is only September and let us see what has happened in nine months. Sariska's tigers went extinct, the PM created a Tiger Task Force, the CM of Rajasthan created a State Empowered Committee—both reports are complete, Ranthambhore lost more than twenty-one tigers, Panna had huge declines, Sansar Chand got caught, a huge sting operation in China revealed the scale of the problem—the tiger slipped away so fast that it was difficult to keep pace with the crisis.

In April 2005 Dr Karan Singh said in a television programme that this is India's terminal tiger crisis and that there will be no solutions. He also said that if Indira Gandhi or he had been Prime Minister many would have lost their jobs and been made answerable or accountable for the crisis. For five months now his words keep coming back to me. And I agree with him entirely. We are in the grip of India's terminal tiger crisis. Nobody in the administration acknowledges it—most are in total denial, many are in part denial, and as their defensive reactions reach a peak, tigers die.

The first part of this book has been mainly abridged from *Battling for Survival: India's Wilderness over two Centuries*. I felt that this was necessary to set a historical perspective for the present terminal crisis. The book concludes with the report of the Prime Minister's Tiger Task Force. As a member of the Task Force, I was bitterly disappointed with the report. The tone of the report is best reflected in the section entitled 'Conserving the Tiger' where it says, 'It is the assessment of the Task Force that every tiger reserve in this country is not facing a Sariska-type crisis.' And a paragraph later, 'A Sariska-type crisis haunts every protected area in India.' So in the same breath you tell the reader that there is no serious problem but that there could be one. This reveals how the task force has been cajoled by the bureaucracy into keeping the enormity of the crisis under wraps. It is this very inability to come out in the open, to acknowledge mistakes, and to work towards solutions, that defeats effective conservation.

The same is true regarding the chapter called 'The Co-existence Agenda'. In one line it recommends that 'the areas which are essential for total protection should be made inviolate'. The next line says that 'in the remaining areas within the tiger reserve and protected areas, the strategy for management has to be inclusive and use of resources must be accepted and allowed'. The Task Force report is thus a mass of contradictions.

It is unfortunate that the Tiger Task Force Report has made recommendations for coexistence between man and tiger since such coexistence is impossible and fraught with problems. The task force should instead have focused entirely on the relocation of villagers for a five-year period in order to create inviolate tracts. After that process a new task force could have come into being focused on people's needs, and to resolve issues concerning coexistence. The Tiger Task Force should not have touched upon the issue; getting into it was a fatal error of judgement that negates the entire report since it blurs the focus on the needs of the tiger. After my dissent note (Annexure 1) the Prime Minister wrote to me since I had sent him a copy of it. In a letter dated 11 August he writes: 'Thank you for your letter...regarding your notes to the Tiger Task Force Report. I appreciate your valuable comments and contributions in the matter.' I was not sure whether by this he was supportive of my dissent or trying to be polite!

Indira Gandhi in such a situation would have convened an immediate meeting to find a solution to the problem. That is why I have dedicated this book to her memory. As far as the tiger is concerned Indira Gandhi's ability to take well-informed decisions in its interest is woefully absent today. Today's political and administrative leadership is ignorant of the needs of the tiger, as are many that are appointed to various committees to deal with tiger protection issues. Decisions are taken in the government's self-interest. That is why governance of the wild is at such a low ebb. Back-stabbing, subterfuge, manipulation, and the defence of untruths have enveloped the governance of the tiger's habitat. Even with the best intentions, our present Prime Minister will be unable to steer a path through this minefield. He does not have knowledge of the natural world like Dr Karan Singh or Indira Gandhi. He is therefore totally dependent on the bureaucracy. And the same is the story of the states that are directly responsible for securing the future of the tiger. Instead of working in the tiger's interest, they prioritize the state government's interest which invariably means the interests of forest dwellers to exploit forest land. Such a strategy suits everyone as it creates a window of opportunity for timber mafias and land mafias to move in—the poor forest dweller ends up with nothing and the tiger dies but there is a lot of romantic nonsense about how forest dwellers will coexist with tigers in the forest and save them.

If to this already grim scenario the repercussions of the new Tribal Rights Bill are added, then it becomes difficult to see any way out. This is a dangerous piece of legislation that thoughtlessly provides forest land to tribals and other forest dwellers. It will just drive the last nail into the tiger's coffin. Nothing short of a miracle is now needed to save it. And I do not believe in miracles.

This is my fourteenth book on the tiger and, I fear, probably my final one. I attract more hatred from the system by speaking the truth than a Sansar Chand or even an identified poacher. This is the level we have sunk to. That is why good people in and out of government no longer want to work in the interests of the tiger; they fear the harassment that will follow. We all must engage with and battle for the truth and hope for the miracle that will keep the tiger alive—if it happens I will write about it.

In a book like this one must acknowledge the efforts of those who have uncompromisingly championed the tiger's cause and fought for its survival into the twenty-first century. In the last thirty years the following names come to mind in India whom I have known: Fateh Singh Rathore for his battles for Ranthambhore, P.K. Chowdhary and R.S. Chundawat for Panna, Shree Bhagwan and Harsh and Poonam Dhanwatey for Tadoba, Rajendra Singh for his lost battle for Sariska, Niren Jain for his battles for Kudremukh, D.V. Girish for his work in Bhadra, Ullas Karanth and Praveen Bhargava for their battles nationally and in Nagarahole, K.M. Chinnappa for Nagarahole, P.K. Sen for his battles across India, Bittu Sahgal for his national interventions, Billy Arjan Singh for his battles for Dudhwa, A.K. Barua and Maan Barua for so much in Kaziranga and the northeast, Belinda Wright and Ashok Kumar for their effort to curb the illegal trade on tiger derivatives, B.K. Sharma for his remarkable efforts in investigation, S.C. Sharma for trying to do the right thing, Mahendra Vyas and M.K. Jiwrajka for their legal interventions, Harish Salve for his enormous contribution as Amicus Curea in the Godavarman case, Justice B.N. Kirpal for triggering rapid action in the judiciary, Jay Mazumdar for engaging the media, the Chief Minister of Rajasthan, Vasundhara Raje, for acting so promptly, Malvika Singh for her effective interventions at so many levels, Debi Goenka for being just who he is, Hemendra

Kothari for his passion and support to the tiger, Dr Karan Singh for always saying what he feels and fighting in the tiger's interest, V.P. Singh, an unusual Parliamentarian who as chair of the Rajasthan Tiger and Wildlife Committee did a remarkable job, G.V. Reddy for his total commitment, integrity and zeal, Kailash Sankhala who fought for the tiger like no one else in the 1970s, S.P. Sahi who believed in the interests of wildlife and did what he could in his lifetime, A.J.T. Johnsingh who inspired so much work in the cause of wildlife, Ajit Sonakia who worked so hard in the 1990s, Karan Thapar who never missed an opportunity to spread awareness about the issue, Pankaj Sharma, whose battles in Kaziranga and Nameri are legendary, Romila Thapar for all her historical perspectives, and P.V. Jaikrishnan for all his hard work.

Outside India, George Schaller, Amanda Bright, Ruth Padel, Geoff Ward, Mike Birkhead, John Seidensticker, Peter Jackson, Peter Lawton, Debbie Banks, John Sellers, David Shephard, and Chris Jordan have been very busy in the tiger's cause.

There are many forest guards like Badhya and Laddu who have in the last thirty years sacrificed their lives for the tiger. There are then scores of people both in the forest service and outside who have fought without recognition. In my own way I salute them.

I would also like to thank Oxford University Press, Manzar Khan and Nitasha Devasar for their unflinching support to the tiger, Belinda Wright for her amazing story on Tibet, and Shalini Shekher for editing several versions of the text.

I have mentioned the few I have known, who made a difference. Many of them go on fighting; some have given up hope; but each has been a soldier in the battle to save wild tigers.

VALMIK THAPAR
October 2005

Photographs

10. A tiger looks out into the sunset. Photo: ©Valmik Thapar.
11. Lying on its back, a tiger stretches out in a clearing in Ranthambhore. Photo: © Valmik Thapar.
12. Well camouflaged by the dense foliage, a tiger waits for its prey. Photo: © Valmik Thapar.
13. A tiger enjoying a cool bath in the river. Photo: © Valmik Thapar.
14. Tiger skin and bones that are so much in demand and have created a vast pressure on the tiger. Photo: © Valmik Thapar.
15. The skull, bones, claws, and teeth of all endangered species fetch a huge price in the illegal animal markets of the world. Photo: © Valmik Thapar.
16. A dead tiger in Ranthambhore National Park. Photo: © Valmik Thapar.
17. Tiger and leopard skins seized from a truck in Ghaziabad, U.P., revealing a sharp acceleration in the trade. Photo: © Valmik Thapar.
18. Tiger traps seized in Ranthambhore. Photo: © Valmik Thapar.
19. A tiger with its leg caught in a vicious trap. Photo: © Belinda Wright.
20. Seized illegal tiger and leopard skins. Photo: © Valmik Thapar.
21. A forest official pointing to the hole made by a poacher's bullet in a seized tiger skin. Photo: © Subhash Bhargava.
22. Forest staff after seizing a tiger skin from a poacher. The tiger was killed by electrocution as live wires are strung across the tiger's lair. Photo: © Valmik Thapar.
23. Tibetan horseman at the Litang Festival. Photo: © Belinda Wright WPSI/EIA.
24. Tiger and leopard skins on display in the open market in Litang, China. Photo: © Belinda Wright.
25. Dancers at a Tibetan festival in leopard skin *chubas*. Photo: © Belinda Wright WPSI/EIA.

The Early Days

E vidence from the rock paintings of the caves of central
India, dating back 8,000 years, suggests that the tiger
was a familiar part of the habitat as it is often shown
walking comfortably around villages. Some paintings do show
tigers being speared by man. On the seals of Mohenjodaro,
dating back 4,500 years, are strange ritualistic depictions of the
tiger. Most of the evidence points to some kind of worship of
the tiger. There was some killing also, but only for special
ceremonial purposes. Professor Romila Thapar says of the tiger
in those early days:

The earliest representations of the tiger were in rock art all over the
Indian subcontinent, although many of the highest concentrations
are in hilly areas with many rock shelters and caves. These were the
natural habitat of both the earliest human society and their predators.
The dates of the rock paintings range over some ten thousand years,
and paintings from prehistoric periods have been juxtaposed with or
overlaid by more recent ones, making any chronology imprecise.[1]

[1]Romila Thapar, 'In Times Past', V. Thapar, ed., *Tiger: The Ultimate
Guide*, Oxford University Press, 2006.

The paintings of the tiger hunt, although infrequent, are curious, as the tiger was not routinely eaten. They suggest perhaps an early use of the tiger's body parts for magical and medicinal purposes. Possibly the claws and the skin had already acquired magical status, and the meat may have been eaten as a special treat. It is well known that pastoralists, for example, do not indiscriminately eat the flesh of even their domesticated animals. The Nuer in East Africa eat cattle flesh to mark special rites and occasions and the same is suggested by the earliest textual sources in India. Moreover, eating the flesh of a valued animal was permitted only to those with special status. Among some Naga clans of north-eastern India, tigers were invoked by the shamans but were killed only on ceremonial occasions.

It can be argued that this was a way of establishing metaphorical boundaries. The tiger within the forest observed the rules of natural order among animals, and from the perspective of human society it was admired and could be an object of worship. But when it strayed into the settlement it was a threat, since the rules of the settlement were different and the tiger's transgression of these rules made it an object of hostility. One may not agree with the starkness of the dichotomy, for in a sense the forest, too, has its rules, but these are not always accessible to human understanding. Nevertheless, the metaphor occurs repeatedly in Indian civilization and it was central to legitimizing the gradual spread, over many centuries, of ordered civilization into areas that were forested and unknown.

In its association with the unknown, the tiger came to be linked with sorcery and power. The *Atharvaveda* mentions the grinding up of the teeth, eyes, mouth, and claws of the tiger, the snake, and the wolf, by the sorcerer. This presumably had something to do with protection through sorcery, and the *yatudhanas* (sorcerers) were much feared. The *Atharvaveda* contains many such references: an amulet is said to be so powerful that wearing it a person can attack a tiger; a household fire is described as a tiger that guards the house.

It was said that when the god Indra drank the hallucinogenic ritual drink, *soma*, parts of his innards became the tiger and his blood became the lion. The tiger was said to be the *kshatra,* the epitome of power, among animals of the forest. Gradually, the chief of the clan, the *raja*, aspired to the power of the tiger. At the royal consecration, his seat was covered with a tiger skin. Since the tiger was said to be born of the deities Soma and Indra, he was formidable, and his strength and power were internalized by the raja at his consecration.

The spread of human civilization entailed that new territories were settled, with agriculturists and artisans contributing to the revenue of the state. The cutting down of forests was the first step in this. Hunts were surrogate raids and also provided training for small-scale campaigns, and particularly target practice. The hunter par excellence was a heroic ideal, and in the forest the tiger was seen as the match for such a hunter.

On other occasions when a tiger threatened a settlement, the man who warded off the predator and was killed in the encounter merited a stone memorial that was ritually installed and worshipped. These 'hero-stones', as they have come to be called, were originally memorials to those who had died in battle. But the defence of the settlement was equally important, and the local hero who protected the village became a legendary figure, the subject of epic poems, immortalized by a sculpted representation of his heroic act.

Despite the tiger being a predator, there was remarkable awareness of its symbiotic relationship with the forest. They are seen as inherently bonded, with the tiger considered to be the animal that protects the forest from desecration. Although the two sets of cousins in the Mahabharata are enemies, the Kauravas are said to be like the forest and the Pandavas like the tigers—the bonding of kinship is implicit. In its natural habitat, the tiger was respected and worshipped as a powerful spirit. The hostility was only to it crossing the boundary of its own habitat and threatening the settlement.

CHANGES IN THE POLITICAL ECONOMY FROM THE LATE FIRST MILLENNIUM C.E.

After about the eighth and ninth centuries, substantial changes occurred in the societies and economies of many parts of the subcontinent. The opening up of new areas to settlement gradually became more widespread and intensified. Land was granted on a large scale, generally as gifts to Brahmans and sometimes in lieu of salaries to officers of the administration. Originally, the grant was largely of the revenue from the land and did not confer ownership rights, but in course of time ownership came to be assumed. There were many categories of land grants: some consisted of land already under cultivation or even villages, where the revenue and dues to the grantee were readily forthcoming; but grants in more remote areas required clearing the land before it could be settled and brought under cultivation. The second category covered either wasteland or, perhaps more often, forest areas. Such grants became the base for the acquisition of more territory and rights by the grantees, who after a few generations set themselves up as rulers. Dynasties claiming Brahmanical origins and associated with forest kingdoms were not unheard of in those times. Some settlements grew into towns; exchange introduced commerce, which meant more routes cutting through forest—all of which contributed to the taming of the forest. A concomitant of deforestation was that more and more tigers were killed.

Tiger hunts are mentioned more frequently in later times. Mughal paintings show royal hunts and all the nobility of the period, Mongol, Rajput, Turk, or Afghan, actively hunted the tiger. This may have been due to the exotic value of the sport, but more likely it was in the tradition of heroism, alluded to earlier, associated with heroic status to a person overcoming a tiger—*vyaghraparakramah*. In the last couple of centuries, the tiger has been viewed either as a predator to be exterminated or as a spectacular trophy of big-game hunting. But the gradual replacement of bow and arrow and spear by guns as weapons of the hunt led to the near extinction of the tiger and those who hunted animals with guns were not heroes but exterminators.

A longer-range view points to a relationship that once existed between the forest, people, and the tiger and many other denizens of the forest. Over the centuries, human activities have changed this relationship, sometimes legitimately but not always so. Perhaps we need to reflect on the nature and reasons for the changes. Should we relentlessly continue to destroy forests and those who live in them, or should we recognize that the relationship remains viable and should be sustained, perhaps to enhance the creativity of human society, as it once did? The modern Indian indifference to forests and their inhabitants is all the more tragic considering that many Indian traditions display extraordinary sensitivity towards the tiger and the forest, as expressed in the Mahabharata:

The forest which has tigers should never be cut, nor should the tigers be chased away from the forest. Not living in the forest is death to the tiger, and in the absence of the tiger the forest is annihilated. The tiger protects the forest and the forest nurtures the tiger.

In my view, by the eighteenth century the hero had turned into exterminator and with the coming of the gun we entered an era of tiger extermination that is still ongoing.

One of the earliest accounts of a grand tiger hunt with elephants was written by Sir John Day in a letter dated April 1784 and published in *Oriental Memoirs* by James Forbes:[2]

Matters had been thus judiciously arranged: tents were sent off yesterday, and an encampment formed within a mile and a half of the jungle which was to be the scene of our operations....

We had now proceeded five hundred yards beyond the jungle, where we heard a general cry on our left of 'Baug, baug, baug!' On hearing this exclamation of 'tiger!' we wheeled; and forming a line anew, entered the great jungle, when...a scene presented itself confessed by all the experienced tiger hunters present to be the finest they had ever seen. Five full grown royal tigers sprung together from running heavily they all crouched again within new covers within the same jungle, and all were marked. We following, having formed a line into a crescent, so as to embrace either extremity of the jungle: in the centre was the houdar (or state) elephants, with the marksmen, and the ladies, to comfort and encourage them.

When we had slowly and warily approached the spot where the first tiger lay, he moved not until we were just upon him; when with a roar that resembled thunder, he rushed upon us. The elephants wheeled off at once and shuffled off. They returned, however, after a flight of about fifty yards, and again approaching the spot where the tiger had lodged himself, towards the skirts of the jungle, he once more rushed forth, and springing at the side of an elephant upon which three natives were mounted, at one stroke tore a portion of the pad from under them; and one of the riders, panic struck, fell off. The tiger, however, seeing his enemies in force, returned, slow and indignant,

[2]J. Forbes, *Oriental Memoirs*, 3 volumes, London, 1834–5.

into his shelter; where, the place he lay in being marked, a heavy and well-directed fire was poured in by the principal marksman; when, pushing in, we saw him in the struggle of death, and growling and foaming he expired.

We then proceeded to seek the others...and with a little variation of circumstances, killed them all; the oldest and most ferocious of the family had, however, early in the conflict, very sensibly quitted the scene of action, and escaped to another part of the country.

The chase being over, we returned in triumph to our encampment.

Thus, from the beginning of time, hunting tigers imparted heroic status on the hunter. At the same time the tiger was recognized as the protector of the forest. Once the use of guns became widespread, trophy hunting of tigers became rampant. The tiger as game had both exotic value for English sportsmen as well as imparting heroic status on the hunter. The status of the tiger as protector of the forest began to be callously overlooked. By the nineteenth century hunting for sport had become so endemic as to warrant some laws to govern it. The protector itself required protection.

The Nineteenth and Early Twentieth Centuries

THE FIRST LEGISLATIONS

The nineteenth century must have opened on an India that was nature's virtual treasure house—rich and dense with a remarkable diversity of wildlife. Accounts of the unbelievable hunts that took place provide some glimpses of India's jungles and its fauna in those times.

One of the early records of the jungles and wildlife of India comes from a remarkable book put together by Captain T. Williamson in 1807.[1] It describes the India of those times and, for me, has always been a fascinating record of those early years when the wildlife of India was as rich and profuse as that of Africa and hunting for sport had only just begun. It is a unique record of India's untamed wilderness. The book also contained a remarkable description of how local people hunted and killed tigers with arrows:

Such is the velocity of the arrow, and so quick does this simple contrivance act, that, tigers are, for the most part, shot near the

[1]T. Williamson, *Oriental Field Sports*, London, 1807.

shoulder. Generally, tigers fall within two hundred yards of the fatal spot, they being most frequently struck through the lungs and sometimes straight through the heart. If the arrow be poisoned, as is most frequently the case, locality is no particular object; though without doubt, such wounds as would of themselves prove effectual, unaided by the venom, give the shecarrie least trouble. The poison never fails to kill within an hour.

As soon as the tiger is dead, no time is lost in stripping off the skin; for, were it suffered to remain until the heat might taint it, nothing could effect its preservation; it would rot of a certainty; and, even were it not to do so, rapidly the hair would loosen and fall off.

The gun was still to become a menace and its technology was still antiquated. This was a great time for jungle expeditions and hunting parties. An English lady describes a shooting expedition in 1837 into the Rajmahal Hills of Bengal with 260 attendants and twenty elephants. Writing to a friend she stated:[2]

They do say that there are hills in Bengal, not more than a hundred and forty miles from here; and the unsophisticated population of these hills is entirely composed of tigers, rhinoceroses, wild buffaloes and, now and then, a herd of wild hogs. There, I'm going to live for three weeks in a tent. I shall travel the first fifty miles in a palanquin and then I shall march; it takes a full week to travel a hundred miles in that manner....

We had thirty-two elephants out this morning to beat the jungles and to be sure, they were jungles that required beating. What is called high grass jungles, the grass being the consistency of timber; it seems to me, so very much higher than elephant, howdah, and human creature, nothing to be seen of them at 5 yards distance, nothing heard but the crunching of reeds by the elephants as they break their way through.

[2]Reproduced in John Murray, *Tigers, Durbars and Kings—Fanny Eden's Indian Journey, 1837–1838*, London, 1988.

What is amazing about these times is the abundance of wildlife and richness of habitat as endless rhinos and tigers got flushed out by these expeditions.

Another diary entry of 1839 states: 'William arrived yesterday; he looks uncommonly well.... He and Mr A have killed 36 tigers, the largest number ever killed in this part of the country by two guns, and his expedition seems to have answered very well.'[3]

It must have been encounters like these in the nineteenth century that turned the thoughts of those in power towards enacting legislation in order to establish their rights over and secure these rich resources for their own use. By the end of the 1860s pressure was building up for legislation to protect wildlife. Interestingly, the first piece of wildlife or forest legislation in India concerned the protection of elephants. The fauna and flora of India from the 1860s till the turn of the century were protected by the following legislations and acts:

1. The Elephant Preservation Acts of 1873 and 1879 (Madras 1 of 1873 and India VI of 1879): These acts prohibit the killing, injuring, or capturing of wild elephants except in self-defence or under a licence. Clearly, the British wanted strict controls on the wild elephant because it was an economically viable asset. With at least 2000 of them being caught each year this was a historic law and functioned to limit the capture and use of elephants. By 1879 this legislation was applicable to all of British India. Shooting was permitted only of individual elephants that were a danger to humans. This law was enacted nine years after the creation of the Imperial Forest Department in 1864, and it probably played a role in strengthening the power of this department. It also

[3]Ibid.

heralded the beginning of a series of acts and legislations that would empower the British to control Indian forests.

2. Madras Act 11 of 1879; the operation of this act is confined to the Nilgiris and provides for closed hunting seasons.
3. There were three other forest acts enacted in British India;
   (a) The Indian Forest Act, 1878.
   (b) Madras Forest Act, 1882.
   (c) Burma Forest Act, 1902.

The Indian Forest Act strengthened the powers of forest officers and the Imperial Forest Department while enabling large tracts of forests to be brought under government control. Clearly it was the wealth of the Indian forests—be it timber, minor forest produce, wildlife, or its derivatives—that the government sought to control. By the turn of the century nearly 20 per cent of British India would be government-controlled forests.

Some other wildlife- and forest-related laws enacted by the British in India were:

4. The Wild Birds and Game Protection Act, 1887.
5. The Fisheries Act of British India, 1897.

These laws came about because a need must have been felt to preserve India's forests and its fauna, and of course control their use since they constituted a significant resource.

THE EARLY TWENTIETH CENTURY

At the turn of the century, stricter rules governed hunting for sport. Some of the first changes were initiated in the Bombay presidency. Clearly, by the end of the nineteenth century and into the twentieth century the system of bounties had been much abused. The gun was much more sophisticated and it was easy to shoot and be accurate. Wolves, wild dogs, and even tigers had been indiscriminately slaughtered. Even before the turn of the century, George Yule had killed 400 tigers and M. Gerrard 227. They were soon to be overtaken by the native rulers of Udaipur and Gauripur who shot more than 500 tigers each. Another ruler, the Nawab of Tonk, crossed the 600 mark. Such hunting records were only the beginning.

As the rules became stricter, some of the slaughter was reined in but it led to much conflict and furore amongst sportsmen who felt restricted. But there were always some who supported the stricter rules. Reginald Gilbert was a sportsman who, in 1907, felt that the drastic reduction of wild animals in the Indian empire required immediate correctives. In the years that followed, it became clear that large-scale deforestation in places like Sind and the Punjab and the pressure of bounty hunting had entirely wiped out tigers from these areas. These are probably the first records of local extinction of tigers much like what has happened in Sariska in 2004–5.

The 1887 Wild Birds Protection Act was amended and repealed in 1912. The Wild Birds and Animals Protection Act (VIII of 1912) replaced it to put wildlife on the country's agenda for the first time ever. These were early efforts to counter the crisis that had been caused by the excessive hunting of animals like the tiger. Addressing these early concerns about the depletion of India's wildlife was a remarkable book by a forest officer called E.P. Stebbing.[4] Published in 1920, it contains some of the most far-reaching and lucid ideas for saving and governing wildlife. Stebbing goes into great detail about the economic value of fauna and is one of the very first strong advocates of creating sanctuaries.

[4] E.P. Stebbing, *The Diary of a Sportsman Nationalist in India*, London, 1920.

What Stebbing was really doing was attempting the prioritization of both forest and wildlife issues by highlighting their economic value in order to draw attention and political will. It is amazing that this was early in the last century. Nearly eighty years later, I do much the same even today!

E.P. Stebbing, in his writings, voiced concern about the effects of poaching on wildlife and felt that creation of inviolate tracts or sanctuaries was an urgent need even at the turn of the last century! Stebbing merits extensive quoting in this regard, especially from a chapter entitled 'The Preservation of the Indian Land Fauna as a Whole: The Permanent Sanctuary':

We have discussed the Game Sanctuary from the point of view of the preservation of animals of sporting interest, i.e., of those usually termed Game Animals. I now propose to deal briefly with Sanctuary regarded from the aspect of the preservation of the fauna of a particular area or country as a whole. A Sanctuary formed for such a purpose requires to have a permanent character. In other words, the area should be permanently closed to shooting and to all and every interruption to the ordinary habits of life of the species to be preserved.

...In some cases the only prescriptions would probably relate to shooting, poaching, egg collection, and so forth. It would be unnecessary to close the areas entirely to man. In others, however, it is certain that some of the larger and shier animals and birds, and, I believe, certain classes of insects and so forth, can only be preserved from inevitable extinction if Permanent Sanctuaries of considerable extent are maintained, solely with the object of safeguarding the species for which they are created. In sanctuaries of this class it will not be merely sufficient to forbid shooting. It will be necessary to close them to man altogether, to leave them, in other words, in their primeval condition, to forbid the building of roads or railways through their vastness, to prevent the Forest Department from converting the areas into well-ordered blocks of forest managed for commercial purposes; in fact to prevent in them all and every act of man. In every case throughout the world such Sanctuaries will require to be under supervision, but such supervision should be entirely confined to a police supervision to prevent poaching, collecting, and any entrance by man into the area....

I think the concluding extract from Dr Chalmers Mitchell's [Secretary, Zoological Society, London, 1912] paper is one of the highest importance both in its wider sense and in the more confined one as regards India.

Sanctuaries such as above sketched are the only possible method of saving from extinction the rhinoceros, bison or gaur, and buffalo, to take three of the best known of the big game animals requiring protection in India. But these Sanctuaries require to be left in their state of primeval forest. They cannot be treated as commercial forests managed from a revenue-making point of view by the Forest Department. The most scientific arrangements for opening and closing the blocks of forest as they come up in rotation for felling and other operations will not avail to make such areas true Sanctuaries....

That in other words a Permanent Sanctuary does not fall within the boundaries of any area worked by Government officials, either for profit or other reasons, on behalf of the Government. Officials would be appointed to supervise the Sanctuary, but their duties would be confined to policing the area in order that the objects for which it was created might be realized to the full.

Mahesh Rangarajan's observation regarding the devastation of the previous fifty years puts into perspective Stebbing's urgent advocacy of sanctuaries at that point in time: 'Over 80,000 tigers,

---

[5]*India's Wildlife History.* Permanent Black in association with Ranthambhore Foundation (2001), Delhi.

more than 150,000 leopards and 200,000 wolves were slaughtered in 50 years from 1875 to 1925. It is possible this was only a fraction of the numbers actually slain.'[5]

The arrangements for the December 1921 shoot held for the Prince of Wales (later King Edward VIII and subsequently, Duke of Windsor) are one of the most extravagant on record.[6]

The greatest attention to detail was displayed in the lay-out of the camp, and every provision was made for the comfort and convenience of the guests. The roomy tents, which were beautifully furnished and fronted by garden terraces, flanked an open lawn scattered with chairs and tables where people might sit in the evenings. Here also a huge bonfire flared all night, and the giant log blazed—quite the biggest I have ever seen. The whole camp, both inside and outside, was lit with electricity, from the great arc lamps, which hung picturesquely from the trees (under which all the trophies shot during the day's sport used to be shown before being handed over to the ministrations of the skinning camp), down to the little reading lamp by one's bedside, which one could switch off before turning in.

The Royal suite of apartments was simple, yet all that could be desired, and ornamented, as befitted the occasion, with emblems and trophies of the chase. The floor of the mess tent was carpeted with leopard skins, pieced together as a great mat; the effect, as can be gathered, was extremely rich and striking. The very appointments of H.R.H.'s writing table were all mementoes of sport in Nepal, being made up from rhino hoofs, horns and hide, and even the waste-paper basket was made from the lower joint of a rhino's leg. The albums on the tables of the mess tent held the photographic record of many a famous shoot in the Nepal Terai.

[6]*Menu and Food at the Hunt of Prince of Wales—H.R.H. The Prince of Wales' Sport in India*, London, 1925.

The menu for the dinner served to the prince in the impenetrable jungle of Nepal, miles from civilization was: Consommé printanière, Saumon à la grand duc, Suprème de poulet mascotte, Selle d'agneau, Perdreaux sur canapés, Haricots verts à l'Anglaise, Crème Viennoise, Petites rissoles Nantua, Dessert, Café. The total 'bags' of the prince and his staff on their Indian shoots of 1921 and 1922 included thirty tigers, six leopards, three bears, three elephants, ten rhinoceroses, twelve sambar, and seven wild boars. Of these, the Prince of Wales himself shot five tigers, two rhinoceroses, and one sambar.

For those who cared, the 1920s and the horrors of hunting over the last decades must have given little cause for hope. The 1920s was also a time of a great explosion in human population, when the sharpest rise in births took place, and mortality levels went down significantly. This naturally resulted in a sharp increase in the pressure on forests.

By 1926 there was much discussion, dialogue, and debate on 'game' preservation in India. But in 1927 few believed that the time had come to create protected areas. The few that were proponents of protected areas were also tiger lovers at heart and must have believed that without protected areas the end of the tiger was in sight.

A CRITICAL PERIOD 1927–47

The period between 1927 and 1937 saw a remarkable spurt in writing about what was considered a rapidly developing wildlife and tiger crisis. The Indian Forest Act (XIV of 1927) had just been enacted with new rules and guidelines. The human population was growing rapidly and infrastructure development was accelerating, especially the railway network with its endless demand for wooden sleepers. Forests were cut rapidly. Discussions about shooting rules, closed and open seasons, the creation of games preservation societies, and how different regions should create new laws to protect species, became widespread. I think one of the primary reasons for the crisis was the development of the motor car and the laying of roads. This caused havoc to wildlife since forests became easily accessible to many, and cars fitted with lights or specially designed hunting cars that were made for the maharajas, entered the forests in great number, especially to hunt tigers.

Wildlife had little chance. Hunting 'bags' grew manifold. Four tigers in one night was the norm. In 1929, just outside Bombay, which was the headquarters of the Bombay Natural History Society (BNHS), a tiger that had swum in from the Thane creek was shot dead. This was the last recorded tiger shot or seen in Bombay.

In nearby Ceylon also there were serious concerns about the state of wildlife. People like Dunbar Brander wrote on the problems of wildlife in the Central Provinces, once again touching on the debate surrounding the creation of sanctuaries and national parks. Brander outlined a detailed plan for a 'Valley Reserve'. Cadell wrote of the predicament of the Indian lion. S.H. Prater wrote of the problems of wildlife both in India and across the world; Milroy, a forest officer from Assam, wrote on the serious problems that afflicted wildlife in that region; and Champion wrote of the concerns of wildlife in the United Provinces. Thus a number of forest officers across India who loved its wilderness were revealing by the mid-1930s the severity of the crisis that was enveloping it.

In a way this was one of the most turbulent periods in the history of Indian wildlife as evidenced by the debates that raged around the issue of protected areas. Whereas on the one hand were a few who pushed for them, on the other was the strong hunting lobby that was loth to part with its turf. At the end of the 1920s the former were a tiny minority and they were opposed by a majority that was backed by even those at home in England who called for unrestricted access to the best piece of hunting turf in Asia. The debate about sanctuaries raged on and more and more people came into the fray to write about the regions they loved and the sorry state they were in. A.A. Dunbar Brander was a remarkable forest officer with a vision for the future who wrote about the preservation of wildlife and especially the tiger in India.[7]

Good game tracts exist both in Indian States and in British India.

There are four main types of country in which game is found and which I have designated as follows:
1. Himalayan
2. Terai
3. Central Plateau
4. Southern
    ...The finest game country in this tract is found in the Central Provinces, and I shall deal at some length with the causes which have brought about this state of affairs in that area, as I believe they have a very wide application....

The Main Reason why the Destruction of Game has Recently Increased.
1. During the war the rules were relaxed. In certain cases the shooting of does was permitted to make leather jackets for sailors. There was a general activity in the trade in the products of game: tanneries came into being, and what was previously an occasional trade has now become an active competitive one with wide ramifications: a

[7]A.A. Dunbar Brander, *Journal of the Bombay Natural History Society*, vol. 36 (1933), pp. 40–5.

slaughtered deer no longer means merely a gorge of meat for the local aborigines; it is an article of commerce and a valuable one.

2. There has been a very large increase in the number of gun licences issued as well as a large increase in unlicensed or illegal guns. It is easy to see that with a large number of guns legally possessed, the detection of illegal guns becomes more difficult. Be the causes what they may, the State forests are surrounded by guns, many of which are constantly used in destroying game both inside the forest and just outside it. In the present political situation any attempt to regulate the number of guns to actual requirements for crop protection is hopeless. The guns have come, and to stay.

3. The Motor Car—This is perhaps the biggest factor of all, in the disappearance of game, although without the two previous causes its significance would be small. Since the war whole tracts have been opened up—in fact no tract is inviolate—cars penetrating along dirt tracks into country in one day which previously took a week's marching with camels and horses. Every car that moves by day or night has one or more guns in it, and practically every animal seen which presents a fair chance of being killed, without further questions asked, is fired at. Moreover, expeditions go out at night with strong moveable searchlights and shoot down whatever is encountered, and the car enables the booty to be removed. The destruction is terrible. I came across glaring cases during my short three months' trip in 1928. The present game laws were framed before this menace arose, and they require to be reviewed and amended in consequence.

Some Remedial Measures Suggested:

1. An attempt to check the increase of guns, even reduce them.

2. Much stricter control and regulation of tanneries and business trading in wild fauna and its products.

3. Complete review of the rules so as to deal with the motor car

amongst other things, and to bring the owner and the driver of any car within the penalties of law-breaking.

4. Press for stiffer sentences in poaching cases and rewards to subordinates detecting the same. These rewards are at present optional, but should be made as a matter of course, save for definite reasons.

5. Establishing associations for the protection of Wildlife and housing enlightened Indian opinion, and enlisting influential men as members of such Societies.

Sanctuaries

As will be seen from what I have written above, the Himalayan and Terai areas are hardly suitable places, even if required, in which to create National Sanctuaries. With regard to the Central and Southern areas, the case is different. In these tracts they will form a useful and interesting purpose, especially in the former, where the fauna can be readily observed, will readily tame, and be a delight to visitors.

My knowledge of the Southern tract does not enable me to suggest any particular area, but as I know every square mile of the Central Provinces I can definitely assert that one area is suited par excellence for a National Park. This is known as the Banjar Valley Reserve....

The Game—In 1930 this tract contained as much game as any tract I ever saw in the best parts of Africa in 1908. Have seen 1,500 head consisting of 11 species in an evening's stroll. It is nothing like that now, but it is still probably true to say that it contains more numbers and more species than any other tract of its size in the whole of Asia.

Legal Position

This area is one of the oldest State reserves and belongs to Government. It contains valuable timber and is policed and administered by the Forest Department. Government would not care to give up working the valuable timber in the area, but this need not interfere with Sanctuary.

It is essential that the area remain State Forest, otherwise the Forest Act would not apply. Also it is absolutely essential for our purposes that the Act should continue to apply. Some form of 'dedication' could no doubt adjust this as there is no incompatibility.

If the Act applies, as it must, and if the Forest Department continues to manage the Forest (timber), as it will, it is clear that our staff must be also the Forest Staff. Otherwise there will be two staffs in the same area, and one will be in opposition to the other. Moreover, the Forest Department has managed the game in India, against great difficulty, with signal success in most cases, and to deprive them of those functions would create resentment, especially, unless it could be shown to be reasonable and necessary.

Banjar Valley

The shooting of game is strictly regulated, but a tremendous lot of poaching takes place. Part of it is always sanctuary, but these sanctuaries which are found in numbers in all districts are merely administrative shooting sanctuaries, resting blocks, pending opening to shooting again. They have nothing like the status of a National Sanctuary.

Some Suggestions

The local Government might agree to the area being declared a National Sanctuary but would, I consider, be more inclined to give the proposal favourable consideration if it was initiated by Indian gentlemen. It might, therefore, be the best course to first obtain the support of the non-official members of the Legislative Council and it is believed that the conservation of Indian wildlife for the benefit of the Indian People is a plea which no party can lightly thrust aside.

Conclusion

I consider that action in India is urgently required, perhaps more so than in Africa. There are I know questions of detail which apply to particular areas and particular species which I have not touched upon but in the above I have attempted to tell you something about India as a whole, and in particular what definite action might be taken in the Central Provinces.

Dunbar Brander was describing the area in and around the Kanha National Park in Madhya Pradesh. He considers this region to have been better stocked with game than the wilderness of Africa; it must have been magical. Seventy-five years ago sanctuaries were being proposed because there was no other way of keeping the tiger alive. Dunbar Bander was never to know that his dream would come true: this area is one of India's finest national parks today. His proposal for the earmarking of this area as a sanctuary is exceptional for its detail. It was such men and their work that made a critical difference to the future of wildlife in India. It was 1933 and Salim Ali's amazingly well-informed first treatise on the protection of birds in India had just been published. Prater was another such scholar, an encyclopaedia of knowledge. He was curator of the BNHS in 1933 and his book on Indian fauna is still as relevant today as it was then. He also wrote on the preservation of wildlife and the solutions necessary to remedy some of the problems. Some extracts from a speech he made in 1933 on the occasion of the golden jubilee of the BNHS are worth quoting here.[8]

Whether our reserve forests remain the principal sanctuaries for wildlife in this country or whether in some of the Provinces the purpose is

[8]S.H. Prater, 'The Wild Animals of the Indian Empire', *Journal of the Bombay Natural History Society*, vol. 36 (1933), pp. 1–11.

effected by establishing national parks, there is need for a real organization whose sole concern will be the protection of wild animals in these preserves. Our efforts to protect wildlife have failed mainly because of the haphazard methods we employ, the lack of any coordinated policy and the lack of any real protective agency to carry that policy into effect. The Forest Department, which ordinarily administers the Forest laws, has multifarious duties to perform and, while the Forest Officer has discharged this trust to the best of his ability, he cannot give the question his personal attention, nor can he find time, except in a general way, to control the protection of wildlife in our forests. Experience of other countries has shown the need of a separate and distinct organization whose sole concern is the protection of wildlife in the areas in which it operates.

Further, the existing laws, as now applicable in many of our Provinces, are obsolete. Naturally, their primary purpose is the protection of the forest rather than its wildlife. These laws require consolidation and bringing up to modern standards of conservation....

Lastly there is the all-important question of making adequate financial provision for carrying out the work of conservation.

In these days of depression, when most Governments are faced with deficit budgets, the apportioning of money for this purpose must be a matter of difficulty but, unless and until suitable financial provision is made by the State for the conservation of wildlife within its borders, the effort cannot succeed.... In the United States and in other countries the problem of financing the work of conservation has been helped by the creation of special funds.

The recent Wildlife Commission of Malaya, which made a careful study of this aspect of the problem, strongly urges the creation of such a fund to be termed the Wildlife Fund to be used solely for the purpose of conservation. The idea is that all fees which could be collected under Wildlife Enactments, including any licence or fees for riverine fishing, as well as revenues from all sporting arms licences, permits, duties on arms (sporting) and ammunition (sporting) should be credited to the Wildlife Fund. If any of these fees are collected by another department, then the cost of collection should be borne by the Wildlife Fund. It is the only means by which financial provision can be made expressly for the purpose of conservation. It is the only means by which the money devoted to this purpose will have a definite relation to the revenue derived by the State from wildlife sources and which, therefore, can be expended with every justification upon the conservation of these sources. It is the only way to ensure an equitable system of conservation; the only way in which a properly organized department can be stabilized. It is the solution advocated in other countries and one which is equally applicable to any country which undertakes conservation of wildlife on sound lines.... The necessity for conservation being clear, the importance of an adequate financial policy to support it cannot be ignored.

We have indicated what other countries are doing for the protection of wildlife but it must be apparent that the measures which they have taken, whether initiated by acts of Government or by private enterprise, must owe their success to the support of public opinion. There is need for the creation of sane public opinion on the subject of wildlife protection in India. At present, such opinion hardly exists and even if it does, in some quarters it may be antagonistic. This is mainly because people do not know, nor has any attempt been made to teach them something of the beauty, the interest and the value of the magnificent fauna of this country.

This was the early 1930s. Prater looked globally at the issues involved and then zeroed in on what India really needed. His appeal for a special organization to defend wildlife is something that even today we are fighting for. We desperately need a centralized organization whose sole job will be to protect the protected areas but the vested interests do not allow it to happen.

Even the Indian Forest Service does not want an Indian Wildlife Service. We have not even got an independent federal structure in place to govern both forests and wildlife. Prater believed it was essential way back in the 1930s. We are now in the twenty-first century, but our political leaders are still deaf to reason. They want to keep the doors to nature's treasure house open so that it can be looted and plundered. Without such reform tigers die in alarming numbers.

The 1930s were a busy time for wildlife activists. In 1935 a major all-India conference to discuss the problems that afflicted Indian wildlife brought people like Corbett, Morris, Champion, and many others together. It also saw the birth of the journal *Indian Wildlife,* the official organ of the All-India Conference for the Preservation of Wildlife. The editors included Corbett and Morris, and an Indian, Hasan Abid Jafry. Extracts from their first editorial, give us a flavour of those times.[9]

We are engaged in changing the mentality of a people, and desire to introduce a new angle of vision—a new system of thought—an altogether new attitude of mind towards the Fauna and Flora of India....

Destructive methods have always been employed in India as elsewhere, but fortunately, the numbers of destroyers and opportunities for destruction have been not too many. Demand for the table was little; firearms were few and shooting was an expensive hobby. Firearms and licences for crop protection were almost unknown, and commercial possibilities were definitely limited. But now, with the introduction of modern firearms, commercial possibilities, gang methods, and the use of motor cars and searchlights, wild birds and animals are alarmingly reduced, and many species are threatened with complete destruction.

[9]J. Corbett, Randolph C. Morris, Hasan Abid Jafry, 'Editorial', *Indian Wildlife*, 1935.

Game was plentiful and was found in all parts of India; but within the last thirty years, it has passed through the most destructive period in history. It is but a modest estimate that within these years it is reduced by 75 per cent! India is blessed with at least 2,700 species of birds alone!! She is richer than Africa in the variety of wildlife, but is certainly poorer in number, though Africa is one of the most heavily shot countries and has been attracting sportsmen and poachers of all kinds from all parts of the world for a number of years. African wildlife is being systematically protected. India is in utter confusion! Inadequacy of legislation, unwillingness on the part of subordinate government officials and public servants to enforce the existing laws and orders, and general apathy of the public, through sheer ignorance and for want of proper educative bodies, India is beset with many difficulties. The problem is acute, and unless bold measures are adopted, no effort on the part of legislators, sportsmen and friends of wildlife will be able to save it.

India is hopelessly ignorant of the significance of her wildlife, and there is not a single Province or State which is contributing anything or making efforts, to remove this ignorance, and educate public opinion to realize its responsibility towards creatures which have played no small part in making the country fertile and inhabitable, by doing positive service in the protection of crop, the growing of fruits and vegetables and the production of beautiful flowers and plants.

We started the Association for the Preservation of Game in U.P. as no one could be persuaded to take up the responsibility of forming and running it. Having done educative work for three years in India, we suggested the formation of All India Conference for the Preservation of Wildlife. Again we were compelled to shoulder the responsibility, and were able to found it with the help and support of friends. Fortunately, His Excellence Lord Willingdon, who has done more than any other Viceroy for wildlife, graciously accepted our humble suggestion through Provincial Governments and was pleased to call the All India Conference for the Protection of Wildlife, in Delhi, in

January 1935. The Conference was an unqualified success and was responsible for excellent resolutions. But the Conference is over, the resolutions are on paper, and although more than a year has passed, we are not aware that any serious effort has been made in any part of India to give practicability to any of the resolutions. The geographical distribution of wildlife is such, that an All-India platform is an absolute necessity, and it is for this reason that we are obliged to keep alive the Conference for the Preservation of Wildlife, and we sincerely hope that we will be able to persuade the Provinces and States of India to take positive steps to save the valuable and wonderful wildlife. The Conference is a representative body and has its members from all the Provinces; in fact, we are flattered with the welcome it has been given by prominent public men and responsible Forest officers.

The first wildlife conference in the history of India was just over and there was already criticism about delays in implementing some of the resolutions. The editors were appealing for immediate action. Obviously those were more optimistic times! For Corbett it was his first entry into serious conservation. Corbett may never have given up the gun but he spent more and more time with a camera. His focus was tigers and how to save them. He bought his first camera in the 1920s and filmed for more than twenty years. His major achievement was his success in getting the local provincial government to create the Hailey National Park in 1935, now called Corbett National Park. By the end of the 1930s the journal he edited folded up because of lack of support. Only three issues ever came out.

By 1939 Great Britain was in the midst of World War II. In a way this was one of the worst times till then for India's forests. It was a period of vast timber felling, and contractors engaged in it went after wildlife and tigers with a vengeance, openly flouting all rules and regulations. After all it was a time of war. The British were preoccupied with the War effort and, on the sidelines, the independence struggle. It is estimated that over 300,000 cu. m. of sal alone was cut in these War years. This was vital tiger forest. In the early 1940s there was little writing on conservation issues and it was only after the War ended in 1945 that writing on these issues started again. But as Indian Independence was round the corner and the British were getting ready to leave, the forests and tigers of India were relegated to the background. In my opinion wildlife suffered the greatest damage during this time.

Independent India: 1947–64
The Nehru Years

In the turmoil of Independence no one had time for wildlife and forests. Forests had been indiscriminately cleared during the War and more were cut just before Independence. If the motor car and its invention had started to take a toll on wildlife since the 1920s, its development, speed, and the four-wheel-drive worsened the picture just after the War. The World War, and India's Independence, changed the priorities and focus to other issues. The forests vanished at an alarming rate and soon after Independence the first alarm bells sounded. In 1948 D. Dorai Rajan wrote an article in the *Madras Mail* appealing for the preservation of wildlife. R.W. Burton, one of the Britishers who stayed on after Independence, was a great stalwart of conservation. Burton was not only writing extensively, but was actually battling a brand new government in post-Independence India and was keeping the flag of wildlife flying against all odds. The effects of the War and the state of wildlife in post-Independence India triggered off another debate. But this time the going would be tougher. The country was now under Indian rule. The British who had stayed on wanted to see wildlife safe, but there were very few Indian voices raised in their support. R.W. Burton continued dauntlessly to battle in the cause of Indian wildlife. But by then Corbett and F.W. Champion (another great forester and conservationist) had left for East Africa. Corbett died there but Champion continued to work as a forester. They both probably did not believe that the wildlife of India would survive. This is what Burton wrote in January 1948.[1]

National Parks

Those who have knowledge of the subject are of opinion that India is not yet ready for these. The Hailey National Park, the situation of which conforms in most respects to conditions laid down for a sanctuary (Smith) is specially situated and may be a success. A full account of it would be welcomed by members of the Society.

The Banjar Valley Reserved Forests area in the Central Provinces is perhaps suited for eventual status of a National sanctuary (no Park). The case for it is outlined by Dunbar Brander. Buffalo, lost to it not many years ago could be re-introduced; otherwise it contains all the wild animals of the plains except elephant, lion and gazelle. Elephants are not wanted as there are plenty in other provinces.

Even fifteen years ago the area was admittedly tremendously poached.

Sanctuaries

All sportsmen are agreed that these are of little use unless adequately guarded and, as that has not yet been found possible in India, such areas merely become happy hunting grounds for poachers from far and near. The constant presence of sportsmen of the right kind has been found the best guarantee for preservation of wildlife in reserved forests.

[1]R.W. Burton, 'National Parks' *Journal of the Bombay Natural History Society*, vol. 47 (1947–8), pp. 602–24.

There are however, tracts and forests where forethought and administration can, with the willing cooperation of the people if that can be obtained, do much to preserve wildlife for posterity.

Wildlife Department

Forest Officers of the regime now ending have been of opinion that animals inside reserved forests should not be removed from the protection of the forest department and placed in the charge of a separate department. Their argument has been that the present system has worked well; such action would create resentment and alienate the all-important sympathy of the powerful forest department; and that a game department would be in no better case than the forest department for dealing with breaches of laws and rules.

On the other hand, sportsmen and others with many years of experience are of opinion that under the present changed conditions forest officers, while not relieved of all responsibility, should be relieved of their present whole-time onus and share the burden of preservation of wildlife with a specially organized Wildlife Department....

In these days of intensive exploitation of timber and forest produce the work of forest administration has become more and more exacting and the officers find it exceedingly difficult to give time in office and out of doors to work which brings it no revenue and is considered of subsidiary importance....

It has been experienced that an unbribable staff of Game Watches has been difficult to procure. That again is strong reason why there should be whole-time Wardens whose interest would be to prevent malpractices.

A Wildlife Department means the continuity of purpose without which all endeavour is of no avail.

Money and Funds—The whole question is a matter of money. Wildlife cannot be effectually conserved without spending money on an organization for the purpose. It is necessary to recognize the fact that there is an intimate connection between the revenue derived from wildlife resources and the amount of money that can be spent on conservation.

This is the basis on which the financial policy should be built, together with the recognization that 'wildlife is a national asset and it is the responsibility and duty of the State to preserve it'. Therefore the fund will need such State grants as may be necessary to make the department effective, especially in the commencing years.

It should not be possible for funds to be cut off, reduced or abrogated by governments. The Wildlife Fund, as it might be termed, should not be within the control of any Finance Department, Central or Provincial. It should be established by law, kept apart from General revenues, earmarked for conservation of wildlife and protected from any possible raiding of it or interference by the Legislatures....

It is commonly said that it will take years and years to arouse public opinion as to wildlife. But we daily see what the present leaders of public opinion in this country can do in many ways vitally affecting the present reaching measures put into motion. There is, for instance, the vast organization for further education of the literates and the initiation of universal literacy for masses. There seems to be no reason why wildlife preservation could not also be given higher priority. Some of the reforms could wait, not that they should, far from it, but the wild creatures cannot wait—and survive.

Wildlife preservation does not only mean the protection of animals and birds, it means a fight against the destruction which is going on at an increasing pace—particularly against deer—and is not of Nature's ordering....

The years are passing; this great national asset is wasting away. It is the duty of every government to preserve it for posterity. The urge should come from the highest levels.

Propaganda Methods

The time is now.

The Ministry of Information and Broadcasting could make it a routine matter to keep this subject constantly before all classes of the people. Special talks could be given on All India Radio, and other systems.

The Educational Department could cause all governing bodies and educational institutions to issue pamphlets, organize lectures, lanternslides, and issue suitable leaflets to all colleges, schools, and primary schools. All this could be worked out on the lines of the anti-malarial campaign which was an India-wide effort. But it must be a continued effort.

For the literate classes there are the newspapers and other publications as media for propaganda; and for all classes there is the cinema screen.

Suitable slogans could be devised and shown as a routine matter at commencement and during intervals of all cinema shows, accompanied twice a week by a short talk in regional languages.

A Brief for Action

1. A decision by the Governments.
2. Issue of a general law to prohibit sale, possession, marketing of meat, hides, horns, etc., of indigenous animals and birds.
3. Enforcement of Arms License rules and conditions.
4. Enforcement of laws and rules under Act VIII of 1912 and Act XIV of 1927.
5. Formation of Wildlife Department.
6. Propaganda.
7. Generally all possible steps towards saving wildlife.

Through the continued efforts of their leaders the peoples of India were roused to political consciousness. Through their long-sustained efforts they attained political freedom. Will the leaders and people not now demonstrate to other civilized nations that they are equally capable of preserving wildlife for posterity? Surely they will. Because they should, and because it is demanded for the prestige of India.

It was the intention of the Society and the writer to submit this pamphlet to Mahatma Gandhi with appeal for his powerful advocacy. Alas! It was not so ordained.

Yet, in view of the late Mahatma's well-known sympathy with all things created, it may surely be hoped that the peoples of India and of Pakistan will respond to this appeal in accordance with what would without doubt have been his wishes and his guidance for the preservation of wildlife in this country.

R.W. Burton had, just after India's Independence, summarized more than fifty years of conservation efforts, and spelt out his recommendations as well. He had observed the devastation and his views were rooted in that knowledge. Unfortunately Mahatma Gandhi's assassination put paid to Burton's plans of enlisting the Mahatma's support in the cause of wildlife. Post-Independence India was a time of great destruction for its wildlife. Now, every forest officer's training commenced with 'shooting a tiger'. Travel agencies mushroomed, seducing the hunters of the world. Forests were rapidly cleared in the name of 'development'. The Maharajas created new hunting records with a vengeance. It was a free-for-all and few laws were followed or enforced.

Burton continued to push for an agency to do the job of wildlife protection. It was now 1949 and India's wildlife was being depleted alarmingly. He therefore battled on, continuously putting pen to paper. His prolific writing was having an impact in the corridors of power in New Delhi. Burton had put two long notes through the system. His solutions to India's wildlife problems were very clearly stated in them and he warned that unless quickly adopted, India would be poorer by a great deal: 'Without a wildlife department as suggested herein the survival of much of the wonderful wildlife of India is inconceivable and a great national asset will disappear never to be regained, as the majority of the unique species will become extinct.'[2]

Sadly, fifty-four years later we are still fighting the same battles as Burton fought (even the Tiger Task Force report of 2005 suggests the creation of a wildlife sub-cadre within the Indian Forest Service); sadder still, the response from senior forest officials of the country is the same stone walling.

Finally, a year after Burton's first note in 1948, the highest forest officer in the country, Inspector General of Forests, M.D. Chaturvedi, was forced by Burton's writing to come up with the first so-called 'plan' to save the wildlife of India.[3]

1. While agreeing with much that Lt. Col. Burton has said in his valuable pamphlet on 'Preservation of Wildlife' and in the supplement issued later, I cannot reconcile myself with the view expressed by him that the interests of wildlife come in such sharp conflict with forestry, that forest officers cannot be entrusted with the task of looking after animals, a task which they have performed so well for the best part of a century. Theirs has been a labour of love. I do not deny our shortcomings, but I do feel that the contribution of several generations of forest officers towards the preservation of wildlife deserves better appreciation.

2. I must confess, I see the advantages of organizing a separate Wildlife Department, the best justification for it being its ability to cover vast areas outside the reserved forests. In the early stages, however, the balance of advantage would lie in enlisting both the services and the cooperation of forest officers in the stupendous task of preserving wildlife. True, forest officers are not conversant with

[2] *Journal of BNHS,* vol. 48, no. 3 (1949).
[3] M.D. Chaturvedi, 'Preservation of Wildlife', *Journal of the Bombay Natural History Society,* vol. 48, no. 3 (1949).

the modern technique adopted in the preservation, control and protection of wildlife. But, what I submit for the consideration of enthusiasts like Lt. Col. Burton is that after all is said and done, an average forest officer knows far more about wildlife than an average civilian or an agriculturist or even a sportsman. One wonders where the game wardens and upper grade assistants will come to be recruited from in Burton's scheme. In no other walk of life is even a nodding acquaintance with the animal kingdom available except in the forestry profession.

3. There is at present neither need nor room for organizing a separate Wildlife Department. Might I urge that the solution of the problem lies in the adoption of a middle course? The cadre of the forest department should be supplemented to enable it to organize wildlife preservation on modern lines. What is needed is not the creation of a separate department consisting of a large number of whole-time officers, a host of clerks, menials, orderlies and other paraphernalia, but the appointment of regional wildlife officers working in close collaboration with the existing forest departments and their vast organization for surveying, mapping, policing and maintenance of roads and rest houses.

4. The sort of organization which I envisage for the United Provinces is as under:

    (i) Provincial board for the preservation of wildlife.

    The Board will consist of the following members:

    1. Honourable Minister in charge of the forests or his Parliamentary Secretary (Chairman)
    2. A member from each of the two houses of legislature.
    3. Enthusiasts from sporting circles.
    4. Chief Conservator of Forests.
    5. Director of Agriculture.
    6. Director of Veterinary Services.
    7. A senior Commissioner.
    8. Provincial Wildlife Officer (Secretary).

The functions of this board should be advisory. It will be a sort of standing committee to advise government in respect of legislation to be enacted for the preservation of wildlife. The board will direct its secretary to advise ways and means to enforce existing game laws to afford facilities for tourists and to secure protection from and for wildlife. The board will meet twice a year. Today this board is called The National Board of Wildlife and sometimes it has not met for years—written policy of this country is hardly ever followed.

Burton's rejoinder to the above was again clear and strong.[4]

In paragraph 4 of his note the Chief Conservator sees the advantages of organizing Wildlife Department. In the next paragraph he says there is neither need nor room for organizing a separate Wildlife Department, and advocates a middle course which he outlines in some detail.

In other countries it has been found that half measures are futile and a waste of time; and that there is in fact no satisfactory middle course.

The Chief Conservator wonders where the wardens and upper grade assistants will come from. Surely it can be envisaged that the bulk of them will be obtained from among those of the Forest Service who have at heart, as has the CCF, the interests of the wild animals, and birds they have seen daily in the forests through the years of their service. Recruitment of staff would be through careful selection of applicants in all grades.

All things have a beginning. Perhaps the scheme drawn up for the United Provinces by the Chief Conservator will herald the commencement of the much needed all-India policy envisaged in Section D of the proceedings of the Conference held at Delhi on the 8th–9th September 1948 to secure the implementation of a coordinated forest policy dealing with Inter-Provincial and national matters.

There is no matter more wholly national than the effective protection

[4]R.W. Burton, 'Comment', *Journal of the Bombay National History Society*, vol. 48, no. 3 (1949).

and preservation of that Wildlife which is the Vanishing Asset of the peoples of this country.

I would agree entirely with Burton. Half measures never work and are a total waste of time. The need of the hour then, as now, was the creation of a full-fledged wildlife department.

The post-War world situation and post-Independence Indian conditions combined to produce a great spurt in writings and interventions in the 1950s, with an impassioned set of people fighting a hard battle. In India at this moment the cheetah was about to vanish. But this state of affairs was not confined to India alone. It was the same all over the world. From the crisis emerged a new organization: the International Union for the Protection of Nature (IUPN), what is now the IUCN (International Union for Conservation of Nature). Lots of new legislations came into force for different areas. In India, in 1952 a Central Board for Wildlife, which is now called the Indian National Board for Wildlife, was created. It was at its first meeting that the creation of a second home for the Gir lions was suggested. Fifty years on we are still discussing the same proposal. The establishment of associations for the protection of wildlife was earnestly advocated by many and even today is an important issue in the NGO movement in India. The movement for creation of national parks and sanctuaries received a great push forward, probably because the rate of loss of forests was so high that it was seen as the only option. There was great concern about the acceleration in the use of both motor cars and searchlights to shoot and hunt, and many who cared advocated a ban on the use of both in forests. The 1950s also ushered in a series of 'State of India's Wildlife' reports, as efforts were made to reveal the tragic state of affairs so as to force the government into taking action. This was true all over the world and even before the beginning of the

1950s the first international efforts to save wilderness across the globe had started. The majority of people fighting for India's wildlife were still British. It would change—but slowly. The first Indian wildlife activists were coming to the fore. But till the 1950s the entire movement for saving wildlife in India was spearheaded by the British and we must acknowledge this fact.

As India entered the 1950s, several changes in law were advocated by wildlife lovers to save India's rapidly vanishing wildlife heritage. Within the pages of the BNHS journal were endless policy suggestions and recommendations. The laws that governed wildlife became the focus as they were recognized as the only real deterrent to the future depletion of wildlife. Again, it was the BNHS which played a unique role in steering through, what was then, a ground-breaking legislation, the Bombay Wild Animals and Wild Birds Protection Act, 1951, which formed the basis of the Wildlife Protection Act, 1972. An Indian, Humayun Abdulali, played a vital role in formulating its first drafts. All the spadework for this Act was done in the early 1950s. This is the kind of work that created the awareness that slowed the rapid pace of extinction of India's wildlife. People like Burton, Phythian-Adams, Morris, Stracey, and of course Abdulali can never be forgotten. Forest officer, J.A. Singh, also played a critical role.

It is very clear from past records that post-Independence India had a very active group of people fighting to preserve its wildlife. In the 1950s, E.P. Gee became one of the most active wildlife conservationists. In many ways, in this sphere, the decade of the 1950s belongs to him and his writings.

The period from 1953 to 1955 in India ushered in big dams and hydroelectric projects. Prime Minister Jawaharlal Nehru believed that these projects were the temples of modern India and would lead to rapid development. These so-called modern temples ripped apart large tracts of splendid forest. In a nation-building environment, Nehru didn't prioritize wildlife or forests at all. So activists like Gee kept on writing to take a stand on a series of environmental issues between 1954 and 1960.

Gee was a prominent figure in these years with his ideas and suggestions. On the Indian Board of Wildlife he took a hard stand; he wrote frequently on a variety of ills that plagued Indian wildlife; and most of all he tried to create political will, particularly with people like Nehru. Thus he once again stressed the economic logic of wildlife tourism. Gee joined issue with the then Inspector General of Forests for his dictat that only if a forest officer had shot a tiger could he be put in charge of a forest division. He came up with the alternative that every forest officer should be able to catch a fish with a rod and line! He wrote: 'Fifty years ago it might have been all right. But if every divisional forest officer in India today were to bag a tiger there would be no tigers left.'[5] Gee, an Englishman, educated at Cambridge and electing to stay on in India after Independence, in my opinion, played a much more stalwart role in conservation than either Salim Ali or M. Krishnan in the 1950s. Let's not forget that Gee started his work as early as 1933 on the hornbills of Assam, much before most of his colleagues.

The 1950s had been a decade of devastation for wildlife and much of the responsibility for that goes to the princes of India. Mahesh Rangarajan describes it succinctly:[6]

Princely India left behind a mixed legacy. There is no doubt that many of today's famous nature reserves from Gir in the west to Bandipur in the south had their origins as royal hunting reserves. But to see the

---

[5]*Journal of BNHS*, vol. 51 (1952), pp 1–17.
[6]*India's Wildlife History*. Permanent Black in association with Ranthambhore Foundation (2001), Delhi.

princes' efforts as conservationists in present-day terms would go against their own records of their deeds. Many exceeded the British in their lust for trophies. They used the rules of the hunt to oppress their subjects at times endangering the latter's lives and much more often offending their sense of human dignity.

The hunting records of the Indian princes far outstripped those of the British. By the 1960s, thus, the situation had become grim enough to spark off widespread demand for curbs on hunting. The hows and how much began to be debated. Shikar travel agencies had flourished and strong will and measures were needed to curb the excesses of this so-called sport. I had the horrific experience of seeing some archival footage of the 1960s from the area around Kota quite close to Ranthambhore. A series of tiger shoots had been organized by the Maharaja's party in broad daylight using buffalo bait. Tigers were picked off like flies. Early 1960 saw the local extinction of the tiger in many of its natural habitats just like in Sariska in 2004–5. In my opinion the so-called sportsmen of those times were much worse than today's poachers.

In the 1960s all the post-Independence ills plaguing wildlife reached crisis point. P.D. Stracey in his book, *Wildlife in India* looks at the crisis of these years:[7]

As one who has been both a shikari and a conservationist throughout a career as a forest officer in Assam and who has witnessed, heard and read of the destruction of wildlife at an increasingly rapid pace during the past few years while being associated with measures for its conservation, I have become gradually filled with the realization that the situation is rapidly deteriorating to the point of no recovery. As a practical administrator I have often been impatient with mere words

[7]P.D. Stracey, *Wildlife in India: Its Conservation and Control*, IFS, 1963.

and latterly I have increasingly felt that while considerable planning for the preservation of wildlife is in the air not much of it is reaching the ground fast enough to be of use....

What India's wildlife now needs is an attempt at a reasoned argument for its correct management and a large plea for its preservation....

The decline started and with greater rapidity from about the middle of the 19th century with the increase in the number of sporting weapons and the development, in succession, of the large-bore rifle in 1840 and the express rifle in 1860. The early British army officers, tea planters and the civil servants were, in many cases, heavy despoilers of game....

...[The] period of 'grow-more-food', coming as it did close on the heels of the war years when heavy depletion of wildlife stocks took place in many parts of India wherever armies were encamped for training or for fighting, has been indeed disastrous for our animals and birds and it is safe to say that more damage has resulted in the last fifteen years than in the previous one hundred and fifty.

To the cumulative effect of the war and the expansion of agriculture that followed it must be added that large numbers of gun licences have been issued since the securing of Independence. Under the British administration such gun issues were restricted, for obvious reasons, but with the passing of the power into the hands of the people it was but natural to expect a much greater degree of leniency in the consideration of applications for weapon licences, whether for display, sport or crop protection. The inevitable result has been the development of a new type of sportsman with a new set of sporting values, whose influence on the status of wildlife has been profound. And when in addition we consider the deadly potentialities of the mighty little jeep in the countryside, one may well doubt the chances of large-scale survival of wildlife....

Fortunately for wildlife, Indian agriculture has not yet reached the stage where thousands of acres are cultivated by machinery and where there are no trees, shrubs or weedy patches to break the monotony. 'Clean farming' is a much more important and insidious enemy of wildlife than are the natural predators....

The need for increasing food production for human consumption in India is well recognized but crop specialists agree that much bigger results can be obtained by selecting better seed and through the use of fertilizers and modern cultivation methods rather than by clearance and ploughing up of every 'marginal' jungle patch, no matter how poor the soil and deficient the water. To the extent to which this is recognized, many species of wildlife will prosper accordingly.

As regards available legislation...generally speaking the Wild Birds and Animals Protection Act or the game laws or shooting rules under the Indian Forest Act, combined with the Arms Act rules, are adequate for protection of wildlife both outside and inside reserved and protected forests, provided there is a determined and efficient machinery to enforce it. While the forest department is specifically in charge within the managed forests, 'what is everybody's business is nobody's business' may well be said of the wildlife protective machinery in areas outside such forests in India. The civil and police departments, whose function it is to administer the Arms Act rules and the Wild Birds and Animals Protection Act where it exists, are generally woefully ignorant of the rules and regulations and far too preoccupied with other duties to pay much attention to game protection. Looking back one can cite many incidents to illustrate this.

In India unless more realistic and positive steps are taken and as speedily as possible, there will be no wildlife left to protect in areas outside the managed forests in a few years and the only stocks of wildlife will be found in the reserved and protected forests, in which are included the sanctuaries and national parks. Even here the comparatively stringent provisions of the Indian Forest Act require necessary modification to suit altered conditions and the normal, long-established system of protection embodied in the forest departments requires reinforcement by special staff. Elsewhere, wildlife can continue to exist only if public opinion is favourable and it is dependent to very large extent on public cooperation. To secure this a cadre of honorary wildlife wardens from among the public should be built up and a vigorous campaign of publicity and education, particularly among the youth of the country, launched.

Lastly, while these measures may be expected to improve conditions in the managed forests and the areas adjoining them, certain long-term measures of insurance are to be implemented, such as the declaration of certain species as protected in areas where they are threatened, their reintroduction into areas from which they have disappeared and the creation of sanctuaries and national parks wherever conditions permit. The main responsibility for all these measures to 'rescue' wildlife will, of course, rest with the forest departments of the States but in this task the assistance, cooperation, and sympathy of the civil administration is essential.

In India, the real threat to wildlife and to game animals in particular, has been the great increase in the number of firearms as the result of a much more liberal policy in the issue of licences to possess weapons, partly as the result of political emancipation and partly for protection of crops in the context of grow-more-food schemes. But fundamentally it is a question of a too rapid increase in population. This has particularly affected the areas outside the Government forests but its general effect has been severe. At the present rate of increase in population there will soon be no room for animals....

The first and most urgent measure is to control the use of crop-protection guns so that they are only used for the purpose for which they are granted and in the correct season. Their withdrawal in the areas where danger to crops is insignificant or where the danger is seasonal should be enforced.

Owners of crop-protection guns and all patta-holders living on the edges of forests should be categorically warned that harbouring of outside meat hunters on their land will result in cancellation of their licences and this should be acted upon.

An efficient organization with a system of rewards for informers should be established between the civil and forest departments, which must both play their part to maintain check over poaching.

Issue of gunpowder and ammunition to licences should be curtailed and the sale of 'buck-shot' banned or severely controlled by district authorities.

A system of rewards and accelerated promotions to lower categories of civil and police officers who detect and report offences against the Arms Act or game laws should be applied.

The trade in netted birds should be abolished or strictly licensed and the serving of game birds in restaurants or their stocking in cold-storage establishments in the close seasons prohibited.

What is really needed is greater vigilance in enforcing the rules of the weapon licences by civil and police authorities. If in addition the forest department introduces more effective protection of the government forests with increased and special staff, the damage now being done by illicit shooting, abuse of the close seasons and killing of protected species and prohibited sexes, can greatly be reduced. All these measures should be accompanied by a vigorous campaign of propaganda and publicity in favour of preservation of game species and conservation of wildlife in general, particularly among the youth of the country.

The sale of the meat of wild animals should be banned, for it must be recognized that such is no longer essential for human existence, as may have been the case when man was more primitive. But even if this is not practicable, stricter control of this trade is essential....

Another direction from which wildlife is seriously threatened is that which is tied up with the habits of certain primitive groups of peoples, such as the Hos and Santhals of Bihar, the Baigas and Gonds of Madhya Pradesh, the Bhils of Bombay, the Kurubas of Mysore, the Chenchus of Andhra, the Pardis and Poligars of Madras, and the Hacharis and other tribes of Assam. These aboriginal tribes, whose passion is hunting, have practically laid waste their jungles in the matter of wildlife and as their diet is practically omnivorous.... The large number of man-eaters reported recently from parts of Orissa can quite easily be accounted for by the destruction of their natural prey, deer and pig, by these people. Tribal people employ dogs and fire to drive game and all manner of traps and devices to capture animals and birds and are expert marksmen with the bow and arrow.... The Kacharis of Assam stretch a long, wide-meshed net across the countryside and then drive game into it; everything living that runs into the net is killed with spears and staves. Other tribes like the Mikirs of Assam poison water with the bark of certain climbers and kill all the fish in the locality. In the North Cacher Hills of Assam there is a practice of destroying birds which are attracted to fires lit at night at certain times of the year for the purpose. The Nagas of Assam have virtually exterminated wildlife, even birds, in their hills particularly since the war when large quantities of weapons came into their possession.

There is no longer any room for these primitive and destructive tribal practices and their eradication is an essential step in the restoration of wildlife in certain parts of the country, though it is realized that this may, as in certain cases like the traditional 'hakwa shikar' of the Hos of Bihar or 'Parad' of the Bastar tribes, impinge on tribal ways of life and result in some curtailment of supplies of meat. Rehabilitation of the several tribes scattered over India who are professional bird and animal trappers and killers and of those tribes who at present live on hunting and forest produce is urgently called for.

Turning to the details of the legislation, we find that wildlife in India had received a fair amount of protection under British administrators.

The Indian Forest Act (1879, 1927, 1950) and its adaptations in States is administered by the forest departments and gives basic protection to wildlife in reserved and protected forests as follows:

Prohibition of shooting, fishing and poisoning water, setting of traps and snares: Section 26(1) Reserved Forests, Section 32(J) Protected Forests.

Prohibition of killing or capturing of elephants or capturing of elephants in areas where the Elephant Preservation Act of 1879 is not in force: Section 33(J) Protected Forests, Section 26(J) Reserved Forests.

The penalties under these sections are imprisonment for a term up to six months or fine up to Rs 500, or both, vide Section 26 for Reserved Forests and Section 32 for Protected Forests. The State Government may make rules 'generally to carry out the provision of the Act' under Section 76....

In addition to the Indian Forest Act there was the 1887 Act for the Preservation of Wild Birds and Game, or the 'Wild Birds and Animals Protection Act' as it became in 1912. This Act is applicable to all types of areas and in areas outside the reserves is administered by the civil and police departments of the States to which it has been extended, though in reality it is a dead letter.... Besides these acts, certain special pieces of legislation have been in existence for some time, such as the Elephant Preservation Act of 1879, the Indian Fisheries Act of 1897, the Assam Rhinoceros Preservation Act and the Bengal Rhinoceros Protection Act.

As the result of the impetus given to wildlife conservation in recent years after the formation of the Indian Board of Wildlife, some State Governments have been overhauling their wildlife legislation. The Bombay Wild Birds and Animals Protection Act of 1951 is an advanced piece of legislation, which has been recommended as a model for other States, and some mention of it is necessary here.

There is great need for the rewriting of the rules concerning wildlife and their compilation in handy book form to show the close seasons, protected species, and prohibited sexes for ready reference. If drawings or photographs illustrating the various species and their local names are added it will greatly assist in their identification. Among the public generally there is great ignorance of the rules while among officials and even staff of the forest departments, there is both ignorance and indifference, which is not aided by inscrutability of the rules in question. Some States publish their rules in handy book form, but they are practically repetitions of the legal provisions and schedules under the act and require considerable study to be clearly understood by the average person. What is wanted is a brief but adequate presentation of all the restrictions on the destruction of wild life in a form that can be readily comprehended.

What is important is the absence of a special organization to protect wildlife in areas outside reserved and protected forests and in this respect the African models are worthy of imitation. When the onerous duties of the existing forest departments and the impossibility of their being able to deal adequately with wildlife protection is appreciated, the seriousness of the position will be realized. Unless the enforcement of existing protective laws is improved the situation will continue to deteriorate until in a short time there will be no wildlife left outside the Government forests, while inside them it will be greatly reduced.

The need for publicity and education in the service of wildlife is urgent. One of the greatest obstacles in India which the wildlife enthusiast has to face is the comparatively uneducated state of the very class of society which he has to convince of the utility of wildlife and the need to preserve it, the man in the street and particularly the rural dweller. And yet it is certain that wildlife can survive only if the people wish it to do so. Top-level planning for conservation of wildlife can be thorough and far reaching but if it is not accompanied by adequate publicity, propaganda and education, the effect will be lost.

Side by side with a strong policy of enforcement of wildlife legislation there should be an intensive campaign of propaganda and publicity, designed to remove false ideas with regard to wild animals and birds and their exaggerated harmful effects on man, his crops and his kin and at same time to convince people in regard to the need for conservation of wildlife for inherent values. This propaganda must be honest and there must be no attempt to conceal or distort facts, while at the same time it must be scientifically based to convince people. It must be particularly aimed at India's youth and the village and rural dweller, who lives more close to wildlife than the educated sportsman. The latter should undertake the task by banding themselves into associations for the preservation of wildlife and for propaganda and education on the need for it. Such propaganda and education can succeed most if directed at the youth of the country, for the 'youth of today are the conservationists of tomorrows'.

E.P. Gee was very pessimistic about the state of wildlife in India at the end of the 1950s. He feared that by 2000 the only wildlife left would be creatures able to adapt to thickly populated areas, as this extract from his book shows.[8]

As I see it, there can be no doubt that, at the present rate of cutting vegetation, overgrazing by domestic stock and killing of wild animals in India, by the time public opinion can rally in support of wise conservation of wildlife there will be practically nothing left to conserve. There will be very little wildlife left by the year AD 2000, only thirty-six years from now, except in zoological gardens.

The first to go will, generally speaking, be the large mammals and birds, especially those which are edible. Smaller mammals and birds, particularly the latter which can escape by flying, will be the last to disappear.

Imagine the year 2000, with the only wildlife consisting of those creatures which can adapt themselves easily to thickly populated areas, such as jackals, rats, mice, vultures, pariah and Brahminy kites, crows and sparrows!

How the inhabitant of the future would miss the lovely sight of a

[8]E.P. Gee, *The Wildlife of India*, London, 1964.

snowy white cattle egret gracefully alighting on the back of a rhino placidly grazing among the flowering reeds and grasses of Kaziranga! What would the Gir Forest be like if, bereft of its stunted trees, there were no noble lions and lionesses with their cubs to enrich our lives? Can one imagine Bandipur without its magnificent 'bison', or Periyar without its lordly elephants, or Kanha without its elegant swamp deer? Or Bharatpur without its wonderful congregation of breeding water birds?

If the spectacular tiger, the proud peacock and all the other splendid denizens of the forests and grasslands were to cease to exist, then how dull life would be!

If nature conservation could be considered important in India as long ago as 300 BC and 242 BC, it should surely be accepted as a first-priority necessity at the present time. The existence of a sound nature and wildlife conservation organization in a country is a reliable indication of a stage of a country's progress, and development. There is very good chance that the leaders, planners and people of India will see the 'writing on the wall', and that they will not fail today in their duty of preserving the country's heritage of forests and fauna for those of tomorrow.

Though we managed to enter the twenty-first century with much of our wildlife intact, Gee was not so far off the mark. Sariska's tigers went in 2005. And I believe many more areas are on the brink.

From 1947 to 1964—the Nehru years—wildlife was an entirely non-priority area and Nehru's understanding of the issues was limited. Wildlife was 'beautiful' in a distant exotic way that had little to do with the hard realities of a newly independent, poor, developing country. There was much rhetoric by Nehru but little action resulted in the field over the seventeen years that he ruled in terms of conservation of forests and wildlife. In these seventeen years the loss of forest and wildlife was enormous.

In fact it was much worse than at any time in the British period. In this period, India probably lost forever more of her natural treasures than at any other time in the last century.

It was soon after this, at the end of the Nehru years, that the American zoologist George Schaller completed his first-ever study on the Indian tiger in Kanha National Park in Madhya Pradesh. This was the same area that Dunbar Brander had advocated be earmarked for a reserve in the 1920s. Schaller's comments are pertinent:[9]

Independence ushered in a period of destruction that could almost be compared to the slaughter on the American prairies in the 1880s. Rejecting shooting regulations as a form of colonial repression and released from restraint, Indians shot down wildlife everywhere, including sanctuaries and private estates. As a result of food shortages the government initiated a national drive to protect crops from depredation of wild animals, and guns were issued freely to farmers, an action which literally doomed almost all animals near cultivation. For instance, G. Singh, Conservator of Forest in Punjab, wrote to me in 1964: 'Blackbuck was found in large number in central and southern parts of Punjab state until 15 years ago. Then it was treated as a crop pest and killed in large numbers. This resulted in virtual extermination of the species.' A new type of hunter emerged, too, a motorized one who drove jeeps along forest roads at night and shot at any eyes that reflected the beam of his light. For about five years the destruction continued unabated. In 1951 Bombay state passed the Wild Animals and Wild Birds Protection Act; in 1952 the Indian Board for Wildlife was formed and in 1958 the Wildlife Preservation Society of India. Conditions improved slowly with each state government making serious attempts to preserve its fauna and to strengthen the existing shooting regulations. A number of fine but small reserves were

[9] G.B. Schaller, *The Deer and the Tiger*, Chicago, 1967.

established. But enforcement against poaching on the local level remained inadequate, with the result that the wildlife continued in its decline.

Coupled with the outright destruction of wildlife by shooting was the indirect method of eliminating the habitat. As late as the sixteenth century, rhinoceros, elephant, buffalo, and other animals characteristic of fairly moist conditions occurred in parts of western India that are now covered with dry thorn scrub (Rao, 1957), indicating a rapid destruction of the habitat undoubtedly caused by misuse of the land by man (Puri, 1960). Chinese pilgrims in AD 600 talked of the dark jungles in the Gangetic basin, and even of virgin forest (Robertson, 1936). Today, the heavily populated Gangetic basin retains sizable patches of forest only at the base of the Himalayas, areas that were uninhabitable earlier because of malaria. Tremendous tracts of grass and reeds in the valley of the Brahmaputra River were put under the plough, and Kaziranga Sanctuary remains as one of the few remnants of a habitat that once covered thousands of square miles. Forests were cleared throughout India for cultivation, and the timber was cut for use in railroad construction. After Independence the drive for more food and the unchecked increase in the population resulted in the cultivation of most marginal land. The natural vegetation cover of India is forest, but less than a quarter of the country is still covered with it.

A great scourge of India's land is the vast numbers of domestic animals which are undernourished, diseased, and unproductive.... India had an estimated 204 million cattle and buffaloes and 94 million goats and sheep in 1956, of which 21 million of the former and 13 million of the latter grazed exclusively without restrictions in virtually all forests and most sanctuaries, and serious damage to the vegetation culminating in widespread erosion is common particularly in the thorn and deciduous forests....

Livestock diseases, especially rinderpest and foot-and-mouth disease, also affect the wild ruminants. There are numerous records of gaur, chital, and others contracting diseases from cattle and dying in large numbers, whole populations having been wiped out in this manner (Brander, 1923, Ali, 1953)....

In one hundred years the combination of land clearing, uncontrolled slaughter, habitat destruction by livestock, and disease have reduced one of the world's great wildlife populations to a small remnant. Yet in spite of a realization that wildlife represents the country's fastest vanishing asset, no detailed studies of any kind have been attempted on the large mammals.

India's wildlife has reached a critical stage in its survival, and the country is fortunate in possessing a sanctuary like Kanha Park, where a remnant of the peninsular fauna still exists in fair number. The park is large enough and ecologically varied enough to support a considerable wildlife population on a permanent basis, especially since the forests surrounding it provide a buffer zone between the park and the heavily cultivated parts of the district. As a potential tourist attraction the tiger has few equals among animals. And the park as a whole can provide future generations with a view of how their country once looked before the forests were overexploited for timber and overgrazed by livestock and before much of the wildlife fell to the poacher's gun. The park can also become a study area unaffected by man's influence where the interrelationships between species and many other ecological problems can be investigated. A national park represents a specialized form of land use in which, ideally, the native flora and fauna are permitted to exist undisturbed by man. This in particular should apply to the predators, which have aroused the antipathy of man for centuries and have as a result been needlessly persecuted on the slightest pretext. Certain management practices in a park are sometimes necessary, and these should of course be based on a thorough study of the situation and be directed at the principal and not the superficial cause of a problem. The evidence presented in this report, for example, indicates that poaching and not tiger predation has been the general cause of the decline of the wildlife in the park. The most effective means of managing the tiger is obviously to manage the prey, which in turn means: (1) curtailing the activity of poachers, and (2) limiting and gradually eliminating all livestock from within the boundaries of the park. Only after these two tasks have been accomplished, and all forms of wildlife have been substantially increased, will the park be able to fulfil its unique potential as a living museum and natural laboratory. Above all, Kanha Park is part of India's cultural heritage, a heritage in many ways more important than the Taj Mahal and the temples of Khajuraho, because, unlike these structures formed by the hands of man, once destroyed it can never be replaced.

Schaller was making the comparison with the Taj Mahal that Jepson had made in the 1930s. Schaller's work on the wild tigers of Kanha was remarkable. E.P. Gee said in his review of Schaller's book: 'For the first time on this sub-continent a dedicated scientist has remained almost continually for 14 months in what is possibly the finest remaining habitat for wildlife found in Asia.'[10] Gee had even visited Schaller in the field, marvelling his ability to sit long hours waiting for tigers.

But there were many Indian Forest Officers who objected to the American connection and gave Schaller a rough time, especially since Gee's review had also recommended that the book, 'should be read and studied by every forest officer both before and after taking charge of a division.' This obviously led to jealousy among forest officers.

Schaller's work came at a time when the tiger was still regarded as a supreme game trophy. A letter dated 6 April 1965 from the Maharaja of Sarguja to Schaller stated:

My total bag of tigers is 1150 (one thousand one hundred and fifty only). I have shot a white tiger also. My shoots have been nearly all

[10] *Journal of BNHS,* vol. 36, no. 3 (1966).

over India including Nepal for tigers. I shot my first tiger when I was
13 years old. I have shot in Kenya, Uganda and Tanganyika and got
there 30 lions. I have never tried to put up my record in papers etc.
but as you have asked I have given you numbers.

Around this time Juan Spillet, another American, undertook a
survey of Indian wildlife. Spillet came to India in the mid-1960s
to do fieldwork. He ended up—within a period of six months—
travelling 13,500 miles across India's forests, 300 miles on foot
and twenty-one days on elephant back. His survey of India's
protected areas for the BNHS produced a report. In 1966 the
BNHS Journal was all about Spillet's surveys. And they had
strong policy recommendations:[11]

India has been richly endowed with precious natural resources. Many
of these however, already have been destroyed or lost due to ignorance,
tradition, apathy or political expediency. On every side the remaining
natural resources of this country are confronted with what often appear
to be insurmountable barriers. Unless the leaders of India are soon
able to implement definitive measures and initiate sound conservation
practices, little more than want and poverty and the eventual weakening
of this great nation can be expected.

He felt that one of the biggest scourges afflicting wildlife in India
was overgrazing and the way things were going, all the desirable
plants would vanish and in the end all that would be left would
be plants animals do not usually eat. He stated:

I am almost invariably told by officials that the problem is realized,
but that it is impossible to control grazing by domestic animals in a
democracy such as India's. This is faulty reasoning. No government,

---

[11]Juan Spillet, *Journal of the Bombay Natural History Society*, vol. 36,
no. 3 (1966), pp. 616–29.

particularly a democratic one, should permit its people to destroy the nation's most priceless possession—its land. Many feel that in a democracy public property belongs to everyone. But this does not mean that the people are free to destroy the public domain. For example, a public building belongs to everyone just as much as does a reserved and it is prohibited to damage such buildings or to remove materials from them for private use.

Further:

India is basically confronted with two major problems. I firmly believe that if these two were brought under control, the numerous other problems which are presently receiving so much attention and publicity, such as the scarcity of food, lack of foreign exchange, poor living standards, and so forth, would eventually resolve themselves....
These two problems are: (1) too many people, and (2) too much domestic livestock.

In my opinion both poaching and illegal grazing went hand in hand and the 1990s would reveal the truth of Spillet's ominous warning about the seriousness of the problem of grazing. Most other social scientists have ignored the problem of grazing even though, I believe, at least 500–600 tigers were poisoned in the 1990s by graziers because they had attacked their livestock. People and tigers can not coexist.

To sum up, the 1950s and 1960s saw an all-time low for India's flora and fauna. Independence had relegated conservation issues to the back-burner for all but a committed few and forest after forest got cut down in the name of development. Shikar agencies mushroomed and every forest officer felt he could only prove himself if he had shot a tiger. However, by the mid-1960s Indira Gandhi had replaced her father at the helm of affairs and where he had been indifferent to India's forest resources, she was strongly committed. Well-informed and involved, she also had the drive to put her views and plans into action. Thus whereas, on the one hand, the 1960s were a time of relentless destruction for India's forests in the name of development, they also gave birth to a leader who, in my opinion, was one of their greatest saviours, one who stemmed the tide before the process had became irreversible.

Countering the first Crisis
A Committed Leader

I ndira Gandhi took over the reins of power in 1966. Even while Gee, Stracey, and Seshadri wrote, she was being groomed as the next Prime Minister of India. She was to become India's greatest wildlife saviour. At the time she took over, the situation was very grim for India's flora and fauna. Indira Gandhi remained in power till 1984 except for a short gap in between. We shall later examine, in detail, the impact of her tenure on wildlife and forests. Let us have a quick look here at what she had managed to do by 1973. By 1968 she had agreed to hold the first IUCN Conference in India. The Conference that took place in 1969 in Delhi, brought the crisis out in the open, and it was followed by an immediate ban on tiger shooting in India—a ban seriously enforced. In 1971 she created a task force to draft the Wildlife Protection Act of India, and in 1972 piloted it through Parliament. Soon a census of tigers revealed that there were just about 1,800 tigers left in the wild in India and Indira Gandhi spearheaded the birth of Project Tiger. India had found a Prime Minister to whom wildlife and forests were a priority issue. She empowered a group of people around her to implement some of her wildlife policies, one of whom was Kailash Sankhala.

Sankhala was a forest officer whom Indira Gandhi liked and in the late 1960s he was director of the Delhi Zoo. In fact his first experience of tigers was through a zoo tiger called Jim. Sankhala was plucked out by Indira Gandhi to be the first director of Project Tiger. She made him a great power of the 1970s. Let us look at how he viewed those years that closed the 1960s and the enormity of the crisis that we faced.[1]

The pace of the person-to-person campaign to stop the heavy drain on our leopards and tigers was too slow for me, and I decided to raise the tempo. But how? I talked it over with my friend Razia, a charming lady on one of the national newspapers, and we devised a plan. She was to pose as a lady shortly to be married in England. A photographer would take a picture of her in the coat in order to get it approved by her brother before he bought it. And so we went from shop to shop, taking stock of the pelts and having a perfect excuse to photograph them.

One shopkeeper informed us he had a regular supply of 1,000 snow leopard skins a year. Another specialized in clouded leopard skins and his annual supply was nearly 2,000. Countless leopard skins were neatly piled up in his shop; he said he had nearly 3,000 on view and double that number in his warehouse. An interesting piece of information came to light: most of the exports were to East Africa. I could not understand this carrying of coats to Newcastle, for Africa has far more leopards than we have in India. I was told that in Kenya leopard skins could be sold at a much higher price because of the numerous tourists who went there; also, the local traders could obtain a certificate of origin for these imports which came in handy for smuggling Kenyan leopard skins. The illegal killings of Indian leopards were being utilized to legalize the killing of leopards in Kenya. The vicious circle had no end, and the leopards of both countries were losing ground.

[1] Kailash Sankhla, *Tiger. The Story of the Indian Tiger*, London, 1978.

I counted 22 tiger heads and all seemed to be laughing at us; probably they were mocking at our mission. There were hundreds of tiger rugs, and I pulled out four and spread them out on the floor. The trader immediately offered me a 30 x 40 ft carpet for $10,000. I asked if one was readily available. 'Yes,' said he, 'but you will have to place a firm order as I have to bring it from a palace.' I found a ready excuse to decline the offer.

The next shop had just as many skins. 'The fur of cubs is softer,' said the shopkeeper, adding that it required nearly 80 skins of leopard cubs to make a coat. After taking photographs of the lady wearing various coats and counting the stock we concluded our investigations.

The soft pelts of snow leopards, which the ladies love best and from which the shopkeepers earn a substantial profit, came in a steady flow of 600–800 skins per year in the fashion market. Snow leopards are so rare that even people living in the Himalayan regions hardly ever see them. They live at an altitude of about 12,000 feet where they prey on marmots, musk deer, and snow hares. Occasionally they come down to the lower pastures but hardly ever have a chance to attack the sheep of the ever vigilant Gujjars. But some of the graziers, renowned as tough walkers and climbers, who for the six summer months live above 8000 feet, are tempted by the lucrative offers of the valleys. Equipped with firearms and living in rugged mountainous areas where there is little chance of the civil law being enforced, these men become poachers and soon run amok, endangering the whole wildlife of the Himalayas. They chase the snow leopards, leopards, lynx and martens for their pelts and musk deer for their musk pods. Down the valley they go to the emporiums, where they get their loans paid off quickly and even obtain the lure of extra money.

The story of the striped skins is equally pathetic. In the Dehra Dun forests I heard of a tiger held in a snare for two painful days. When the Wildlife Officer came to dispatch the beast it broke its paw and ran off into the jungle to die an agonizing death. Another tiger was stoned to death in the Umariya forests of Madhya Pradesh in 1912. Sometimes villagers trap tigers and invite influential persons to shoot them at a point-blank range.

This large-scale poaching, especially by poisoning, has proved fatal to the big cats of India. I put the most blame on the traders who purchase the pelts and are quite unconcerned how they were obtained. The price of a tiger skin in the late 1950s was hardly $50; ten years later it had risen to $559. This was too much of a temptation for habitual poachers to resist, particularly when the average annual income of a man working in the forests is less than what he could make by selling one raw uncured tiger skin.

The results of my investigation with my lady accomplice were published on the front page of the *Indian Express* in 1967. It was followed by numerous letters to the Editor and led to questions in Parliament. A ban was immediately imposed on the export of all kinds of spotted skins, and the firms concerned raised a tremendous hue and cry, presenting their pre-ban commitments for not less than 20,000 skins. Many tigers and leopards not yet born were destined to honour these commitments. The case was presented to the Indian Board for Wildlife with a plea to the Grievances Committee of the Government. The Chairman of IBWL, a young and effective minister, Dr Karan Singh, reacted sharply: 'In that case we have grievances against the Grievances Committee.' The ban on the export of skins was imposed effectively in 1968.

Indira Gandhi and Dr Karan Singh made Kailash Sankhala a really powerful figure in those times. Sankhala did not like foreigners doing wildlife research in India, but was fully committed to protecting India's wildlife, and especially the tiger.

Like Kailash Sankhala, another forest officer of those times committed to the protection of wildlife was S.P. Shahi. He also records a series of events during the late 1960s and 1970s that highlight the extraordinary role of Indira Gandhi in protecting India's wildlife.

It was in 1968 that the IUCN held its tenth General Assembly in New Delhi. In her inaugural speech Indira Gandhi declared: 'We need foreign exchange, but not at the cost of the life and liberty of some of the most beautiful wildlife habitats of this continent.'

Indira Gandhi had also given teeth to the Indian Board of Wildlife and its Chairman, Karan Singh, was one of the most dynamic persons ever to head it. This period provides great examples of political will. Karan Singh said:[2]

The steady decline in the tiger population of our country has been causing great concern. The Prime Minister has expressed her anxiety over the situation and has suggested a complete moratorium on the killing of tigers for 5 years.

This problem was also subsequently discussed in the executive committee of the Indian Board for Wildlife, and it was decided to recommend that there should be a complete moratorium on the shooting of this beautiful animal with effect from 1 July 1970 for five years so that the declining trend is arrested.

This was the same Dr Karan Singh who in 1968 as chairman of Indian Board for Wildlife had successfully managed to ban the export of skins. Just in the nick of time for India's wildlife, a committed and well-informed team was in charge at the very top. It was 1970 and according to Shahi few cared for the order, but Indira Gandhi's pressure mounted. One of her typical remarks of those times was: 'Forestry practices designed to squeeze the last rupee out of our jungles, must be radically re-oriented at least within our National Parks.'[3]

[2]Minutes of IBWL—Karan Singh, Chairman 1969—Speech—personal.
[3]All quotes from Indira Gandhi, correspondence, addresses, etc. cited here are from the author's records and the book, *Safeguarding Environment—Indira Gandhi*, New Age, 1984.

By September 1970 the concept of a Wildlife Act was mooted. At an informal meeting of conservationists held by the Prime Minister in September 1970, it was resolved that the Union Government should bring forth a uniform enactment relating to wildlife conservation. Since wildlife was a state subject, before such legislation could be enacted in Parliament the Legislative Assemblies of at least two states must adopt a resolution under Article 252(1) of the Constitution delegating the power of passing such a law to Parliament.

On 29 March 1972 F.A. Ahmed, then Minister of Agriculture, wrote to Chief Minister of Bihar, Kedar Pande:

No nation has such a rich and varied fauna as India and yet to date the rapid decimation of India's wildlife has few parallels. Areas once teeming with wildlife are quite devoid of them and the few sanctuaries and parks where wildlife now seeks refuge have a tenuous state. Some animals and birds are already extinct and certain others are on the verge of being so.... It is therefore imperative that the country should have a uniform Wildlife Conservation and Management Bill which would make provisions for the control of not only hunting but also of trade and traffic in wildlife produce, and for the conservation and management of the wildlife habitats.

Indira Gandhi personally pushed the details of this bill through. In her letter of 12 April 1972 addressed to Kedar Pande and several other chief ministers she stated:

I have written to you in the past about wildlife conservation and management. Although there is now greater consciousness about this problem than a few yeas ago, we have not been able to significantly arrest the continuing decline of our fauna, including many endangered species. Poaching is on the increase, and we continue to receive reports of a lucrative trade in the furs and pelts of even those animals, like the tiger, whose shooting is in law prohibited throughout the country. Regrettably some State emporia are also involved in this business.

My colleague, the Agriculture Minister, has already written to you about the difficulties of controlling trade and taxidermy in the absence of uniform Central law applicable to the entire country. Experts are unanimous that only an integrated and country-wide policy of wildlife conservation and management can arrest the present precipitous decline. I have also received urgent appeals from the World Wildlife Fund.

It is for these reasons that we now seek your cooperation to enact Central legislation on wildlife conservation and management. A new Bill incorporating the most recent thinking on wildlife management has been prepared. The Bill also provides specific remedies in the Indian context which will make it possible for the Central and State Governments to deal effectively with the more insidious threats to our fauna.

This is not a political issue. It concerns the survival of our famous natural heritage. It is hard to think of an India devoid of its magnificent animals, of the hard-pressed tiger, for instance, going the way of the now extinct Indian Cheetah. Past experience reveals the limitations of the regional approach, with State laws frequently at variance with one another and all the attendant difficulties of implementation. The Centre and the States must now act in concert on the basis of common legislation which should be strictly enforced.

In April 1972 again, she appointed Dr Karan Singh as Chairman of a tiger task force to create an action plan to save the Indian tiger. Kailash Sankhala was appointed Officer on Special Duty. It was the proposal which was handed to Indira Gandhi in September 1972 by the tiger task force that gave birth the following year to Project Tiger.

In June 1972 a prominent member of the Congress Legislature Party in Bihar wrote to Indira Gandhi about the tragic release of 100 acres of land from the Madanpur forests: 'Madanpur forests in my district of Champaran are still rich in wildlife with a concentration of over a dozen tigers. I am distressed to write to you that there are very disquieting reports about releasing forest land to different persons in this forest.'

This member asked for help and he got it. On 5 July 1972 his letter was forwarded to Chief Minister, Kedar Pande, with a covering letter from Indira Gandhi that stated:

I enclose copy of a letter which I have received regarding the preservation of wildlife in Bihar. You already know of my interest and concern. The Bihar Assembly has not yet passed a Resolution in favour of Central legislation on this subject about which I wrote to you on 12 April 1972. I hope you will get this expedited.

I am disturbed by what the letter says regarding the release of forest land. Please look into this personally and stop it.

It is interesting that this letter was written from Simla at a time when the Prime Minister was having her historic talks with Mr Zulfikar Ali Bhutto, Prime Minister of Pakistan. In the midst of the most hectic and historic summit in Simla, to take time off to send a letter regarding the Madanpur reserve forest division, points to Indira Gandhi's enormous political will in the interest of wildlife.

In the mid-1970s, she approved of a proposal to set up 'wildlife wings' in the states. S.P. Shahi wrote in this regard:[4]

Much will also depend on how we go about the business of setting up a suitable administrative machinery for wildlife management in the country. The notion that wildlife should be looked after by an altogether separate service and that the present forestry personnel are ill-equipped for it, has been debated for quite some time. To support this argument, it is often stated the East African countries have different personnel

---

[4]S.P. Shahi, *Backs to the Wall: Saga of Wildlife in Bihar—India*, Delhi, 1977.

for their reserves and their forests. But few people realize that, in those countries, the wildlife live in open grassy savannahs, unlike India where the bulk of wildlife lives in forests. Wildlife and forests have to co-exist in this country.

Even if a separate wildlife service is created, I doubt if it will attract men with the necessary aptitude and dedication. As it is, the Indian Forest Service is less glamorous than the other two existing All-India Services. A Wildlife Service will be still less so. The Indian Forest Service was conceived so that available talent could be dispersed and in the hope that meritorious youngsters would join this service. But this hope, unfortunately, has been belied. In the seven two-year courses between 1968–70 to 1974–76, out of the 116 persons who were selected for training at the Indian Forest College, Dehra Dun, for the IFS, as many as forty left during the course of the training for other services. Not only that, they left largely for the Indian Administrative and Indian Police Services, a few of them went to the State Bank, and the Central Engineering, Revenue, Indian Ordinance and Railway Services. The situation in the country at present is such that it is not only the salary but the pomp and power that goes with a service that also influence meritorious young men wanting to join it. As long as such a situation exists, the Wildlife Service will continue to be unpopular, and will mostly attract the leftovers.

Considering all the pros and cons of the matter, certain guidelines have very recently been issued to the State Governments by the Government of India to establish immediately a separate Wildlife Wing under the overall charge of the Chief Conservator of Forests. An officer of the rank of Additional Conservator of Forests will head this wing. An officer of the rank of Additional Inspector General of Forests at the Centre is to coordinate and direct the activities of the Wildlife Wings in the various States. It is envisaged that members of the Forest Service trained or experienced in wildlife management will join the new wing without loss of rank.

The Prime Minister approved this proposal for organizing a wildlife wing in the various states in a note dated 18 September 1974—sadly she did not go as far as a wildlife service. Today these wildlife wings are redundant.

Training the next generation of wildlife managers is critical. I am not sure whether we have the necessary expertise within the country. We should not hesitate to look abroad for the skills we may need. Possibly UNESCO or UNDP could help in providing a small group of foreign experts to be deployed both at the Forest Research Institute, Dehra Dun, and the Centre to help in training and to keep a watchful eye on our evolving wildlife programme.

In order to maintain performance standards, all persons directly or indirectly concerned with wildlife management should be regularly assessed in their annual reports for the performance in wildlife conservation work.

The Unit at the Centre will have an important role to play, especially in the early stages. It should be staffed at a high level by specially selected officers, so that it has the means to persuade and assist the States.

By the 1970s, the British conservationists committed to India's wildlife had all gone but they had been replaced by an equally committed home-grown cadre. Some like Sankhala and Shahi operated within the system, others like M. Krishnan and Billy Arjan Singh outside it but with the full backing of the Prime Minister. In different ways, they all drew their strength from a close association with Indira Gandhi. Billy lived in the wilderness of Dudhwa on the India–Nepal border and was obsessed with tigers. Indira Gandhi really respected him and was fascinated by his wild ways. It was she who made Billy famous in the late 1970s by permitting him to import a captive tigress from Europe to reintroduce in the wilds of Dudhwa. She supported Billy's experimentation in this sector, something that would be unthinkable today. Billy battles on in his efforts to save both forests and wildlife. In his 80s, he continues his work in Dudhwa and is a pillar of strength for all conservationists.

He is one of the greatest advocates for an Indian Wildlife Service. In 1979 he articulated his views eloquently in a note for the government. Most of the Indian Forest Service did not agree with him but I think he came very close to persuading Indira Gandhi to create such a service. It is really regrettable that he did not ultimately succeed.

The year 1969 is a vital year in the history of India's forests and wildlife. Indira Gandhi had come to power in 1966 and in 1967 to 1968 she had just started restructuring all the forest and wildlife policy-making bodies. She had early associations with wildlife. She was once President of the Delhi Bird Watchers Society and has also loved the wildlife of Africa when she had toured Kenya as a young member of Parliament. She came to the job of prime minister with a love for the wilderness. Till 1968 hunting was rampant, there was a flourishing trade in skins, and there were very few laws to check the sad state of affairs. On 8 July 1969 Indira Gandhi made a pertinent address to the Indian Board of Wildlife—gone were the lacklustre and superficial addresses at such meetings, gone was the lack of priority attached to such meetings as was the case in the Nehru era. Indira Gandhi had made the young and dynamic minister of tourism, Dr Karan Singh, the chairman of the Indian Board for Wildlife in 1968, and the meetings were suddenly important in the corridors of power. I reproduce Indira Gandhi's inaugural address to the 8 July meeting which shows her depth and understanding of detail on this issue in the first years of her prime ministership.

I am happy to have this occasion of saying a few words to this reconstituted Board for Wildlife. I am here not as Prime Minister but as one who loves nature and feels deep concern for the manner in which it is being gradually destroyed, not intentionally but through, perhaps, lack of knowledge on the part of public and people who live around.

Forests and wildlife that exist in them are not only beautiful to see but they are also of great value to us in a variety of ways. In some countries, there is a debate going on as to what effect the extinction of certain species of birds or insects is having on the human beings, on crops and on many other parts of our daily life. As Jagjivan Ramji has said India is indeed fortunate in having a great variety of plants, trees, and animals. This should have been a source of pride and joy to us. But, unfortunately, there is hardly any appreciation of this bounty and beauty. We should aim at conserving what is available to us and, if possible, to add to it, so that the coming generations do not have less but more.

The two great enemies of wildlife, or amongst the enemies of wildlife, are economic progress and, perhaps, greed. Also, of course, ignorance and insensitivity. But if progress is well planned, there need not be a danger to wildlife or natural beauty. Sometimes our engineers or administrators or dam builders do not have any reverence for nature.

Of course, it is not quite enough to designate some areas as national parks and sanctuaries. We should ensure that they are really sanctuaries. I must confess that I have not seen all our national parks but I do not know if they are run as well as they ought to be. I have seen several of the game sanctuaries in Africa. The atmosphere there is entirely different to what we find in India. The first thing you notice when you happen to be there is that the wardens have genuine love for animals. They know the individual animals. They can recognize by their pug marks. The whole atmosphere is one of convenience of the animals first and of the tourist and of the human being second. Although cars are allowed on various roads, they are not allowed to blow horns or to do anything that might disturb the normal routine of the animals or to frighten them in any way and that is important if the parks are to continue to be natural and not have a kind of atmosphere of a zoo.

In order to preserve wild game one has also to preserve smaller animals that have grown in the forests because it is on the smaller animals that the larger animals live. Tigers and leopards are big animals who, when cannot pursue their normal hunting habits, start attacking domestic cattle and perhaps become man-eaters.

I made some reference earlier to greed as one of the enemies of the wildlife. Now we all know that in the last century many countries have suffered because of the impatience of those who traded in animal skins, furs, and so on. Even the need for foreign exchange does not justify the killing of tigers and leopards and other such valuable animals in a manner that become extinct.

A few months ago I received a cable from the International Conference on Game Conservation and Wildlife Management on this subject and I believe that this is one of the items on your agenda.

Last March I was very sorry to read about the devastating fire in Corbett Park. A place cannot be called a National Park if lorries and jeeps are running around and timber men and traders are swarming and disturbing the life there. The new Chairman of the Board also happens to be our Minister of Tourism and I hope that this coincidence will lead to greater tourist facilities in our national parks and sanctuaries, but as I have said, without disturbing animals.

If I may give personal experience in one of the Parks in Uganda. They have built very small cottages. From outside they look like mud huts. I do not know what they are really made of. Very early in the morning I heard a noise outside my door I thought that somebody is disturbing me with morning tea though I do not take it and I was prepared to go out and shout at the person for waking me up early. But when I looked out I saw a lot of small animals who had come to lick something that was put near about. In the pre-dawn light they were playing perfectly free from all fear of human and other people and it was really one of the most unforgettable sights. This is an atmosphere which we should try to build up in our own parks....

Sometimes I have been grieved to receive complaints that even forest officials and district officers have turned poachers. I do not know whether there is any truth in it, but it certainly deserves to be fully investigated.

I find you have proposal for an All India Wildlife Service and for the training of guides. There is certainly need for guides who are well-trained in the art and science of preserving wildlife and who will be able to indicate their love for animals and their enthusiasm to the public.

At this point in time Karan Singh's role was really important. He was the Maharaja of Kashmir and ranged against hunting. Most other Maharajas had huge hunting records to their name. The Maharaja of Surguja, for example, had killed 1,100 tigers by then. Cleverly, Indira Gandhi empowered Karan Singh to protect and neutralize some of the hunting lobbies of the royals in India. We will see later that they both succeeded.

At the 1969 IUCN Congress later that year, Indira Gandhi delivered another hard-hitting speech on the state of India's wildlife and the need to conserve it:

I am delighted that the International Union for Conservation of Nature and Natural Resources is holding its General Assembly in our country. May I extend a warm welcome to all the delegates on behalf of the Government and the people of India.

I have special pleasure in coming to your Conference for, if I may strike a personal note, as an only child whose childhood was invaded by the turbulence of a vast national upheaval, I found companionship and an inner peace in communion with Nature. I grew up with love for stones, no less than trees, and for animals of all kinds. I have always felt that closeness to Nature helps to make one a more integrated personality. I say this especially because of the general lack of concern or feeling for these things nowadays, at least in my country.

India is a country in the throes of change. And to be a conservative is not popular. Nor am I one, for, our conditions demand that we speed the process of social and economic transformation. Yet, there are some things which I would not like to change—which I would like to conserve—our beautiful craft, the rural folk's instinctive feel for line and design and, of course, the natural beauty of our wildlife, our forests and our mountains. This is not merely for one's aesthetic sense, though that is important enough, but also for our future well-being.

As one looks around at the Universe, one marvels at the order and the balance. How beautifully everything fits in. How remarkably well everything is organized. All creatures must struggle against Nature to survive, and each species has equipped itself in some special way for self-preservation. Man developed his brain and today has transcended the limits of sound and space. He is the professor of undreamt knowledge and power. In the struggle for survival, he has gained the upper hand. One should have thought that, with this knowledge at his command, man would have learnt to live at peace with himself and with Nature. Yet, no matter where one goes, one sees the needless and wasteful destruction of plant and animal life for the sake of a moment's pleasure or a temporary gain, with no heed to the balance of Nature or the disturbance of its serenity. It is a sad commentary on our attitude towards Nature that we still talk of 'exploiting' its resources. This is an unpleasant word, for it implies taking an unjust advantage. Instead, we should think of the 'development' of resources, of using resources with care. We all work for progress, but progress has its ugly side also. The steady growth of population and the economic needs which it imposes, have gradually encroached upon forest resources. Mankind looks at animals, at flora and fauna, for what it can get out of them.

In the last century, and especially during the last three or four decades, India has been denuded of her forest wealth. The wanton felling of trees has changed the landscape, affecting climate. Deforestation is creating a major problem of soil erosion. A massive campaign is necessary now to educate our people in the first principles of natural conservation.

We must teach them, from their early school days, to become planters and protectors of trees and to care for animals.

When forests are cut down, wildlife is naturally threatened. Some beautiful and interesting species have become extinct. At the rate at which secret poaching and shooting are taking place, the rhinoceros, the famous Bengal tiger, and even the elephant might disappear unless we take vigilant and drastic steps to preserve them. Fortunately, we have an enlightened forest service but its strength is not adequate to the size of our country. Thanks to pioneers, who were impelled by a missionary zeal, we have set up several parks and wildlife sanctuaries. We have a Wildlife Board, which has placed a ban on the export of the skins of tigers and leopards. We do need foreign exchange, but not at the cost of the life and liberty of some of the most beautiful inhabitants of this continent.

From 1969 onwards, Indira Gandhi took several immediate and decisive steps towards wildlife protection that were rigorously enforced—whether it was the ban on tiger shooting in 1970, the creation of a tiger task force, the passing of the Wildlife Protection Act in 1972, or the launch of Project Tiger in 1973.

In June 1972 at the United Nations Conference on Human Environment she stated:

I have had the good fortune of growing up with a sense of kinship with nature in all its manifestations. Birds, plants, stones were companions and, sleeping under the star-strewn sky, I became familiar with the names and movements of the constellations. But my deep interest in this our 'only earth' was not for itself but as a fit home for man.

One cannot be truly human and civilized unless one looks upon not only all fellow men but all creation with the eyes of a friend. Throughout India, edicts carved on rocks and iron pillars are reminders that 22 centuries ago the Emperor Ashoka defined a King's duty as not merely to protect citizens and punish wrongdoers but also to preserve animal life and forest trees. Ashoka was the first and perhaps the only monarch until very recently, to forbid the killing of a large number of species of animals for sport or food, foreshadowing some of the concerns of this Conference. He went further, regretting the carnage of his military conquests and enjoining upon his successors to find 'their only pleasure in the peace that comes through righteousness'.

Along with the rest of mankind, we in India—in spite of Ashoka— have been guilty of wanton disregard for sources of our sustenance. We share your concern at the rapid deterioration of flora and fauna. Some of our own wildlife has been wiped out, miles of forests with beautiful old trees, mute witnesses of history, have been destroyed. Even though our industrial development is in its infancy, and at its most difficult stage, we are taking various steps to deal with incipient environmental imbalances.

The launch of Project Tiger in March 1973 afforded her special satisfaction. In fact it was her political will over the previous five years that had finally led to Project Tiger. In a strongly-worded message she stated:

Project Tiger abounds in irony. The country that has for millennia been the most famous haunt of this great animal now finds itself struggling to save it from extinction. The Project is comment on our long neglect of our environment as well as our new-found, but most welcome, concern for saving one of nature's most magnificent endowments for posterity.

But the tiger cannot be preserved in isolation. It is at the apex of a large and complex biotope. Its habitat, threatened by human intrusion, commercial forestry, and cattle grazing must first be made inviolate. Forestry practices, designed to squeeze the last rupee out of our jungles, must be radically re-oriented at least within our National Parks and Sanctuaries, and pre-eminently in the Tiger Reserves. The narrow outlook of the accountant must give way to a wider vision of the recreational, educational, and ecological value of totally undisturbed areas of wilderness. Is it beyond our political will and administrative ingenuity to set aside about one or two per cent of our forests in their pristine glory for this purpose?

Project Tiger is a truly national endeavour. It can succeed only with the full cooperation of the Central and State Governments and the support of the people. It has my very best wishes.

In December 1973 she detailed her views on wildlife personnel and wings.

In the last few years wildlife conservation has made significant progress. A new legal framework has been enacted in the shape of the Wildlife (Protection) Act, 1972. Project Tiger is under way and the States are more responsive. There is also large financial allocation for wildlife programmes in the Fifth Plan.

I feel that the time has now come to introduce more specialized management for our parks and sanctuaries. At present, personnel are posted there in a haphazard manner without regard to expertise, aptitude or special dedication. Also postings are of such short duration that experience and expertise cannot be adequately built up. Many officers who have received wildlife training abroad or in Dehra Dun are being used for other jobs.

Throughout the world, wildlife management is becoming increasingly specialized. Our conservation efforts cannot yield the desired results without a similar effort on our part. One possible approach with which I am in broad sympathy is enclosed. I have asked the Department of Personnel to examine it further in consultation with the Inspector General of Forests in order to give it more concrete shape before commending it to you. It would be helpful if your Forest Department could also apply its mind to this problem from now and keep in touch with the Inspector General of Forests.

There is one other matter to which I would like to draw your attention. Despite the enactment of the Wildlife (Protection) Act 1972, enforcement at the field level leaves much to be desired. It seems that none of the State Governments has so far recruited additional staff whose sole duty would be to enforce the Act, to patrol wildlife areas and sanctuaries and prevent violations of the law. I continue to receive reports of even endangered animals listed in Schedule I of the Act being killed illegally. The tiger and leopard have received considerable publicity in this connection. The black buck merits similar vigilance. It would be desirable to set up black buck sanctuaries wherever sizeable herds of this rare and beautiful animal remain.

To

Chief Ministers of all State Governments and Union Territories, and Governors of Orissa and Manipur

1. Creation of a Wildlife Department under the Forest Department at the Government level in those States which have large and important areas of wildlife. In the other States, there may be a separate wildlife wing under the Chief Conservator of Forests.

2. Forest officers and field staff may be given option to come to the Wildlife Service. Some special pay may be offered as an incentive. However, once having opted for it, these officers will not be allowed to go back to the regular forest line unless their promotion prospects are available. Alternatively, an officer may be given promotion in the Wildlife Service as and when his promotion in his parent Service becomes due. This will ensure long tenure, specialization as well as attract people with the necessary commitment and enthusiasm.

3. Personnel may be drawn from the Indian Forest Service, State Forest Services and to the extent that there is a shortfall from the open market or from other services. Special training will be imparted to these personnel in wildlife management. In addition,

Govt. of India could offer to provide specialists on deputation as Consultants of Advisors.

4. National Parks and Sanctuaries will be managed by the Wildlife Service exclusively, and all staff and activity will be under their control.

5. If for commercial reasons, a State Government is unwilling to stop exploitation within a national park or sanctuary, it will be the duty of the Wildlife Service rather than the Forest Department to conduct and supervise timber felling etc. Such an arrangement will ensure that damage to wildlife is minimized.'

Indira Gandhi was finally trying to put into practice what Burton had suggested in 1948.

In 1976 she continued to pursue the states on the issue of wildlife wings in her endeavour to bring urgent reforms in this sector.

On 27th December, 1973 I had asked you to look into the possibility of establishing a Wildlife Wing within the Forest Department. The aim was to provide specialized wildlife management, without which our conservation effort cannot prosper.

Since then, a scheme has been drawn up by the Department of Personnel and circulated to all State Governments. However, the feedback from the States shows that progress has been disappointingly slow. In some cases, Wildlife Wings have been established on paper, but remain ineffective. Elsewhere, even preliminary steps have not been taken. In all cases there is a marked shortage of trained wildlife staff, and no evidence that the few people available have been deployed to maximum advantage.

I cannot avoid the feeling that Forest Departments continue to treat wildlife as a peripheral and unimportant matter. If such an attitude of indifference persists, attempts at conservation will not succeed.... Throughout the country there is new emphasis on the need for compassion towards animals and for environmental conservation. A good share of the burden must necessarily fall on Forest Departments, which should be alive to their responsibility.

I should like you to ensure that departmental apathy and resistance to the effective functioning of Wildlife Wings are to be overcome. Cadre management must be adjusted to reflect the new priorities. The Planning Commission will be responsive to properly conceived schemes, so shortage of funds need not be an undue inhibition. Detailed practical suggestions have already been conveyed to you: what remains is to put them into practice.

Please keep me informed of progress.

By the end of 1976, Indira Gandhi had put forests and wildlife on the concurrent list of the constitution so that the central government could play a more active role in preservation. And this was essential because the Constitution of India, adopted in 1950, did not have any specific provisions relating to the protection of the environment or the conservation of nature. Indira Gandhi realized this problem and quickly rectified it.

The forty-second amendment to the Constitution would play a critical role in the decades ahead in protecting our beleaguered wildlife. For the first time, a specific provision was made to protect and improve the environment and both the state and its citizens were put under the fundamental obligation to do so. The environment includes forests, lakes, rivers, and wildlife.

Between 1977 and 1979, Indira Gandhi lost power to a united Opposition and the focus and passion-driven concern for forests and wildlife which had characterized her government was lost for a while. But even in the interim, Morarji Desai, the new Prime Minister, was forced to continue the policies started by her government. He stopped the trade in rhesus monkeys in 1978 and tried to mount a rescue operation for three crocodile species. From 1947 to 1977 two million rhesus monkeys had been exported for foreign exchange. Morarji Desai had to follow the law that Indira Gandhi had put into force, that is The Wildlife Protection Act, 1972.

By 1979, on her return to power, there was much debate about restructuring the forest and wildlife departments which thus far had been housed in the Ministry of Agriculture. In the early 1980s she also stopped the Silent Valley Project, in an effort to protect the rain forests of the Western Ghats. Again in 1979–80 she got the Forest Conservation Act drafted and piloted it through the Parliament—a piece of legislation that can be largely credited with keeping our forests alive to date. Most greedy politicians hate it because it empowers the Ministry of Environment and Forests only to release forest land on a case by case basis. Without this Act it is doubtful whether we would have had any forests left today. Starting on these very positive notes, the early 1980s saw some strong measures, displaying the greatest degree of political will in the area of environment and conservation to be seen in the last century in India.

On 23 January 1980 the President of India addressed the joint houses of Parliament and referred to the need to set up a specialized machinery with adequate powers to incorporate all planned development measures to maintain an ecological balance. These first years of the 1980s were to be memorable in the history of our forests and wildlife. The President had declared national commitment to the subject, and by the end of February Indira Gandhi had set up a high-powered committee on environmental protection under the chairmanship of the Deputy Chairman of the Planning Commission. The committee would recommend legislative measures and the administrative machinery necessary to ensure environmental protection. Its final report, which we shall later look at, was published in September 1980.

On 6 March 1980 Indira Gandhi launched the World

Conservation Strategy of the IUCN and stated in her keynote address:

The need of the poor for livelihood, the greed of middlemen for quick profits, the demands of industry, and the short-sightedness of the administration, have created ecological problems. It is sad that even scientists, because of their collection activities, have contributed to the disappearance of several species of orchids and other plants in our Himalayan foothills. The manner in which we are encroaching upon our forests and mountains and are permitting the indiscriminate cutting of beautiful and useful old trees is alarming. In spite of the Government of India's Forest Policy Resolution, we have lost large areas in the last 30 years. As a result, there have been soil erosion, floods, and the silting of reservoirs and rivers. Large tracts of land have become saline or alkaline. One of our immediate tasks is to restore the eco-systems of the Himalaya and other mountain ranges. Can we ensure that by the end of the century, the Himalaya will have the same extent of vegetable cover as prevailed at the beginning of this century?

Nature is beautifully balanced. Each little thing has its own place, its duty and special utility. Any disturbance creates a chain reaction which may not be visible for some time. Taking a fragmentary view of life has created global and national problems.

In his arrogance with his own increasing knowledge and ability, man has ignored his dependence on the earth and has lost his communion with it. He no longer puts his ear to the ground so that the earth can whisper its secrets to him. He has cut his links from the elements and has weakened resources which are the heritage of millions of years of evolution—all those living or inanimate things which sustained his inner energy—(earth, water, air, the flora, and fauna). This loosening of his intuitive response to nature has created a feeling of alienation in him and is destructive of his patrimony. So, while we have to think of conservation, we must ask whether man himself is growing into a being worth saving.

On 20 April 1980, Indira Gandhi wrote a detailed letter to all the chief ministers and governors of the states reflecting her concern about the state of affairs in forest India and asking for immediate correctives. Some important points that she made were:

1. Officers with the right attitude should be posted in reserved forests and sanctuary areas; if possible, a special corps of such officers could be identified for duties relating to wildlife and forest and environment conservation.

2. Forest development corporations or similar agencies should be asked to take up plantations on steep hill sides, catchment areas and clear-felled forest areas so that productive forestry and protective forestry go hand in hand.

3. A massive programme of social forestry should take up specified schemes. The wastelands in villages, all community lands, field bunds, canal bunds, etc., should be clothed with fast-growing species under this useful scheme.

4. In areas where tribals depend heavily on forests for their livelihood, they should be involved in replanting the species that they are already exploiting. A scheme of forest farming should be undertaken. Particular attention must be paid to the replanting or fresh planting of fruit trees.

5. The existing regulations and security arrangements in sanctuaries should be tightened and personal interest must be shown by top people in administration to see that poaching activities are ruthlessly suppressed.

6. The system of contracting away forest areas should be replaced or modified to see that every tree felled should be replaced by the planting of at least another one if not more.

7. Tree plantation programmes should be undertaken by schools and other institutions. Some countries have initiated a programme of a tree for every child.

8. Serious attempts must be made to change the orientation of all persons working in the Forest Service and Forest Administration with a system of rewards and incentives for those who do better in preserving or extending the forest areas.

We should also give thought to some other measures needed to preserve our environment. Please devote some time every week to review the developments in this field personally or through one of your senior colleagues. I shall be glad to have your suggestions as also an indication what your State proposed to do or has done in this field.

Thus Indira Gandhi showed her far-sightedness in this regard. Unfortunately, after her death in 1984, never again has the kind of political will that she showed towards conservation measures been replicated and in the twenty-five years that have passed since she wrote this letter, most of what she aimed for, tragically, has never come to pass, except for bits and pieces of social forestry and plantation work and that also in the most haphazard of ways. I am, from the outside, still fighting for reform in the forest service and for a sub-cadre of forest officers to focus their work in protected areas. There are so many vested interests in the system at play that any effort at change is fought tooth and nail. Suffice it to say that we still fight for the same things today that Indira Gandhi wanted done twenty-five years ago.

In May 1980 Indira Gandhi again wrote to all governors and chief ministers following up on the progress of measures suggested in her earlier letter. Her focus was on the improvement of the infrastructure that governed wildlife and forests. She suggested that 'Wildlife Advisory Boards in your states should meet regularly to review the progress in the preservation of sanctuaries and stopping the exploitation of game'.

She wanted the leaders at the top to take personal interest in this matter. She would have been shocked to learn that in 2005 there was a 30 per cent vacancy in forest staff who are the guardians of India's Forests. Wildlife Boards in the states hardly ever meet today. This is because nobody in power really cares any more.

Though she could not bring reform in the forest service, probably because forest officers did not want it, she was, shortly after this letter, able to bring to Parliament the Forest Conservation Act in 1980—the most comprehensive piece of legislation in the field ever to be enacted in India.

For Indira Gandhi, it was an extraordinarily active time in relation to forest protection. On 15 September 1980 the committee for recommending legislative measures and administrative machinery for environmental protection submitted its report to her. N.D. Tiwari (presently Chief Minister of Uttaranchal), then Deputy Chairman of the Planning Commission and Chairman of the Committee, stated in his letter to Indira Gandhi:

Under your leadership, the National Development Council at its recent meeting has also, for the first time in the history of Indian planning, approved the following major objectives for the Sixth Plan: 'Bringing about harmony between the short-and the long-term goals of development by promoting the protection and improvement of ecological and environmental assets.'

Further:

We need a suitable institutional arrangement in the form of a properly structured government department for ensuring that this objective is translated into reality. Since such a department will require for its successful functioning the cooperation of all other departments of government, we have proposed that you may be good enough to keep such a department under your direct charge.

Tiwari knew that Indira Gandhi had the political will to ensure that the Department of Environment would work and therefore he wanted it to be in her direct charge.

The Committee asked for the immediate creation of a

Department of Environment under the charge of the Prime Minister. The Prime Minister accepted the report of the Tiwari Committee, as it was called. In November 1980 the Department of Environment was set up as the focal agency in the administrative structure of the central government for planning, promotion, and coordination of environmental programmes. At long last the subject was separated from the Ministry of Agriculture.

At this point, Billy Arjan Singh was most vocal about the creation of an Indian Wildlife Service. He believed that if wildlife was to be protected, there had to be a cadre for it:[5]

I maintain with absolute conviction that the fragile status of wildlife, which has deteriorated to crisis proportions due to abusive practices as a State Subject, should be immediately taken over to by the Department of Environment to be administered by a Central Wildlife Service. Wildlife has no fear imperative to assist in its future survival, and I feel that once the euphoria of creative effort is over, the preservation of wildlife may once again be relegated to its pristine state in the order of priorities.

The draft Sixth Five-Year Plan 1978–83 recommends that 25 per cent of forest area should be taken over for wildlife preservation, and this area should be identified immediately for management by the Wildlife Service, with the present Parks and Sanctuaries as a working nucleus.

A moratorium should be declared on commercial operations in all forests, and fresh priorities for the functioning of the forest department should be laid down for wildlife management.

However to this day this demand of wildlife activists for a separate wildlife cadre hasn't been met. There is no wildlife service or national park service in the country. The reason for this is that the majority of forest service officers do not want it.

[5]Minutes of IBWL, 1980.

By November 1980 India had its first ever Department of Environment. Looking at it from the perspective of today, it was a remarkable achievement. The subject of forests would continue to remain in the Agriculture Ministry but wildlife would become a part of the new Department of Environment.

On 14 September 1982 Indira Gandhi once again wrote to the chief ministers reminding them of their priorities.

For over a decade, I have been emphasizing the need for special attention to wildlife conservation and specialized management in this field. This is the reason for the enactment of the Wildlife Protection Act in 1972 and this subject was included in the Concurrent List of the Constitution in 1976. Simultaneously, specific guidelines for the formation of separate wildlife wings in the States and Union Territories were circulated by the Ministry of Agriculture. At the same time the Department of Personnel and Administrative Reforms also wrote to all the States on this subject.

Thereafter, the matter has been pursued at various levels. In 1980, shortly after we launched the World Conservation Strategy in India, I wrote to you on the 20 April and again on the 2 May. More lately, the Indian Board for Wildlife has expressed serious concern about the lack of attention by State Governments to the formation and working of separate wildlife wings in the States. The Board wanted the Ministry of Agriculture to examine the position carefully and specially review the working of wildlife wings in some bigger States which claim to have set up such separate wings within the Forest Departments. This exercise has been done in the last few months and the overall picture is most disappointing. Most States have not set up proper wildlife wings, as visualized in the guidelines circulated by the Central Government. Where this has been done, these are not being manned by properly selected and motivated officials. The detailed review with regard to some bigger States has revealed a number of deficiencies. The main points are given in the attached summary.

The forthcoming Wildlife Week is from the 1 to 7 October, 1982. Please see that concrete action on each point contained in the attached summary materializes by that time, and that a report on the action taken is sent to me urgently. Please also keep in close touch with the Department of Environment here which has been asked to deal with the wildlife matters in a more intense manner.

Indira Gandhi was thus continuously pushing the chief ministers to prioritize wildlife protection.

On 1 October 1982 the fifteenth meeting of the Indian Board for Wildlife was held.

In her opening remarks, the Prime Minister emphasized the importance of the meeting since it was the first time that a meeting of the Board was being held during Wildlife Week, and also because it had come up soon after the transfer of wildlife as a subject at the centre to the Department of Environment. She expressed the hope that the new arrangement would help in giving much-needed closer attention to the subject and lead to quicker results, which would be possible if the field-level agencies worked in harmony and in a spirit of mutual cooperation.

Stressing the need for a nationwide effort based on active public interest and involvement, the Prime Minister laid down that the strategy and action programmes for wildlife conservation in the country should aim at:

1. The establishment of a network of protected areas such as national parks, sanctuaries and biosphere reserves, to cover representative samples of all major wildlife ecosystems and with adequate geographic distributions;
2. The restoration of degraded habitats to their natural state, within these protected areas;
3. The rehabilitation of endangered species and their restoration to protected portions of their former habitats, in a manner which provides some reflection of their original distribution;

4. The provision of adequate protection to wildlife in multiple-use areas (such as production forests and pasture) so as to form 'corridors' linking up the protected areas and providing for genetic continuity between them;

5. Support for the management of botanical and zoological parks and gardens and undertaking captive breeding programmes for threatened species of plants and animals;

6. The development of appropriate management systems for protected areas, including a professional cadre of personnel fully trained in all aspects of wildlife and sanctuary management, as well as the provision of proper orientation to all officers concerned with wildlife;

7. The development of research and monitoring facilities which will provide a scientific understanding of wildlife populations and habitats essential to their proper management;

8. Support for wildlife education and interpretation aimed at a wider public appreciation of importance of wildlife to human betterment;

9. The review and updating of statutory provisions for protection to wildlife and regulating all forms of trade, as to ensure their current effectiveness;

10. Assistance in the formulation and adoption of a National Conservation Strategy for all living natural resources on the lines of the World Conservation Strategy launched in 1980;

11. Participation in international conventions designed to prevent the depletion of the wildlife resources and to provide protection to migratory species;

12. Long-term conservation of wildlife based on the scientific principles of evolution and genetics.

Tragically, twenty-three years later none of these twelve objectives has really been met. Indira Gandhi was in a continuous process of countering crisis—crisis could thus never envelope her or the nation. That kind of unrelenting commitment is absent today and therefore we are deeply plunged in a wildlife crisis of enormous magnitude.

At the conference of state forest ministers in New Delhi on 18 October 1982 Indira Gandhi's address was sharp and precise:

As the Minister has just said, I have been writing repeatedly to Chief Ministers on different facets of forestry in these last three years. This was to convey our collective anxiety on the rapid depletion of our forests and the ill effects that this would have on our climate—is already having—our economic development and our future itself. Fortunately today there is greater awareness all around regarding this problem and a few steps have been taken for the conservation of this precious resource. However it is obvious and a cause for distress that these steps do not go far enough. The Minister was pleased to say that I was a saviour of forestry and wildlife, but I will be saviour only if they are actually saved. So far, they are not saved.

Yet when it comes to taking a concrete decision either to stop the cutting of trees or to preserve endangered species of animals or to put down poaching or smuggling of rare species, we waver. The initiative is left often enough to people who depend upon such activities for their living. I am certain that a total change can be brought about in our whole approach to forestry only if all those who are responsible for decision, whether they are politicians or officials or non-officials, are imbued with a strong commitment to conserve our environment. These ideas will prosper if there is a genuine feeling for them and not merely because it happens to be part of a programme. Perhaps you remember Gandhiji saying that when any major decision is to be taken we should recall the face of the *Dharidranarayan*. Similarly when any decision about felling of trees or allowing wildlife to be overrun is taken, we have to think of the life of the tree and the lives of wild animals and how intimately these are bound up within human living.

I know that there is tremendous pressure on our forest resources for timber, fuel, forest produce, fodder etc. I don't minimize the importance of these needs but they should not result in indiscriminate felling of forests. Some hard measures like a ban on felling in all critically affected areas like hill-slopes, catchment areas and tank-beds are inevitable. The avarice of the contractor must be recognized and dealt with firmly. Only a few States have dispensed with the contracting system. Even in those States, it is necessary to have another closer look as to how the new system works, whether it has resulted in slowing down the rate of depletion.

I have received many complaints that State Forest Departments have totally clear-felled areas before starting plantation. When degraded areas, deforested areas and other vacant government lands are available for plantation, they should be taken up on a priority basis.

So far as wildlife is concerned, recently we have decided to entrust the subject to our Department of Environment. The objective is to ensure that the scientific management of wildlife, which is an integral part of the environment, gets more specialized attention. The intention was not to divorce wildlife from forestry—that cannot be done as the two have to go closely together. But forestry practices in wildlife areas must change. Much more attention has to be paid to endangered species and to wildlife outside sanctuaries. There is a strong demand that forestry also should be removed from Agriculture, because of what is now happening, and put along with environment. This will depend on how the forest departments function. If we find that they are not changing their ways, then we will have to review the whole situation and if necessary change the whole concept of the service and the way it functions. But it simply cannot continue as it is going on now. That is one thing on which we are all quite definite.

The feeling that wildlife is only a matter of curiosity which can be preserved through ecological parks must go. Wildlife has to be wild and it has to survive. I would like to say that I am quite unhappy at the way, for instance, the Gir lions are now treated. They have become quite tame and are no longer wild. They are fed and now they have got no capacity to hunt for themselves. That is not anybody's concept of wildlife nor of a sanctuary. I think that some of our wildlife wardens have been to Africa and seen how beautifully this is managed there and how natural the surroundings are. There the animals come first, not the visitors, no matter how important the visitor is. You are not allowed to make noise—there are so many rules, not for animals, but for the human beings. I think we will have to adopt some of them here.

There are good scientific reasons for taking special steps to preserve wildlife. Of course, it has to be managed properly so that no particular species overruns another because that would create the same sort of problem which man has created by overrunning his forests. It is distressing that many people still treat the wildlife wing in a perfunctory manner. All posts where important work has to be done relating to working plans on wildlife are not filled up by highly motivated officers with good experience on the subject. There is too high a turnover of personnel in these jobs. The Indian Board for Wildlife has repeatedly drawn my attention to this. As I said earlier, changes have to come from a heartfelt recognition of the importance of the subject. Many State Boards for Wildlife have not met at all. If State Forest Ministers and senior officers of the forest departments devote time to wildlife management only on symbolic occasions like the Wildlife Week, we cannot ensure survival of important species. Our country has a rich variety of flora and fauna, the like of which may not be found in many places. We should be proud of this heritage and try to preserve it. Doubts have been expressed about the preservation of species like crocodiles, elephants, tigers, etc., which sometimes overrun their territory and are considered inimical to human population. It is well known that when these or any other animals are properly managed, they do not pose any threat to human life, and in a way they ensure the survival of the forests themselves. I would like to suggest that in these matters you should be guided by scientific assessment rather than lay beliefs.

It would take another two-and-a-half years for forests to be pulled out of the Ministry of Agriculture and for the creation of a Ministry of Environment and Forests but discussions on it had started. One rather interesting fact is the impact of Africa on Indira Gandhi. She seems to have been vastly impressed with the rules that governed African wildlife. She always wanted to adapt some of them to India. Alas, she did not succeed. The system is immune to taking on board good and innovative ideas.

In 1982 she piloted the first amendment to the Wildlife Protection Act, 1972, in order to further strengthen it, by further empowering chief wildlife wardens. In 1983 she gave her full support to the creation of the Wildlife Institute of India which started its first operations in that year.

Before she was assassinated she stated in a message for a book:

Our forests are shrinking, and many species are endangered by growing towns and cultivation, not to speak of human greed. This is an irreplaceable loss for the world. Now we must look ahead. There is still hope. We have saved the tiger, the lion, the rhinoceros and the bustard. Across the country larger numbers of people are making it their business to come to the rescue of animals.

With Indira Gandhi's assassination in 1984, India's forests and wildlife lost their greatest saviour and spokesperson. In any reckoning of the accounts of Indira Gandhi's reign, a very big entry on the credit side must surely be her work for the forests and wildlife of India.

Indira Gandhi's long stint in power stopped the complete wipe-out of forests and wildlife in the nick of time. The laws or amendments to laws that were made in her time were like checks and balances to the total anarchy that followed. These laws have been the only consistent factor providing safety to Indian forests in the decades that followed. Every political party and all governments have had to follow them. Many have tried to tinker with them and dilute them but in the absence of political will, judicial will has luckily come to the fore to interpret them correctly and keep the forests protected. The Indira Gandhi era left a solid base for future leaders to build on. However, only her son tried to strengthen the environmental laws of the country when he was Prime Minister by bringing in the The Environment Protection Act 1986 and amending the Forest Conservation Act in 1988. After his party lost the election in 1989, little has happened except for some controversial amendments to the Wildlife Protection Act in 1991. In fact much has been diluted administratively and through government orders.

We should be very clear about one thing. If we have any ecological security left as a nation it is because of Indira Gandhi. Her vision surpassed that of all the conservationists around her. It is because of this vision that in the present century we have something left to fight for. In the 1960s Indira Gandhi steered India on a course that saved the forests and wildlife of the country for at least another fifty years.

When Indira Gandhi was assassinated she left many environmental measures in the pipeline. Probably the most important was the creation of a new Ministry of Environment and Forests out of the Department of Environment. There was also, just before she died, much discussion on the legislation of an Environment Protection Act that could ensure control on industrial pollution and minimize the negative impacts of haphazard development.

A fresh general election at the end of 1984 resulted in Rajiv Gandhi coming to power. One of the first events of his prime ministership was the creation of the new Ministry of Environment and Forests which had two departments: one for environment and another for forests and wildlife. This was a most sensible decision but sadly, in April 1985, a series of administrative adjustments merged both departments into one. In my opinion, this was a fatal administrative mistake. As the years went by environmental issues became so time consuming that in the process forests and wildlife got relegated to the background. This 'one-department' concept has been a disaster. It is only after the 17 March 2005 meeting of the National Board of Wildlife (NBWL) that Prime Minister Manmohan Singh has agreed to address this issue.

Unlike his mother, Rajiv Gandhi's focus was environmental issues. His concerns were about environment and development—about climate change and pollution. There was much less directly addressing wildlife and forests. Rajiv was much more sympathetic than his mother towards the rights of tribal and forest communities over forests. He wanted to follow the process of 'humane conservation.' There was an innocence and lack of cynicism about him. He had great belief in some of his own government schemes like the Ganga Action Plan which he thought would clean the Ganga by the year 1989. It never did.

As far as forests and wildlife are concerned, Rajiv was not in his mother's league. His focus was environment and Anil Agarwal of the Centre of Science and Environment, whose speciality was urban and industrial environment, advised him on green concerns. But forests and wildlife were truly Indira Gandhi's domain.

It is my view that by 1987–8 Indira Gandhi's policy of 'protection' of wildlife and forests was giving way, under Rajiv, to more environment-focused concepts and the approach of involving tribal and local communities in managing forests, be it through joint forest management techniques or something else. This was, however, easier said than done and the 1990s would reveal how some of the most damaging initiatives got disguised and clothed in tribal 'apparel'. Such approaches only led to the creation of mafias in villages around forests and countless armchair environmentalists fuelled the process. A great tragedy!

Rajiv Gandhi was assassinated in 1991. Even though during 1984–9, the years of his prime ministership, he was nowhere near as focused as his mother on issues concerning forests and wildlife, he did manage to sustain an interest and concern in green issues, especially concerning the environment. If Indira Gandhi was responsible for the base on which all our forest and wildlife policies stand then Rajiv Gandhi was responsible for the base on which all our environmental policies stand. Between them they were responsible for creating laws and policies for the protection of India's natural resources and environment. Every political party even today is forced to follow these policies.

The Second Crisis
The end of a century 1990–2002

L et us now look at the period 1991–2000 which started with Narasimha Rao taking over as Prime Minister after Rajiv Gandhi's assassination. He was a staunch supporter of the Gandhi family. But he was totally unconcerned with green issues and the beginning of the decade signalled the end of the Gandhi era and their protection of the forests of India. Rao's tenure was the beginning of the end for India's forests. I doubt if Rao even realized this. I saw this era very closely since at this time I got sucked into the Ministry of Environment and Forests and all the numerous committees that surround it. This is my story of the last decade of the twentieth century.

By late 1989 the champions of both forests and wildlife—the Gandhis—had all but vanished from India's political scene. I was following tigers in Ranthambhore National Park, one of the smallest of the Project Tiger Reserves that were set up in 1973. I had been doing that and little else since 1975. And it was clear to me that at the end of the 1980s Ranthambhore had become one of the great success stories in tiger conservation. Tigers literally spilled out of everywhere. I had, in the decade of the 1980s, written three books about wild tigers. Looking back, these were the glorious years of Indian wildlife—years in which the impact of Indira Gandhi's policies and concerns could be felt in the field.

In fact, sometimes when I visit Ranthambhore today it appears that the 1980s were another and better world, a time gone by and difficult even to explain to someone who has not experienced it; this is so at least for the forests of India. It was a time when I could see sixteen different tigers in one day. It was in 1988–9 that I got down to the hard work of setting up an NGO that tried to involve local communities in the protection of the park. I idealistically, and with the benefit of hindsight, naively believed that the future lay in this work. Many still believe that this is the way forward. I am not so sure any more.

Narasimha Rao's tenure as Prime Minister in 1991 started with a clear focus on changing the economic policy to usher in India's new free market economy and 'green' concerns were one of the victims of this policy. In a way, Rao was only pushing ahead. Rajiv Gandhi's economic agenda. Rajiv had laid the foundation in the late 1980s to liberalize India's economic policies. But unlike Rajiv, Rao had no green concerns and therefore the new economic policy took no account of the impact of various measures on India's forests. Had Indira Gandhi's laws and regulations of the 1970s and 1980s not already been operational, the consequences of an unchecked liberalization would have been catastrophic. As it is in 1991 one of the worst-ever amendments to the Wildlife Protection Act took place. The 1991 amendment made it much more complex to notify protected areas and was totally counterproductive for our forests and wildlife.

'Money' and consumerism could after 1991 be unashamedly pursued in India. They were the new Gods and there were no checks on greed. In Ranthambhore there were endless rumours of poaching. Few wanted to believe them, but in 1992 the arrest of a poacher led to revelations from which it was clear that from late 1990 poaching gangs had wiped out 15–20 tigers and hundreds of other animals. It was a similar story right across India. In the pursuit of quick money, nothing was sacred and inviolate any more. The plunder of India's forests was in full swing. Laws or no laws, there was no commitment of the Prime Minister to forests and the state governments were permitting all sorts of activities in the forests that were unfriendly to its denizens, to bring in money. By 1992, hopelessness pervaded the ranks of wildlife activists and few believed that tigers would survive the turn of the century or that any decent tracts of forest would remain intact. Many lamented the passing of the Gandhis. It was all about greed now, and the corporate world entered forests with a vengeance, be it for mining, river valley projects, or anything that could further their exploitative agenda.

From 1992, I, quite inadvertently, got sucked into the Ministry of Environment and Forests and ended up working really closely with the then minister, Kamal Nath. Ranthambhore's poaching crisis had blown up and forced me to enter the arena of government and decision-making and all the endless committees that go with it. A friend of my father's had taken me to see the minister and soon after that the ministry literally gobbled me up. From the steering committee of Project Tiger to the Indian Board for Wildlife to the Tiger Crisis Cell, to the expert committee on River Valley Projects, to international conferences on the tiger, I was doing hundreds of things in an eighteen-hour working day. It was crisis time and much like being engaged in battle. I did not even have time to think where it would all lead to. Without the Gandhis we were totally dependent on the political will and power of the Minister of Environment and Forests who had made some of us NGOs all-powerful in the ministry. And 1992–3 were tough years. The large-scale seizures of skins and bones of tigers made headlines across the world and the mechanisms of government were ineffectual to counter this menace. We, as a bunch of conservationists, ran around like headless chickens. We thought that we were making a difference. Looking back I doubt if we did.

I remember the enormous pressure created after the exposé of the Ranthambhore poaching incident in the media. We fuelled the pressure to force decisions. Finally a meeting with the then Chief Minister of Rajasthan was arranged for me. He flew me to Jaipur in his little plane. It was during the monsoons, and it was a frightening experience. When we finally arrived in Jaipur, I was asked to acquaint a group of bureaucrats with the realities of the situation. I did so in the Chief Minister's office. Soon after I was asked to go to Ranthambhore and set in motion some correctives. But it was all an eyewash aimed at neutralizing my critique. For a while, the Chief Minister probably succeeded in this objective. But the crisis was bigger than all of us and the impotent institutions that existed. Geoffery C. Ward provides a picture of these years.[1] The following extracts show the uncanny similarities of the causes, reactions, and proposed solutions with the present crisis in 2005:

In late June 1992 I received a letter and a set of newspaper clippings from Fateh [Fateh Singh Rathore]. Several poachers had been arrested at Ranthambhore; they had confessed to the police that they had shot more than fifteen tigers there over the past two years. And they were not alone. Several other poaching gangs, they said, were at work in and around the park.

Rumours of tiger poaching had swirled around Ranthambhore since 1990, but the Chief Wildlife Warden of the state had dismissed them

[1]Geoffery C. Ward and Diane Raines Ward, 'Massacre' in *Tiger Wallahs: Saving the Greatest of the Great Cats*, Oxford University Press, 2002.

all as 'baseless', 'the products of vested interests' (by which he seems mostly to have meant Fateh, without a job again and noisily unhappy at what was happening to the sanctuary he still considered his). Some 31,000 tourists, more than half of them foreigners, visited the park during the winter of 1990–91, an all-time record, and a good many complained that they had seen no signs of tigers, let alone the tigers themselves. Noon—the tigress that had mastered the technique of killing in the lakes, the animal I had watched, feeding with her cubs, in the grass two years earlier—seemed suddenly to be missing. So was the magnificent tiger called the Bokhala male. So were other individual animals well known to Fateh and Valmik [Thapar] and to the guides and jeep drivers who made locating tigers their business....

The rumours persisted. During our visit to Ranthambhore that winter, the corpse of Badhiya, a forest guard who had been one of the most knowledgeable and dedicated members of the forest staff, was found sprawled along the railroad tracks outside the park. There were whispers he'd been murdered because he knew too much about poaching.

Something was very wrong. Even the Forest Department began to worry, and when the census was undertaken the following May, Valmik Thapar was asked to help conduct it. The results were devastating: he could find concrete evidence of only seventeen tigers in the park, and tentative evidence suggesting there might be three more. Again, the Chief Wildlife Warden denied everything. The census was faulty, he insisted, botched by the same amateurs he himself had asked for help.

But then came the arrests. Gopal Moghiya, a member of a traditional hunting tribe who ordinarily worked as watchman for local herdsmen, was seized by the Sawai Madhopur Police, along with the skin and bones of a freshly killed tiger he had shot....

Gopal Moghiya's confession led to the arrests of several others, including his own brother, a Muslim butcher, and four Meena herdsmen who admitted killing four tigers to protect their livestock.

Again, the Forest Department's initial instinct was to cover things up. One or two animals might have been killed, it said, but poaching on such a large scale was impossible. (Gopal Moghiya did eventually recant his confession, yet he had airily bragged of his poaching skills to several disinterested journalists before doing so.)

But the facts could not be denied: eighteen tigers and leopards were already gone from Sariska, perhaps twenty tigers missing at Ranthambhore, and reports of more poaching were filtering in from everywhere. In Uttar Pradesh, for example, where the Forest Department stubbornly insisted that Dudhwa and its adjacent forest still held one hundred and four tigers, Billy [Arjan Singh] estimated there were now no more than twenty.

Valmik did a hasty calculation of the total number of tigers thought to have been poached, based on just five years' worth of official seizures of skins and skeletons. It came to one hundred and twenty animals. And it seems reasonable to assume that several times as many more went unreported.

At that rate, the Indian tiger is surely on its way out. (So, evidently, is the Nepalese: Twenty-five tigers disappeared from the Royal Chitawan Reserve between 1988 and 1990 alone, so large a percentage of the park's resident population that it may be impossible for it ever to recover.)

Tigers have always been poached. Villagers poison them to protect themselves or their livestock, and some skin smuggling has continued despite an international ban on the trade. But compared to the twin menaces (of expanding population and dwindling habitat) poaching has been a relatively minor threat to the tiger's survival. Now that has changed. If allowed to continue at its current pace, poaching will swiftly undo whatever good Project Tiger has managed to do over the past two decades.

The immediate crisis was caused by the peculiar demands of Chinese medicine. For hundreds, perhaps thousands of years, tiger bones and other tiger by-products have played an important part in Chinese healing....

The Chinese themselves have finally run out of tigers. Wild populations that once ran into thousands have been reduced to fewer than one hundred animals and so they have begun importing tiger bones on a massive scale, ignoring the complaints of conservationists and willing to pay prices smugglers find irresistible....

The Ranthambhore scandal could not have come at a worse time for Project Tiger. The year 1993 was to be its twentieth anniversary, and a celebration was already planned at which a brand new national census figure was to be announced: 4,300 animals, almost two-and-a-half times the number there had been when the project began.

All the old problems still persisted. The hostility of local people had intensified: arsonists had recently set fires raging through the hearts of Kanha and Nagarhole, where K.M. Chinnappa, the ranger responsible for defending it for so long, had been forced to flee for his life. And there was already one disturbing new problem, a sad side effect of the national struggle with sectional and ethnic separatists that threatens to tear apart the Indian Union. Armed militants of one kind or another had taken shelter in seven of the nineteen reserves, intimidating forest staff, slaughtering animals for fun or food or profit, making a mockery of the parks' supposed inviolability.

Now, massive poaching has been added to that already bleak mix. A three-day International Symposium on the Tiger was to be held in New Delhi in February 1993. Nearly two hundred and fifty delegates were coming from every region of India and many parts of the world, and the government's more strident critics predicted little more than a desperate exercise in defensiveness.

They were wrong. The new all-India census figures of 4,300 was bravely announced, though almost no one believed it; 3,000 tigers seems a far more realistic figure, according to most of those with whom I spoke, and even that may now be far too high. And the delegates were made to sit through an appallingly self-congratulatory film: 'Foster cover is increasing' the narrator intoned. 'The tiger reigns supreme'; and in the reserves, 'all is well'.

Everyone in the hall already knew that all was anything but well, and for the first time in my experience Indian government officials were willing to say so in front of one another and in public. The Forest Secretary, R. Rajamani, set the tone of candour: 'The anniversary conference,' he said, 'should be an occasion for introspection, not celebration.'

For three full days, the tiger's champions talked and argued and agreed to disagree....

Everyone seemed to agree that a much greater effort had to be made to involve local people in the creation and management of parks. The poaching crisis would never have occurred had local people felt they had any stake in the tiger's survival. And both Central and state government seemed serious about undertaking ambitious eco-development projects—electricity, water, alternative forms of fuel—to provide benefits at last to the people who live in and around the parks. Some plans seemed so ambitious, in fact, that Ullas Karanth gently pointed out that the government already had access to 96 per cent of the country on which to experiment with economic uplift, and might do better to leave alone the mere 4 per cent left over for wildlife while one field director suggested that before government came to the aid of the herdsmen he'd been trying to keep out of his park, he hoped it would at least provide trousers for his forest guards.

There was also a good deal of what seemed to me to be very romantic talk about the importance of maintaining intact the ancient 'sustainable lifestyles' of the tribal peoples who live in and around the besieged reserves. I couldn't help but remember the gujjars whose herds I'd seen avidly eating up what was left of Rajaji National Park. Their lifestyle was ancient all right, but it was no longer remotely 'sustainable'; if Rajaji is to survive, some creative alternative will have to be found for them.

If it is not found, the forest will vanish, and so will they. And though every park is unique, it is hard for me to see how the same won't ultimately be true for most if not all of the people now living within India's reserves.

From 1992 to 2000 I worked as hard as humanly possible. I visited, on various missions, more than thirty protected areas in India, wrote 286 notes, papers, and interventions to the different ministers that came, and to one of the Prime Ministers I had known from my childhood. I even handed the Prime Minister 320 signatures of Members of Parliament for radical change in policy to save the tiger and forests. Of course, Parliament dissolved a month later and little happened. But I left no stone unturned. In between government missions, committees, and endless parleys with ministers, I directed the NGO I had founded, Ranthambhore Foundation, and completed three more books and over a dozen films for the BBC as a presenter and a voice, and life was as full as it could be. I also wrote scores of articles. I believed somewhere that information would aid effective conservation. So books, films, articles, and the media were vital to inform and create both public and political will. I thus carried on much like a steam engine that never runs out of steam. But success in the interventions I made remained elusive.

Inadvertently I learnt a great deal about the ills that afflict the system—enough to stun me. On the trail of the tiger I learnt about the scams, the dirt, and the politics that afflict India. It was like living a nightmare. My peace was shattered. Ministers came and went. The horrors continued. The tiger walks the richest part of India. Everyone wanted a piece of it in the form of mines, minerals, minor forest produce, timber, large river valley projects. And land was in short supply and the land mafia had become expert at using forest communities to encroach on forest land that years later would be legalized in the so-called interests of the 'poor'.

Missions for the Ministry of Environment and Forests were always full of surprises. I remember once going to Tadoba Tiger Reserve and driving around with the field director and discussing the menace of poaching when suddenly six dogs and two men came running out of the bush and pounced on what we discovered was a wild boar. It was the first time on inspection I had witnessed a hunt in progress. On another occasion I was on an inspection of Ranthambhore with the Inspector General of Forests from the Ministry of Environment and Forests. We both had woken up early and therefore decided to drive around the park without all the encumbering official paraphernalia. Twenty minutes later we were confronted with hundreds of cows and buffalos and a threatening bunch of graziers that abused and tried to intimidate us. The IG was shocked—it was a moment of sad mismanagement in Ranthambhore's history. On another occasion, on an inspection of Nagarahole, somebody whispered in my ear that there was a big illegal timber camp operating in the heart of the National Park. We went to the site and saw the horrific remnants of the slaughter of trees that man does so well. A sawmill-like situation had been created in the forest and the local forest officers had preferred not to inform us.

On another occasion, while on an inspection of both an irrigation project and some mines around Madhav National Park in Shivpuri, I realized, looking at the map, that something was wrong. I asked a young forest officer near me about the location of a dam. He whispered, 'Yes, it is inside the national park.' Enquiries were ordered on my return but there were violations of laws everywhere. At the end of the 1990s, the murder of nature by open flouting of norms was rampant. None of the big projects followed their mandatory conditions. They violated the

Environment Protection Act of 1986 and the Forest Conservation Act of 1980. There was little will to enforce. Chief Ministers did not fear the Prime Minister as in Indira Gandhi's time. The state governments were major culprits, tinkering with the laws and dismantling the systems that existed. In fact, in a letter dated June 2001, Sonia Gandhi had to ask her party's Chief Ministers not to 'tinker' with the laws that Indira Gandhi had made. Such was the state of affairs! The makers of the law had become the breakers of the law. In the 1990s dozens of protected areas had been denotified without following the due course of law. My missions to the field gave me a lot of insight on 'non-governance' of forests but at the same time there were wonderful encounters with wildlife. There were countless days and nights spent with an array of forest officers and staff that were a great learning experience in the ways and language of forest India. It brought me the wisdom to never act in haste but always strategically. I had also realized by the end of the century that in 1992 I had known nothing about the functioning of the system. Today some of my colleagues deem me an expert. It is an expertise I would, on the whole, rather do without because it has made me aware of the terrible loopholes in the system and shattered my peace. Indira Gandhi's absence was being felt desperately by the denizens of India's forests. Out of the 1,800 odd ministers at the centre and in the states there were few that cared or inspired decision-making. Probably Maneka Gandhi, Sanjay Gandhi's wife and Indira Gandhi's daughter-in-law, was one such. She was the only one in the 1990s who cared enough to 'get things done' on the environmental front. How I wished her passion was wild tigers and not domestic animals. Moreover, sadly, Prime Minister Vajpayee never gave her the ministry of her choice and she was moved to several different portfolios but not the Ministry of Environment and Forests which was her great desire. He was probably worried that the corporate world would frown at such a move. The big business interests of India were, in the 1990s, at their exploitative best, taking what they could from the forests without putting anything back. They were backed by the new economic policies of the decade. They took every short cut they could find and fully exploited the loopholes in the laws. In fact, the biggest players sank vast oil pipelines into one of the very few marine national parks in India against all the laws that govern our national parks—but with total support from some of our critical functionaries of the law. The Chief Wildlife Warden in this case had stated that the land along the proposed pipelines was degraded and in fact such pipelines would benefit the marine area and therefore a 'no objection' certificate was provided. Such was the hopeless state of affairs that we tried to work in at the turn of the century.

If you were too critical of what was happening you ended up being warned off. I had over the years fought endless battles with the system and some individuals in the government resented my 'power'. They harassed me repeatedly in many ways—through trying to have an inquiry instituted into the NGO I had founded; by accusing me of being, of all things, a poacher who should be investigated by one of their agencies (this two-page note would be used against me whenever I was perceived to have got too close to the powers that be, as was done in 2005 to discredit me with the Prime Minister); and even through the scare of a midnight arrest. On the last occasion I was really frightened. It was later found that a local judicial official had intentionally or otherwise made a 'clerical error'. Luckily none of their efforts succeeded. If you make enemies while fighting for what is just and right you also make friends and the experience of the 1990s was an abject lesson in how to find a path through the complex maze of official 'conservation'. I learnt the hard way that when you battle, you must watch your back and protect it; otherwise you get knifed.

There was much wheeling and dealing in the politics of conservation. I have kept a record of it but most of it for the moment must remain unwritten and off the record. Suffice it to say that ideas, committees, strategies, cells, interventions, etc. travelled through a series of ministers representing different political parties in our efforts to find correctives to the problems of both forests and wildlife. Everything at our command was used—every contact tapped. We were a group of four or five and without a person like Indira Gandhi at the top, our efforts were geared towards strengthening the conservation lobby. There was no other choice. But it changed us, it certainly changed me. It killed my innocent joy in wildlife and made me manipulative and calculating, trying to match my wits against a system that is all-powerful. We learnt the hard way that for the government the best way to neutralize criticism was to create committees, with our small group either participating or helping in the creation of more than thirty such committees, cells, forums, and such like in those years between 1992 and 2000! What a waste of time it was! But it took us some years to learn this. In the mid 1990s I believed that a combination of protection infrastructure and interventions of local NGOs with community conservation could make a difference. Rather than raise money for the NGO that I then headed, I was directly responsible for recommending protection infrastructure to Sitanadi and Udanti Sanctuaries in Chhattisgarh, Ranthambhore and Sariska in Rajasthan, Satpura, Bori, Panna in Madhya Pradesh, Kaziranga in Assam, and NGO activity in West Bengal, Maharashtra, Karnataka, and Rajasthan. And all this to the tune of nearly Rs 1 crore. Later I realized that much of this was pointless till we got better governance and reform of the institutions responsible.

Life and work are about triumphs and failures. But in this
line of work there are more failures. If I was able to collect 320
signatures of Members of Parliament to a petition to save wild
tigers and hand them to then Prime Minister, I.K. Gujral,
Parliament dissolved within months of handing over those
signatures. I.K. Gujral was a great friend of my father and I had
known him since I was a boy. From 1989 the Indian Board for
Wildlife had met only once—in 1997—chaired by Deve Gowda,
who had sadly dozed through much of the meeting, in which
I had participated as a member of the Board. In 1998, I thought
that we could create new policy in the forest and wildlife sector
and managed to persuade Prime Minister I.K. Gujral to convene
a meeting. I briefed him a bit and he asked me to spend thirty
minutes with him before the meeting commenced for a more
detailed briefing. However a 'brief' two minutes while he walked
from the car up to the meeting room is all I got before we entered
the meeting room. And then to my shock I.K. Gujral also dozed
through parts of the meeting! I had watched two consecutive
Prime Ministers of India nap through meetings of what was the
most important policy-making body for forests and wildlife,
what I considered critical meetings. I had missed my moment
and I.K. Gujral, with all his good intentions, had barely one
year in office before the politics of the time forced a change in
government.

I tried everything in the late 1990s and another of my father's
old friends, Jaswant Singh, Finance Minister in the NDA
government, received a volley of letters from me about reform
and governance and what was needed in the forest sector. But
my efforts were largely to no avail. I was more and more
disillusioned with the state of affairs. Prime ministers and
cabinets came and went and with everyone endlessly shifting
around the issues of forests and wildlife which were nowhere on

the agenda. Governance was at its lowest ebb. This was probably why the courts were more active.

I spent much time between 1995 and 1998 attempting to activate NGO movements both in India and abroad in the interest of both forests and tigers. In that period there was great zeal for the objective and I must have managed to requisition more than sixty jeeps, trucks, and motorcycles for different areas in order to strengthen protection. There was lots of excitement, lots of meetings, and a belief that a bunch of concerned citizens could trigger effective action. Those were hectic years but I was to realize later that such efforts are not very fruitful; they only minimize damage, if you are lucky. One good thing that did come out of the hectic activity of the 1990s was the realization that information is the spearhead of effective action. This came in the form of a fifty-page newsletter with detailed information on the state of the tiger that was transmitted to over 1,000 people every four months. I think this was useful. In a way it minimized damage. That is why it continues to come out. But at this time I realized that those that eventually make a difference are forest officials committed to the job. These handful of government officials are actually in the field with the power to act, and, if supported, can deliver magical results. Working closely with good committed officials can do wonders for both forests and wildlife. NGOs in India cannot on their own make a difference. They can make a hue and cry about a crisis and collect funds but without committed forest officers, they achieve little. I saw the mushrooming of NGOs but with little achieved; money was wasted and few created strategies that were practical and effective. That was the tragedy of NGOs as we entered the twenty-first century.

Ultimately, a real difference can only be made if certain vital questions regarding the service conditions of forest officers are addressed: How do you develop a small band of forest officers as a committed corps? How do you prevent their unnecessary transfers? How do you create political will for them and the areas they administer? How do you build the infrastructures they want? If some answers can be found to them, we would be a few steps closer to effective action.

We limped into a new century. Some extracts from a piece I wrote about the end of a century and the beginning of another reflect the sombre mood of the times.[2]

I thought I would end this century feasting on the extraordinary recovery of the wild tigers of Ranthambhore Tiger Reserve in the state of Rajasthan....

But I was rudely awakened on 19 December 1999 to the grim horrors of what is happening to the wilderness when purely by accident the sales tax inspectors in Ghaziabad, a small town in north India intercepted a truck and found, instead of illegal garments, fifty leopard skins, three tiger skins, and a handful of other skins... We remained in shock for a couple of days. After all it was probably the second largest seizure of big cat skins since independence and brought home the fact that our previous wilderness was vanishing....

I was with the Inspector General of Forests and as we stepped out of the car and walked a few yards around a corner, there in front of us were laid out the skins of so many dead leopards that the first sight of it took the breath away and stunned all of us into silence. In a numb state we moved looking slowly at what must be only the tip of an iceberg in the ongoing massacre of India's wildlife—how many thousands of mornings I have waited even for the faintest sign of a leopard in India's forest! I have craved to see even a glimpse of them. I have probably seen about twenty-eight leopards over the last twenty-five years and here I was surrounded by fifty dead ones....

[2]Valmik Thapar, 'The Big Cat Massacre', in Valmik Thapar, ed., *Saving Wild Tigers: 1900–2000—Essential Writings*, 2001.

My vision of the end of the century had been ripped apart, torn in pieces; it was covered in blood. There was no doubt that hundreds of leopards and tigers were being decimated by the coordinated working of poaching gangs right across India....

I did not realize that the beginning of the twenty-first century would get even worse. On 12 January 2000, a day I will never forget, acting on a tip that must have resulted from the 19 December seizure, a police party with wildlife inspectors raided three premises in Khaga, Fatehpur, in the north Indian state of Uttar Pradesh, and seized seventy leopard skins, four tiger skins, 221 blackbuck skins, 18,000 leopard claws, 132 tiger claws. It appears that both seizures are linked. The three premises were illegal factories that were tanning and curing skins. By 15 January, from around these premises more than 185 kg of tiger and leopard bones were recovered, revealing the horrifying state of affairs. Wildlife governance was in a complete state of collapse and clearly 'operation wipe-out' was on. As if it was not enough, by May two more seizures in Haldwani resulted in a recovery of eighty more leopard skins and endless other skins....

We are already losing at least 10,000 sq. km of dense forest each year to timber mafias and so-called developers. We believe that at least twelve billion dollars worth of forest is exploited from India's natural treasury each year, and I am convinced that hundreds of tigers and leopards are trapped, poisoned, and poached so that their skins, claws, and other derivatives feed the international market. The skin market across the world is booming with demand and the planet is losing the best of its natural treasure. This is not just India's failure. We have failed globally. Much of the responsibility must fall on our international organizations, both inter-governmental and non-governmental....

I have followed the trail of the tiger for twenty five years and it has led me over the richest part of India—Forest India. In this forest land there is a vast amount of timber, marble, gems, manganese, iron ore, bauxite, and so many minerals that everyone's mouth waters. Minor forest produce abounds and everyone wants a bit of the land. Big dams, infrastructural projects, and land mafias want their piece too. It is India's natural treasury and this natural wealth is under so much pressure that its very survival is threatened.

This is 20 per cent of India, and the most neglected sector of governance, probably by the explicit preference of our ignorant or mischievous political leadership. In this country we do not create mechanisms for protection but we excel at creating mechanisms for exploitation. We must work out ways to stop it and put public pressure on our political leadership to restructure existing mechanisms and focus on real issues. For instance, take the federal arm involved with saving tigers in the Ministry of Environment and Forests: 95 per cent of its time, effort, and money are spent on clearing public and private sector projects and dealing with city pollution. The 20 per cent of India which is Forest India has been allocated a tiny insignificant 'wing' to deal with its issues. Can you imagine the richest part of India having only a 'wildlife wing'? The richest part of India never has a decent allocation of money from the Planning Commission. The richest part of India has no ministry to protect it....

How do you save tigers in the twenty-first century? We must start from scratch and restructure all our mechanisms for wildlife and forest administration. To start with we need:

(a) A new federal ministry for the protection of forests and wildlife;
(b) A review of the Indian Forest Service for encouraging specialization in the protection of biological resources;
(c) A national armed force for the forest officer, on call like a Forest Police Force, to minimize the enormous damage to our natural treasury;
(d) Rapid financial mechanisms to disburse money from the federal structure to the field for better management;

(e) A declaration of this sector as *essential* so that the huge vacancies that plague forest staff are filled and the gates to looting are closed; and

(f) Disbanding Project Tiger. The time has come in the twenty-first century to disband Project Tiger that over the decades has become only a disburser of money and has no power to govern. Instead, under this new ministry a 'Tiger Protection Authority of India' must be created that is empowered under the law to appoint, recruit, transfer, and assess all officers in tiger reserves from the rank of ranger upwards. This 'Authority' must also be able to disburse money directly to the field and have the final say in the management of all our twenty-seven Project Tiger Reserves.

We entered a new century but little changed—an endless stream of meetings and little field impact. It was clear that little of what we had fought for was ever going to see the light of day. Few wanted to change and reform the system of governance. In January 2002 Prime Minister Atal Behari Vajpayee chaired a rare meeting of the Indian Board for Wildlife. It was a good meeting. I had worked closely with the ministry for it. We had an excellent secretary in the ministry at this point and it was a pleasure working with him. Our minister was also an efficient and no-nonsense person. What probably tipped the scales in our favour was that a bunch of children had a couple of days earlier gone to meet the Prime Minister and asked him to save the tiger. I was also present and I watched him squirm. He did not know the answers to the children's questions. It must have been an embarrassing experience and probably led to the positive energy in the subsequent meeting. Vajpayee promised to declare forests a priority sector and announced a series of other exciting interventions. I was able to bring up at this meeting the urgent need for a separate ministry. I did not realize then that when the NBWL was reconstituted, I would be dropped from it as would other experts for having spoken out too forcefully against a string of projects in North-Eastern India. It would be Dr Manmohan Singh who would reinstate me in 2004 in the middle of the tenure of this board in what I consider was a most unexpected move. Again, we concluded the meeting in an optimistic mood, but till this book went to press only a Forest Commission had been set up under the chairmanship of a dynamic former Chief Justice of the Supreme Court. Our biggest problem of the last decade had been follow-up. There was lots of rhetoric, paperwork, promises, recommendations, and noise but action at field level was missing. Follow-ups were dismal. Persistent political will was absent and the resultant frustration enormous.

One of the big stories of these crisis years is the functioning of one of the largest NGOs in the sector. In a way, as the crisis became more severe it functioned least effectively. The NGO was basically run by one of the larger corporate families in India and in 2001 I was asked to join the board of trustees. This process was accompanied by top-level changes in this organization since all its chapters across the world were complaining about its inefficiency. I thought that things would change for the better but the discussions held with me over lunch by the chairman and some of the trustees surprised me. This was before I got a formal invitation to join. It was like a businessman's club, clueless about conservation but trying to preach to me. I was asked to control my criticism of the government since I would now be a 'prestigious' trustee of a large organization. I realized that the chairman had no spunk and lived in fear of the system. But the letter sent me was even funnier:

The Trustees would expect you to work together and speak in one voice on all joint and common endeavours.... [The organization] cannot be made into a forum for individuals to express their own personal views which may be in divergence with the view of [the majority].... Any public statement made by a Trustee must essentially express the view of...the majority of Trustees.

I do hope that you will accept our invitation bearing in mind that our strength arises from our common endeavour and unanimity on issues of national and international importance.

I replied: 'I hope that my public statements not only touch the heart and soul of conservation and naturally therefore the views of...but also inspire the team...in our common endeavour to protect and save the natural world.'

Finally, I joined, but lasted only a few weeks since the then CEO, a lady to whom I had given my support for the last few months, was so rude that after a telephone conversation I decided that it was not for me. A year later, in 2002, in response to a letter from her asking me about what the organization should do, I replied: 'All those without experience in conservation on the Board of Trustees and herself included should step down.' I was also elected to be a part of the executive committee of the Bombay Natural History Society yet another large NGO but again in less than a year I have resigned. There is too much politics in big organizations and the intrigue is counter-productive to effective conservation.

By 2002, the crisis was snowballing. What provided some relief in the absence of political will was judicial will and especially that of the Supreme Court of India. In the absence of good governance in the forest sector, it stepped in with a series of radical decisions to save India's forests. In fact, Case No. 202 as it is known would go down in the history of the country as a case that gave the forests of India, at a most critical juncture, some 'breathing space'. While the courts, at least the Supreme Court of India, moved in the interest of forests and wildlife, many forest ministers of state governments showed total insensitivity to the problems at hand. Rajasthan and

Karnataka during the past few years had forest ministers who lacked any commitment to the natural heritage of the country. In Rajasthan a bunch of good and honest forest officers faced a lot of harassment. Many false inquiries were instituted against the Director of Ranthambore. Most of my efforts in 2001–2 were directed towards trying to keep the damage to good individuals within the forest service and some of the institutions down to a minimum. An endless round of meetings with politicians and bureaucrats ensued.

My friend Ullas Karanth in Karnataka, known for his remarkable scientific work on tigers, had all his permissions for research withdrawn. In the early 1990s his research on tigers had been stopped, now ten years later his research permissions had been withdrawn. In the 1990s he had been accused of killing tigers. The fact is that the government and especially some forest officers hate the truth. Forest researchers have always been hounded in independent India. This is true from the time of George Schaller's publication of his research in 1964,[3] which caused him to be black-listed in the country which he could only revisit twenty years later. In the late 1970s a Harvard University study on the *langurs* of Ranthambhore was given short shrift with questions being asked in Parliament about the researchers being allowed to take blood samples of the Gods! Any attempt to confront the system and present unpalatable facts has always led to harassment and persecution in this country. And then of course there are the whims of ministers and the disasters they trigger! As I write this there is a big male tiger in Nagarhole walking around with a foot trap on its front paw, with a few days to live, and there must be many more like him all over India. And who is to blame? Ignorant politicians, forest ministers who cannot see beyond their noses, and key bureaucrats who could not care less are to blame. Controversies, violations of the law, scams, and maladministration

[3]Schaller, *The Deer and the Tiger*.

have neutralized field action, integrity, and commitment. Our academic institutions that teach wildlife have become commercialized. The institutions that govern forests and wildlife at both the centre and in the states are becoming steadily more ineffectual and apathetic. There are still a few honest and tough officers who have the courage to fight both those who break the laws as well as the system itself. Forest tracts that have done well in the last decade have done so because such men survive and ensure correct postings. This is vital. Some of the best conservation work, as far as I am concerned, was done by individuals who quietly and invisibly ensured that good people were posted to the right jobs, not by 'grand' projects or donor-led initiatives. And this quiet work is still vital—the right man in the right place at the right time. The NGO movement in India has failed in the last years to deal with the issues in conservation. Most of them have got richer with funds as the crisis has ballooned but few have had the wisdom to do the right thing at the right time. The apathy of government and the apathy of the NGOs have gone hand in hand. If they do not have any understanding of the crisis, the role of NGOs can be counterproductive and I think that this has happened in India.

A RAY OF LIGHT

In all this mess the Supreme Court provided a ray of hope. In June 2002 it came to the aid of India's forests by creating a Central Empowered Committee (CEC): I was also on it. I had always hoped for something like this where a small group of people or even an individual could be empowered by the Supreme Court of India to resolve some of the all-encompassing problems. Looking back, it was clear that from 1996 when the governance of our forests was at its lowest ebb, the Supreme Court had played a vital role in protecting the nation's natural treasures.

Two writ petitions had triggered Supreme Court Case No. 202 of 1995 and Case No. 171 of 1996. The first dealt with deforestation in the Nilgriris and the second with deforestation in Jammu and Kashmir. During these two hearings the Supreme Court realized that deforestation was a critical national problem and notices were issued to all the states. In the last six years at least 150 interim orders have been passed, beginning with the well-known order of 1996 wherein forests were redefined to plug any loopholes in the law that permitted felling of trees or indulging in other exploitative activities. Felling was stopped throughout India except in accordance with a working plan approved by the central government, that is the Ministry of Environment and Forests. The Court was empowering the ministry to act in the absence of political will. All non-forest activities on forest land such as mining, sawmills, and wood-based industries were stopped pending approval of the central government and clearance under the Forest Conservation Act. The felling of trees was totally banned in the tropical evergreen forest in the Tirap and Changlang areas of Arunachal Pradesh. All sawmills 100 km on either side of the border between Assam and Arunachal Pradesh were ordered to shut down. The movement of timber from the north-eastern states was also stopped. In subsequent orders the removal of trees and grasses from national parks and sanctuaries was banned. The definition of forest land covered all wildlife habitats of the country, be they private or protected. The Supreme Court had done a remarkable job. I have to confess that at the time I was ignorant of the kind of forceful orders that were emanating from the Supreme Court. It was these orders that saved the wilderness of India in the last decade when political will was so invisible.

Though the Ministry had a large role now because of the court orders, few of us believed that it could play its part in enforcing all this. Did it have people who had the courage to act? In 2002, the Court thus created the Central Empowered Committee to ensure that there was compliance by all parties with its orders, and it empowered the Committee to act much like a court.

At the time, the Committee gave me hope when I was despairing about the state of both forests and tigers in India. I wrote a piece about this in September 2002. I reproduce extracts here:[4]

It is the eve of the thirtieth anniversary of Project Tiger. When Project Tiger started in 1973 the population of India was about 780 million; today it is nearly 1.1 billion. From nine tiger reserves in 1973 it has come to twenty-nine in 2002. When Project Tiger began there were an estimated 1,800 wild tigers. I believe today nearly thirty years later there are about the same number alive—maybe a few hundred more. So is it success or failure? This is the really difficult question that faces us. In 1992 when poaching scandals swept across India I did not believe the tiger would survive the turn of the century. It did. So at some level the 'tigers' present state is a sign of success.

Let us quickly glance across to where these 1,800–2,000 tigers live:

1. I think, one of the best populations of wild tigers live off the western coast of India where the forests of Karnataka, Kerala, and Tamil Nadu meet in the protected areas of Nagarahole, Bandipur, Madhumalai, and endless tracts of connecting reserve forests. Somewhere between 4,000 to 5,000 sq. km of superb forest could house more than 300 tigers. This is the best tiger turf in India today.

2. Another large chunk of more than 3,000 sq. km of forest, bordering the states of Madhya Pradesh and Maharashtra in central India right from the Satpura and Betul forest to Melghat, could house more than 150 tigers. This is a lovely forest but densities of both tiger and prey are on the low side.

[4]Written for *Sanctuary Magazine*, September 2002.

3. The Sundarbans right across eastern India and Bangladesh on the edge of the sea and covering nearly 5,000 sq. km of fantastic mangrove forests could have more than 300 tigers....

Single large protected areas like Kanha, Corbett, Kaziranga, and a few others and their surrounding forests could have 100 each.

And then there are some tiny gems, little islands of tigers like Ranthambhore, Panna, Bandhavgarh, and Tadoba that keep smaller tiger populations alive. At some level the overall situation is bleak. The larger populations of tigers over contiguous forests are declining. Keeping them alive is one of the biggest challenges for the government since they have to deal with complex issues across states and countries. The forests are fragmented to a much greater extent than ever before and connectivity from one to another has nearly vanished. The levels of illegal encroachments have been enormous eroding the corridors. In the last five years local extinctions of tigers have started to take place and in my opinion the population declines by 150–200 each year....

I have spent twenty-seven years of my life working with and for wild tigers. Over the last two years I have tried to assess what really works and what does not work in saving tigers. It is clear to me that whether it is non-governmental organizations or indeed the government itself spending large sums of money is not the answer. In fact money does not in itself solve the problem or save wild tigers. So what does?

1. In India one of the most vital strategies for individuals, NGOs or others to follow is to get the right man posted to the right job, be it the director of the protected area or even the ranger. The team that governs an area must be handpicked.... And, then the right teams need to be inspired by recognition and awards.

2. When and only when such a team is in place, should international NGOs come to assist, be it for any bit of infrastructure that is necessary. The Indian counterparts should only focus on ensuring that the team remains in place without its personnel being transferred....

3. Equally important is to fund and support good scientific and field research in protected areas where the team in place is good.... This is what international organizations should focus on, in terms of maximum funding.

4. Legal efforts, public interest litigations, interlocutory applications have all played a vital part to save the tigers' habitat in the last decade. The Supreme Court of India and some of the High Courts have played critical roles to keep tigers and forests alive....

5. Records, films, books, the media, good information, and its dissemination are all vital in the above strategies.... It is through an information cell that you can increase awareness and engage more and more people in the battle ahead. Good authentic information and documentation are vital for the law courts. Information and documentation centres are essential for saving wild tigers. This area has been much ignored by international organizations. Sadly they do not realize its significance.

6. Encourage individuals (not NGOs) to deal with all these issues as stated above. Individuals should firstly have a special interest in wildlife watching and commitment to the cause of the wilderness. It is these people that could make a difference and determine if tigers live or die. They need small sums of money to keep them going. It is time to provide 3–5 year grants or stipends to individuals more like a tiger fellowship or monthly wage that allows the person to focus fully on the issues at hand. They could also run and update the information centres. This will be vital to strengthen networking across the region....

For the moment nothing else should be considered by all those in and outside India who wish to save tigers. Wind up the other projects. The reason why many large international NGOs have had little impact in the last decade is that they chose the wrong things to do and both their Indian counterparts and themselves gave little time to assessing the impact of their work or evaluating their interventions—few of them turned tiger literate, be it in India or outside.

It is remarkable, but as the year 2002 draws to a close there is both hope and despair. They cling together over the fate of both forest and wildlife.

Late in 2002 the Supreme Court did the forests and wildlife of India a supreme service and a series of landmark judgements/orders were given based on the recommendation of our Committee.

As far as I am concerned, I learnt a lot about the legal system and its impact on our wilderness in 2002. I also realized that without legal intervention nothing is safe. If there is a fear in the enforcer of law or even the violator of law it comes from the courts. My work with the Central Empowered Committee has been a great learning experience. By November 2002 and after the Kudremukh judgement there were efforts to disband the committee. It is typical of India that when important work is being done someone somewhere wants to neutralize it. But we carry on.

In December 2002 just before the year ended I received the terrible news of the snaring of a radio-collared tigress in Panna, Madhya Pradesh. I knew her well and had watched her closely with my friend Dr R.S. Chundawat. Poachers had killed her and left her two seven-month-old cubs orphaned. Man has remarkable ability to destroy. As the year drew to a close, I mourned her death. Her death would, furthermore, trigger the collapse of good management in Panna. Only weeks before, a tigress had been poisoned in Ranthambhore, also leaving behind two helpless cubs. The battles for securing the wilderness of India in the twenty-first century would be enormous. The only hope for the future is a younger generation of forest officers and non-governmental interventionists finding ways to work together strategically—a well-bonded team that enforces new laws and court orders, with a spirit of togetherness.

The Third Crisis

The second crisis never really got resolved. As in the case of a malignancy, the measures taken to counter it checked its growth for a while but it then attacked with a renewed virulence, since the counter-measures had not been radical enough to begin with and had further lost their edge because of weakness of implementation and follow-up

Sadly, by 2003 the crisis rapidly accelerated. Something was desperately going wrong. The forest protection machinery was totally demoralized. Thirty per cent of posts were vacant; there had been no recruitments for sixteen years, and the average age of the forest guard was 50 plus. I think the political and administrative neglect had triggered an immense crisis. Loot and plunder of forests were rampant. Those who had the courage to confront the system were harassed. In late 2003 one of our top tiger scientists in Karnataka faced a barrage of queries by a forest officer that resulted in raids and the filing of more than sixteen criminal cases against eighteen senior conservationists, all on the grounds of 'trespass' on forest land, probably the only grounds on which it is easy to file a case that can result in the arrest. These false cases were trumped up because this group of people had dared to put up a fight to end a mining lease in a national park. For the next year these defenders of wildlife would be entirely caught up in fighting their cases. The tiger and wildlife in general would suffer enormously. In fifteen years of research, the tiger scientist had faced four serious rounds of vindictive harassment. Even his permissions to research were suspended and the CEC had to step in to redress the situation.

By 2004 another top tiger scientist working thousands of kilometres away also fell foul of the authorities since he reported mismanagement of the park. This was in Panna in central India where he had been tracking radio-collared tigers for eight years. He reported rampant poaching of tigers and was soon charged with going around at night 'without necessary permission' and his jeep was seized. This was a world-renowned wildlife biologist, married to a British lady. The rumour mill was activated to accuse her of acquiring property illegally, making films illegally, and transporting tourists for money—the stories kept coming and the press had a great time maligning the couple. Later I learnt that at least twenty other top researchers in the country have suffered similar fates for coming out with the truth. The usual method of harassment was to charge retrospective fees for their stay or work or use of elephants—all things normally given gratis by park managers. This demoralizing harassment is aimed at making those who have dedicated their entire lives to working in the field, feel so discouraged as to leave it.

THE CAMPAIGN

From about July 2004 till April 2005—till the Tiger Task Force (TTF) was declared, I launched a campaign which involved endless letters and recommendations to, and meetings with, political leaders as well as Members of Parliament. I think that I started the process with a meeting with the Prime Minister and since I had just had a new book out it was a good moment to connect about the tiger problem. In this period I met the Prime Minister thrice and must have sent him a dozen letters including one after the Sariska debacle, proposing the creation of a core group and a Tiger Task Force. I think the Sariska calamity triggered some receptivity in the political leadership. At least they were willing to listen. I met Shri Jaipal Reddy, Minister for Culture and Information and Broadcasting; Shrimati Renuka Chowdhry, Minister of Tourism; Shri Somnath Chatterjee, Speaker of the House; Shri L.K. Advani, leader of the Opposition, and also at least twice in this period Shrimati Sonia Gandhi, Chairperson of the UPA. On three different occasions I met the Chief Minister of Rajasthan, Vasundhara Raje and at least on one occasion the Chief Minister of Madhya Pradesh, Shri Babulal Gaur. All these people were sympathetic to the tiger's needs depending on their levels of awareness. While all this was going on I was also meeting Shri J.M. Scindia, and I began pushing him to start a Green Forum across party lines in Parliament for the protection of wildlife and forests. It finally did start in March and through its medium I met a series of other MPs from Rahul Gandhi, Suresh Prabhu (whom I had known earlier as Minister of Environment and Forests [MEF]), Yadvendra Singh, Natwar Singh, Dr Karan Singh, Shri Jai Panda, Shri V.P. Singh, Shri Anand Sharma, Shri Manavendra Singh, to Shri Rajiv Pratap Rudy (Shri V.P. Singh was also Chairman of the Empowered Committee of the State of Rajasthan and we had been having very constructive meetings together.)

The discussions were fresh and interesting. Dr Karan Singh, whom I had known throughout my life, was made Chairman of the group and its first mission was to express its concern to the MEF on the state of the tiger; this was followed by a meeting between Dr Karan Singh and the Prime Minister on the tiger issue. It was even invited to interact with state forest officials by the MoEF. At the second official meeting of the Forum I gave a presentation on the serious implications of the Tribal Bill after which the MPs went into a close-door meeting. They realized the gravity of the issues involved but because of the political repercussions, there seemed a reluctance to enter this debate in any public manner. Of course the media did not help in any way by centre staging Rahul Gandhi and trying to insinuate that it was he who would sabotage the Bill. They called it a *babalog* group inspired by a group of wildlife activists. In any case, irrespective of the media controversy, whatever happened helped in a way to put the Tribal Bill up for public scrutiny and make it transparent. It couldn't be quickly pushed through Parliament and I am certain that by the end of it the Bill will be much changed. I keep my fingers crossed that the green forum created by the MPs doesn't wind up. This campaign I had launched was with help from many, especially Malvika Singh who also had countless meetings with senior bureaucrats and media persons. I also gave two public talks in Delhi and Mumbai on 'understanding the crisis of the tiger'. There were also numerous television shows to further awareness and information.

SARISKA

We are in the grip of the country's third tiger crisis—its worst ever. Over the last thirty years I have been fortunate enough to spend considerable time in the superb tiger habitat of Sariska. From December 2004, reports of the absence of tigers in Sariska had been reaching Delhi. I could not believe it but in February 2005 our worst fears came true and the Chief Minister of the state created a committee to look into the issue. I was a part of it and when I reached the canopy of this forest to enquire into the disappearance of its tigers, I could not believe the calamity that had struck. There was no trace of its tigers; the tigers of Sariska are extinct. How many areas are we going to lose before we wake up? How many Sariskas do we need before our administrators act? Sariska is a national shame and what is more chilling is that it is symptomatic of several tiger reserves across India. We are facing a breakdown of the entire forest-protection machinery; there is negligence at every level. Sariska was the first wake up call to the emergency we face.

Over the thirty years I have spent working with the tiger, India's wildlife, and its habitats, I have never before encountered a crisis of this magnitude. The roots of the crisis lie in the complete breakdown of governance. The present Ministry of Environment and Forests is dysfunctional and the deterioration started more than two and a half years ago. Because the MoEF doesn't function, the state governments are complacent. Few care about wildlife and seldom is it given priority.

The MoEF was created by Rajiv Gandhi in 1985, soon after his mother's assassination. In the Indira Gandhi years the country was enveloped in its first tiger crisis. Indira Gandhi dealt with it decisively by banning tiger shooting and the export of skins with immediate effect; she then piloted through Parliament the Wildlife Protection Act in 1972, and in the next year created Project Tiger to save India's wild tigers. Nobody has been able to match the kind of political will she exercised in this field and for the next twenty years our forests remained secure and tiger populations shot up. So strong was her political will in the area that state governments found it difficult not to fall in line. In 1992 a second tiger crisis enveloped the nation. Kamal Nath as Minister of Environment and Forests engaged in immediate dialogue and created a Tiger Crisis Cell. He spearheaded the process of finding solutions, and wildlife matters were prioritized.

Twelve years later, we have the worst-ever crisis on our hands but there seems to be no sense of urgency towards finding solutions. In the last few months we have lost an entire population of tigers in a premier reserve like Sariska. This would have been unimaginable a few years ago. The MoEF went into denial mode initially and refused to accept that a crisis even existed in Sariska, and talked of 'tigers migrating', 'tigers in the plateaus', and 'tigers will come back'. Then came a flurry of letters—nearly ten in one week—to the poor Field Director of Sariska regarding the monitoring and patrolling that was required. To this day (July 2005) none of the monitoring protocols or daily register entries have been followed in Sariska or Ranthambhore. Few care!

In March 2005, a team of ten scientists from the Wildlife Institute of India spent ten days in the reserve trying to trace its tigers. They combed the Park but found none; in fact they found clinching evidence of poaching in the form of a wild boar with its leg stuck in a tiger trap! The Zoological Survey of India (ZSI) announced a faunal survey and the state called in its experts. The Central Bureau of Investigation (CBI) was sent in by the Prime Minister to investigate—all this 'investigation' months after the tigers were dead.

All this would seem to suggest either that the poachers moved in suddenly and in one fell stroke killed all the tigers or that the forest officials posted at Sariska were completely dysfunctional. In fact I discovered that the alarm signals sent out by them had been ignored. On 25 May 2004 the Field Director of Sariska sent a census report to the Chief Wildlife Warden (CWLW) of the state which showed a drop in tiger population from twenty-five to sixteen and expressed serious concern; the Field Director asked for help from experts to analyse the results as it could lead to a 'controversy'. No action was taken on this letter.

In August 2004 the CWLW sent a letter to the MoEF with

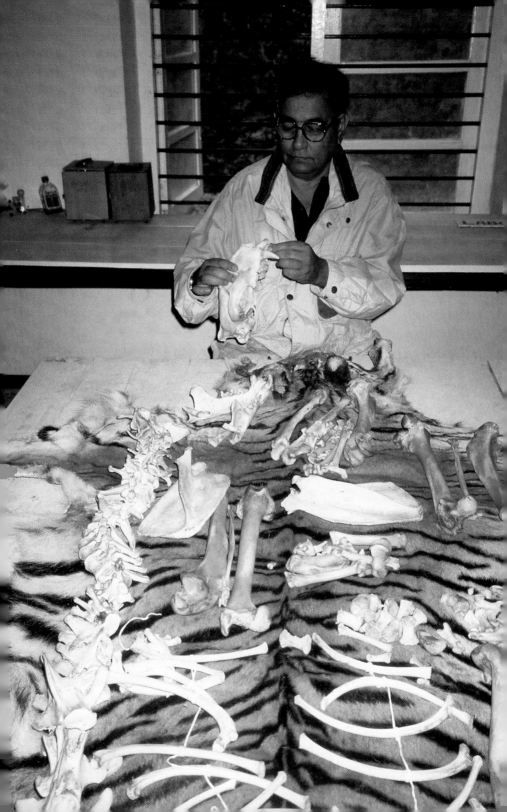

the census results and with a tiny note on the decline of tigers that stated: 'Due to recurring bad weather most of the Pugmark Impression Pads were damaged and it obstructed effective trekking and collection of evidence.' Anyone in the MoEF knows that you cannot do a census with damaged soil straits so such a census had to be immediately rejected and a new one ordered. Obviously Sariska had problems. The state made critical mistakes in its interpretation of a declining census number and may even have misled the centre on the reason for the decline, but how did Project Tiger come to ignore this letter of August 2004? Why did it not ask for a fresh census? This was the time to send a team of scientists down—not some months later when all the tigers were dead. Our systems were malfunctioning big time.

It was in August 2004 again that a letter on record in Sariska provided the director information relating to the 'wipe out' of tigers by poaching in Sariska, and there was little or no action taken on this letter (probably sent by a rival gang) either till February 2005. The result of the inaction is that pretty much all of Sariska's tigers had been poached by October 2004. I have heard some of the gruesome details provided by the Forest Department of the agonized roars of tigers caught in iron traps. Poachers even had the audacity to take in live bait and shoot tigers over their kills. A retired forest guard had informed the forest staff in Sariska in January 2005 that all the tigers had been poached by a gang of fourteen to sixteen poachers; yet the MoEF team that visited the site weeks later told the head of the Rajasthan Forest Department that 'the tigers had migrated and they would return'. This is what it also told the MoEF which happily swallowed it. Only today, when it is far too late, has it changed its tune.

Early warnings were given; sadly the institutions at central and state levels were deaf to them. And this is not true just of Sariska. There was also advance warning of the decline of

Ranthambhore's tigers in the summer of 2004 and clear warnings of massive problems in Panna by early 2004 issued by the CEC on a site visit and in its subsequent report. But was there anyone to listen? Instead the entire system rallied around in a bid to prove that there was no problem, to the extent that in Panna a new census has been undertaken using staff of other forest areas. Of course the results of the new census (based on old flawed methodology) place the tiger population at exactly the same level as before, even though twenty tigers are clearly missing. The response is appalling, showing distrust and subterfuge rather than willingness to confront the problem and find solutions. The effort now is to prove Sariska an isolated incident. I knew instinctively in 2004 that something was desperately wrong. Poachers were having a field day and something had triggered a new demand in tiger skins. But what?

I was responsible, along with Kamal Nath, for having Panna declared a Project Tiger Reserve. I know the place inside out. It is now in shambles and there are innumerable reports and records to prove mismanagement. There are a host of other Project Tiger reserves falling apart, be it Palamau, Indrawati, Manas, Dampha, Srisailam, Namdapha, or Valmiki. In my opinion nearly twelve of twenty-seven tiger reserves are overcome with severe problems that have accelerated over the last few years because of political and administrative neglect.

There are scores of reasons for this but a vital one is that there has been no fresh recruitment of forest staff for twenty years and we now have a 50-plus brigade protecting the finest natural treasures of our land.

Project Tiger Reserves have also suffered because of the failure of the MoEF to engage with or confront issues head on. No meeting of the SCPT was held for two and a half years! It finally met on 13 April 2005 at the Prime Minister's instructions. How can you engage with the crisis without dialogue or consultation? The Steering Committee was created in order to discuss the health of Project Tiger. In my opinion it is a dereliction of duty on the part of the MoEF not to have convened it.

AFTER SARISKA

This is a turning point in our nation's history. If we choose to save our wilderness, we must act now before it is too late. Places like Ranthambhore are very fragile. They are tiny islands in the midst of very populated territory. Nearly 100,000 people with 40,000 livestock live on the immediate periphery of the National Park. It is still the finest place in the world to see wild tigers. It can only survive if we engage with the issues on hand. This is vital since there are, in 2005, three tigresses with cubs in Ranthambhore and our effort must be to ensure that they survive through the troubled years ahead.

Every institution connected with the protection of the tiger desperately requires reform. Some new institutions must be created urgently. The monsoon of 2005 is a critical period for the tigers of India. It is at this time that poachers try to strike. They must be stopped. We will have to deploy forces immediately to the rescue of some of our most troubled habitats. This has to be a first and most necessary step in this enormous crisis.

The agenda of the 17 March meeting of the NBWL prepared by the MoEF also shows its unwillingness to confront the issue of poaching. There is no mention of the word in the agenda. Does the MoEF not know that in the last few years dozens of lethal tiger traps have been seized in both Sariska and Ranthambhore? In fact the third tiger crisis is all about traps and not guns. Hundreds of foot traps are used to disable tigers who are then shot at point blank range. Hundreds of poaching cases have been recorded in the last years across northern India—in Sariska, Panna, Ranthambhore, and elsewhere. Has the MoEF not scrutinized the offence records of the national parks in India? Has it not seen images of the tiger at Nagarahole walking with a trap stuck to his leg? Even after Sariska, the agenda for the NBWL did not include the word 'poaching'—as if it is a dirty word. The Deputy Conservator of Forests (DCF) Sariska has written: 'Hunting, shikari habitation viz Bawarias, banjaras etc. present all along the boundary of the Park. These communities have been traditionally engaged in shikar.' What more does the MoEF want? If it is not willing to even recognize the most potent threat to wildlife parks today, how is it going to deal with it. This unwillingness to call a spade a spade is only going to lead to more tiger deaths. Sariska cannot be made out to be an isolated example; it is reflective of all our reserves.

I serve on the Empowered Committee for Forest and Wildlife Management for Rajasthan constituted by the Chief Minister. We have already stated that poaching has wiped out all of Sariska's tigers. It is the first time in the history of this country as an independent nation that such an event has taken place. And it has created a national and international outcry. The CBI has stated much the same in its report on Sariska.

What is interesting about the CBI report is that it clearly states that Sariska is symptomatic of the state of affairs across India. The main conclusions and observations of this report are:

1. The census figures have been grossly inflated since 1995.
2. Glaring failure of the intelligence machinery.
3. 75 per cent of the staff entrusted with the responsibility of protection are aged between 45 and 50 and are unsuitable for on foot patrolling.
4. Enforcement and prosecution did not receive the priority of the tiger reserve staff for years.

5. Negligence of the staff is evident and overwhelming and collusion with poachers needs further probing. Also suggested is the administrative overhaul of the reserve.

I think the CBI did an excellent job of investigation into Sariska's missing tigers. The Prime Minister must give it the mandate to cover all the tiger reserves in the country.

The Empowered Committee has declared a state of red alert and emergency in Ranthambhore because we are seriously concerned about the linkages between poachers in Sariska and poachers in Ranthambhore. This is especially so, after the interrogation of the poachers in Sariska who claimed to have gangs working in Ranthambhore. The Park has been sealed against intruders. But in a major part of the Ranthambhore Tiger Reserve, the Kela Devi Sanctuary, tigers had already gone missing for many months. Even while MoEF officials were sitting in Ranthambhore during the last week of February congratulating themselves that all was well, the six tigers of Kela Devi had vanished. In fact because of this misinformation the MoEF report on Ranthambhore in March 2005 has glaring flaws in it.

The Field Director of Ranthambhore knew this but failed to inform Jaipur or Delhi till 31 March 2005. One part of Project Tiger doesn't know what the other part is doing! Poachers had struck in Ranthambhore as well. The only way to save what was left in Ranthambhore was by deployment of armed forces. Nearly 200 men are now posted round the clock in the Park to prevent any intrusion. There are three tigresses with cubs still in the National Park area. With strengthened protection they may survive into the next season. Unbelievably, the MoEF is still maintaining a resolute silence on the existence of a crisis. The actions of the state's Empowered Committee saved Ranthambhore's tigers. God knows what would have happened without the red alert.

While serving on the CEC constituted by the Supreme Court of India, I have had ample opportunity to see the growing list of ills afflicting our wildlife areas. Inept decision-making, illegal mining leases, felling, and poaching have created a crisis of unimaginable magnitude. I have listed 200 odd sanctuaries that are in dire straits, suffering from every disease in the book; in fact they are even regarded by some as paper sanctuaries. We need to act before it is too late. But the MoEF has not even accepted what the Prime Minister stated in his letter to the Chief Minister of Rajasthan on 1 March 2005: 'In this situation perhaps it would not be an exaggeration to say that since the launching of Project Tiger, the current situation presents the biggest crisis in the management of our wildlife.'

The Prime Minister even wrote to the MoEF on 4 March 2005 asking that:

immediate action be taken on the reports regarding disappearance of tigers from Sariska. In this regard, Ministry is requested to take the following action.

Short Term Measures:

The CBI could be directed to take up the investigation of the disappearance of Tigers from Sariska through a Special Investigation Team (SIT). The gamut of investigation should cover the possible role of criminals (poachers) and the connivance of Forest Department Staff. The meeting of the Steering Committee of Project Tiger may be convened before the end of March 2005 by MoEF.

Long Terms Measures:

[The CBI report is done and the SCPT met finally on 13 April.] Introduce amendments in the Wildlife (Protection) Act, 1972 (and in any other relevant Act) to provide for:

- Special Courts in Delhi and in some other cities for speedy trial of wildlife related cases.

- Mandatory post mortem and enquiry for every death of a tiger, lion, leopard or elephant that occurs inside a National Park or Reserve.
- Mandatory independent audit once a year of every National Park and Reserve by a group of outside experts to be picked in rotation from a panel prepared by the MoEF and approved by the National Board for Wildlife chaired by the PM. The panels should be revised every 3 years. The findings of the independent audits should be placed in Parliament in a consolidated report every year. They should also be posted on the website of the MoEF.

   This may be brought to the Cabinet in time for the Bill to be introduced in the next session of Parliament. [No action has taken place on this.]

(b) MoEF may:

- ensure the long term management plans are prepared for every Park and Reserve within the next one year;
- prepare and bring to the Cabinet a proposal for the establishment of a Directorate of Enforcement for Wildlife Crimes by 30 April, 2005;
- Examine how the procedures for release of Project Tiger funds can be streamlined (perhaps by releasing directly in the Project authorities), how greater accountability can be established for the proper utilization of funds, and how the salary component can be drastically reduced by 30 April, 2005;
- prepare a scheme for encouraging and funding independent research on wildlife and its habitats by 30 April, 2005.' [Little has happened!]

The PM did all this before the NBWL meeting on 17 March 2005. Let us now take a look at the MoEF and the meeting of the NBWL on 17 March 2005.

MINISTRY OF ENVIRONMENT AND FORESTS AND NATIONAL BOARD OF WILDLIFE

There are several other problem areas in the MoEF which have surfaced over the last year and we need to track back and analyse them. The MoEF is the federal arm of governance and it is vital that it function effectively if we are to resolve the problems that face us.

1. For the last three years the Additional Director General (Wildlife) has been holding a dual charge in Delhi and Dehradun and therefore shuttles back and forth between the two places (hopefully this has been addressed now!).
2. Four Wildlife Inspector posts in the MoEF are vacant, so is the post of Deputy Director General (Wildlife) and several lower staff positions.
3. One person looks after the entire 'Project Elephant' (That post is now vacant.)
4. Wildlife matters get scant attention. Everyone in the MoEF is obsessed with the mega projects that require environmental clearance. Governance of wildlife is minimal except in a crisis.

The MoEF style of functioning can be seen most clearly in the way it handled the latest NBWL meeting. This board is chaired by the Prime Minister. This is the most prestigious policy-making body of this nation in the field and houses independent experts chosen for their lifelong devotion to wildlife. The MoEF is supposed to facilitate meetings of this Board. A year had gone by without a meeting. Each Prime Minister I have known says he will have a meeting every six months but never does. In October–November of 2004 the MoEF asked for agenda items that were duly sent. In February 2005 it announced the date of the meeting and sent agenda notes that did not include the agenda items of the members. In fact 85 per cent of the agenda items were of the MoEF which is not even a member of the NBWL. The deletion of items was done without intimation to members. The members complained. They then received letters two days before the meeting saying that this had been done with the Prime Minister's approval, but on the same day the MoEF was asked by the Prime Minister to include the agenda items of one of the members (me)! And on 17 March, with the Prime Minister's permission, I spent eighteen minutes giving a presentation on the tragic state of affairs and the problems with the MoEF. (I must thank my friends in the MoEF who will remain unnamed who helped in this.) The gist of my presentation was about the functioning of the MoEF. Let us examine it in detail. Two ministers and the entire MoEF senior staff were present and I think I will never be forgiven for this attack—but it had to be done. I had heard only a few days earlier how some officials had tried to tell the Prime Minister's office that I could be a poacher and should not be given ear to. They had even pulled out an eight year-old document that describes me as bald, 6 foot tall, the owner of a hotel, and with a series of other inaccurate facts in order to create suspicion about me at the highest level. The system was jealous of my links with the Prime Minister and was doing everything it could to malign me. These details were even given by senior ministry officials to selected journalists and at the same time the only two tiger scientists of our nation were called 'criminals' in an effort to prevent them from being appointed on any committees. In fact it was at this time that I suggested the constitution of a tiger task force to the Prime Minister and the ministry had vehemently opposed it. The MoEF attacked my idea on record and said that there was already another committee to deal with the issue.

My letter to the Prime Minister and the MoEF's comments were part of an agenda item placed before the NBWL meeting on 17 March 2005. I reproduce it here.

Proposal to PM

1(a) Reform measures are urgently required in the Ministry of Environment and Forests. The first step is to split the Ministry in two:

   (i) Ministry of Environment
   (ii) Ministry of Forests and Wildlife

This will make the federal instrument of governance more streamlined and efficient to tackle the prevailing crisis and problems that afflict 20 per cent of India which is forest land.

Comments of the Ministry

The TORs of the National Board for Wildlife are as follows:

- *It shall be the duty of the National Board to promote the conservation and development of wildlife and forests by such measures as it thinks fit.*
- *Without prejudice to the generality of the foregoing provision, the measures referred to therein may provide for—*
  - *framing policies and advising the Central Government and the State Goverments on the ways and means of promoting wildlife conservation and effectively controlling poaching and illegal trade of wildlife and its products;*
  - *making recommendations on the setting up of and management of national parks, sanctuaries and other protected areas and on matters relating to restriction of activities in those areas;*
  - *Carrying out or causing to be carried out impact assessment of various projects and activities on wildlife or its habitat;*
  - *reviewing from time to time, the progress in the field of wildlife conservation in the country and suggesting measures for improvement thereto; and*

- *preparing and publishing a status report at least once in two years on wildlife in the country.*

It does not seem appropriate within these TORs for NBWL to take up this item. In any case Government of India have set up a National Forestry Commission headed by Justice B.N. Kirpal to go into all matters relating to various aspects of administering Forestry in the Country. This issue is also under consideration by the Forest Commission. The Commission is likely to give its report by August this year. It has obtained views of various sections of public, institutions, public servants etc. on these matters and is likely to come up with some constructive suggestions.

Proposal 1(b): 'Reform of the Indian Forest Service so that a sub-cadre is created which will be like a National Park Service where inter-state transfers will be permitted so that interested and competent officers can function effectively as a director of Ranthambhore can be posted as director of Kaziranga since the skill is not site specific. This is the only way to prevent the present 'dead wood' from functioning in our Parks and this process will result in the "right man being posted to the right job."'

Comments: The Indira Gandhi National Forest Academy has undertaken an exercise on professionalizing the Indian Forest Service. This includes identifying various schemes of specialization including several focused on wildlife. The Forest Commission is also considering the matter. We may await both these reports before taking a view on the proposals put forth by Hon'ble Member.

Proposal 2: 'The immediate commencement of a Wildlife Crime Bureau with a full-fledged staff and infrastructure to commence immediate operation against illegal wildlife trade.'

Comments: The Cabinet note for establishment of Wildlife Crime Control Bureau is under circulation for inter-ministerial consultations and it is also a part of the agenda for this meeting.

Proposal 3: 'The reactivation of the Steering Committee of Project Tiger which was created by Indira Gandhi to guide and steer Project Tiger in the right direction. The Committee with reputed experts has not been permitted to meet by the Ministry of Environment and Forests for the last $2^1/_2$ years. The result has been that there is no early warning system to the prevailing crisis.'

Comments: The Ministry has appointed in August 2004, five independent Monitoring Committees consisting of two experts each selected vide the guidelines of MoEF which have received the approval of the Supreme Court to review the functioning of all the Tiger Reserves in the country as per methodology formulated by IUCN. These independent Monitoring Committees are expected to give their reports shortly. The deadline for submission of the reports by Monitoring Committees is 30th April 2005. The meeting of the Steering Committee will be held soon after the receipt of the monitoring reports to have a worthwhile review of the entire Project.

Proposal 4: 'Financial Institutions—There appears to be no shortage of funds especially in the light of recent Supreme Court orders that have made it necessary for the state governments and other project proponents to deposit money in a trust fund. New mechanisms to transfer this money without delay to the field where it is required must be created.'

Comments: On the initiative of Ministry of Environment and Forests, the Hon'ble Supreme Court in a ruling dated 21st February 2005, have already directed that the financial assistance sent to the States under the Project Tiger, must reach the Park Manager within 15 days of receipt of the grant by the State Government. Compliance of these directions will be monitored by MoEF and if further steps are necessary, the Hon'ble Supreme Court will be approached again.

Proposal 5: 'While all the above starts to take place a special Core Group (mainly of outside experts with the ability to undertake independent assessments of different problems) should be created under your chairmanship to ensure:

(a) that the reform process is carried through.

(b) that the serious crises in places like Sariska, Panna, Damdapha, Indrawati, Srisailam, Palamau (this is nearly 25 per cent of Project Tiger Reserves) can be dealt with on a war footing by the Core Group.

(c) The Group will also facilitate the immediate creation of Wildlife Crime Bureau.

(d) It will also direct state governments to fill all vacant posts and urgently start fresh recruitments so that average age of forest guards can come down from the present average of 50 years. No fresh recruitment has been done for 17 years.

(e) The Core Group will immediately encourage scientific research into some of the very important issues that require urgent answers.

(f) The Core Group will meet once a month with or without the presence of the Chairman and attempt to resolve all the serious crises faced across India. This will also include all the problems related to financial disbursement.'

Comments: The two High Level Committees, namely, Standing Committee of the National Board of Wildlife, a Statutory Body—and a Steering Committee Project Tiger are headed by the Minister of Environment and Forests. The terms of reference of these committees cover the entire issue related to the conservation of Wildlife in the country including the ones flagged by the Hon'ble Member. These Committees comprise of Members of internal as well as external experts, NGOs, Members of Parliament etc. Such high level Committees being already in place, there does not seem to be any need for constitution of another 'Core Group'.

The TORs of the Standing Committee are as follows—

* *The Standing Committee shall ordinarily meet once in three months at a place to be decided with the approval of the Chairman.*

* *The Member-Secretary shall prepare agenda items for the meeting, obtain approval of the Chairman and circulate it to all members at least fifteen days prior to the date of such meeting.*

- *The Member-Secretary shall prepare the minutes of the meeting and circulate it to all members within thirty days of the meeting after obtaining approval of Chairman.*
- *The Member-Secretary shall also initiate follow up action on the decisions of the Standing Committee.*

The TORs of the Steering Committee of Project Tiger are as follows—

- *To guide the activity and watch the progress of the Project.*

This is a typical example of the MoEF's response to any outside intervention. And for the Prime Minister's reference, what they have failed to mention is that both the SCPT and the SCNBWL (Standing Committee of the National Board for Wildlife) are not dealing with any of the issues in the terms of reference. The SCPT hadn't met for two and a half years. The Prime Minister's intervention forced a meeting of the SCPT. Looking at its comments, if we followed the MoEF's logic nothing would ever have happened. Irrespective of all this, the Prime Minister took some action after my presentation.

The Prime Minister accepted the constitution of a tiger task force twenty minutes after I presented the idea but on 13 April when it was announced, the victory was the ministry's since all the genuine tiger experts were kept out on one pretext or the other. Apart from one other member and I, the others came from walks of life unrelated to tigers. Thus a great opportunity to make a difference was lost. But irrespective of all this I received support for my blunt presentation on 17 March 2005 to the National Board of Wildlife. Sonia Gandhi some days later was very congratulatory for this 'hard hitting' presentation to the NBWL which she felt had resulted in the necessary action by the Prime Minister. She felt that the facts reveal a 'truly alarming picture' and she was sure that my recommendations would be given serious consideration.

In 2005 the MoEF has become a *khitchdi* of hundreds of different things. Forests, wildlife, and the environment are all part of a single department. Let us look at its mandate. Forests make up 21 per cent of India's land mass—from forest protection, the conservation of all the wildlife that lives in them, maintaining ecologically fragile areas, and governing institutions for research like the Indian Council for Forest Research and Education (ICFRE), Botanical Survey of India (BSI), Zoological Survey of India (ZSI) and Wildlife Institute of India (WII), to river cleaning operations, afforestation of land, coastal regulation zones, ecodevelopment, environmental research and education and the huge National River Conservation Directorate (including building 3,600 toilets, believe it or not!), hazardous substances management, pollution control boards, clean technologies, water quality monitoring, fly ash utilization, climate change, externally aided projects, animal welfare matters, the administration of zoos, legal cells, global conventions are all a part of the parcel. Projects concerning river valleys and hydroelectric power, thermal power, mines, infrastructural and miscellaneous projects, and nuclear projects (315 such were cleared in 2003–4) have expert committees that provide environmental clearance to project proponents.

In the 1990s there were still some experts on these committees but in the last few years they have been stuffed with all kinds of people (more than 100 'experts' must work on these committees) who are not too critical and can be 'persuaded' to accelerate the endless process of project clearance. Each of the projects is cleared subject to conditions, and sometimes 10–15 such conditions are imposed. Few of the conditions are ever followed by project proponents—they 'run away' after the clearance. Prestigious committees of the MoEF like the Steering Committee of Project Tiger haven't even met for two and a half years. The mechanisms of the MoEF have become antiquated and rusted. It is governance at its lowest ebb.

The list of MoEF activities is endless. Can you imagine the mess! It is a busy churning mass with little thought to quality or content. Generally environmental issues are looked after by 800 staff and 80 officers and forest matters by 200 staff with 30 officers. And there is just one Secretary who deals with the pile up of files from toilets to CNG to National Parks!

There are six regional offices of the MoEF supposed to ensure that projects follow their environmental conditions but when I served on two of the expert committees in the 1990s, the regional offices reported that there was an over 90 per cent violation of conditions! The mandatory conditions are never followed by the projects and effective monitoring by regional offices in detecting violations receives no priority whatsoever in the MoEF. Little action is taken against the violator. Another invitation for disaster.

When the MoEF was created in 1985 it had two departments—forests and the environment—to streamline functioning. At the whim of a bureaucrat one got disabled. Now because of a rivalry between the Indian Forest Service (IFS) and the Indian Administrative Service (IAS), there is no progress in terms of reform. The MoEF spends approximately Rs 1,000 crore a year. The 21 per cent of India, forest India, gets Rs 255 crore a year and a large chunk of this is allotted to research institutions like the ICFRE which is MoEF's own baby. Environment, River Conservation, and Eco-developmental boards get nearly Rs 740 crore a year. In this crazy swirl of activities much confusion reigns in the corridors of the MoEF. Ministers come and go. Repeated dilutions of notifications under the Acts continue to afflict our natural world.

Under the Forest Conservation Act, 1980, a statutory committee, the Forest Advisory Committee, is supposed to decide on what forest land can be diverted and used for development. Again, some of the decisions taken by this committee are in gross violation of the law of the land, for example mining leases in sanctuaries like Jamua–Ramgarh Sanctuary, Barda Sanctuary and Madhav National Park. Many such decisions have now travelled to the apex court. In one case more than 500 violations of the Act were brought to the notice of the Supreme Court. But even after this the MoEF is inert and little action has even been considered against the violators, let alone taken. There are huge pressures and lobbying for the release of forest land. As a senior forest officer who was in charge of this area in the Ministry told me: 'Those with the power to get their projects cleared manage to but those who are simple project proponents without powerful connections suffer.' Recently, against the spirit of the Act, a 21 December 2004 directive from the MoEF states clearly that illegal encroachers are not to be evicted from forest land! There are a string of strange directives and orders by the MoEF in 2004, especially in February just before the general election. Many of these have been stayed by the Supreme Court. Inept decisions are a fact of life. So the MoEF has a grave wildlife crisis on its hands, with wetlands like Bharatpur (a World Heritage Site) short of water and tiger reserves like Dampha, Indrawati, Palamau, Srisailam, and Sariska bereft of tigers. In the last decade there have been dozens of amendments/dilutions of the Environment Protection Act.

The natural world deserves the best the country can give. The present structure and functioning of the MoEF would not be acceptable to anyone with common sense, especially our Prime Minister. Firstly, the MoEF needs to be sliced in two: a Ministry of Environment and a Ministry of Forests. It is ridiculous today to keep such diverse activities as dealing with Compressed Natural Gas (CNG) and automobile exhaust fumes to building toilets and saving our wilderness under one umbrella. It is disastrous for governance. The bifurcation will streamline it and create new structures, especially in the vital area of enforcement. It will create efficiency and provide priority to a hugely neglected area. If the Prime Minister does not act rapidly, the machinery that governs our natural world will remain stagnant and be an invitation to more natural disasters.

With this must come change in the Indian Forest Service (IFS). The IFS has, over the years, been involved in too many diverse activities especially 'development', resulting in little focus on protection. Today the forest officer is busy either making revenue from wood or planting trees but seldom is he interested in the good governance of India's protected areas which are in dire need of a committed cadre of men who can be transferred across the states. This service should have its own norms and rules for recruitment and the men and women who join it should be permanent recruits. By this process the right person can be placed in the right job and it will therefore be a vital reform of the prevailing system in order to effect positive management of these areas.

But even in the face of the Prime Minister's obvious concern, the MoEF is inert. Clearly in its present form it is incapable of handling the grave situation. The MoEF must be split in two and until that is done two departments must be immediately created as was done in 1985 when Rajiv Gandhi was Prime Minister: one for forests and wildlife and the other for the environment. This is the only way to prioritize decision-making and ensure quick action. It will also prevent the endless goof-ups that are taking place.

The wildlife of this country will not live for long in the present climate. Our natural treasures are the country's most valuable resource and surely they deserve better. There is much work to be done and we need unity of purpose in and out of government. To create new institutions requires the political will of the Prime Minister and he has indicated that he recognizes the grave necessity. In states across India little recruitment has been done in the last twenty years, making the guardians of our forests an ageing force. The defenders of our wilderness are in no position to defend it, ageing and short staffed as they are; some are valiant and dozens lose their lives each year, but they are fighting a losing battle. So what do we do?

ACTION PLAN FOR CHIEF MINISTERS

1. We need to act immediately and on a war footing modernize our forest staff of over 1,75,000 men who are directly responsible for the protection of both tiger and forest. This protection force has been thoroughly neglected for decades and has gone to seed. Thirty per cent of posts are vacant and there has been no recruitment for twenty years as an 'economy' measure. It is this measure that must bear the brunt of the blame for the vanishing tigers and forests of India. The average age of the forest guard is now touching 53. He is not fit to patrol his beat and defend it against armed poachers. We have, by virtue of the ban on recruitment, left our nation's natural treasures open to rampant looting. Today the forest staff is totally demoralized and lacks motivation. They require an urgent dose of inspiration. We need to fill all vacant posts with fresh recruits and provide arms and other infrastructure right across the country so that the forest staff is fully equipped to deal with the present threat. This first step must be taken immediately by our Chief Ministers, since forests are a state subject.
2. Equally vital is for all the state governments to provide for all the forest staff the best training capsules that money can

buy. The protection machinery needs to be lean and mean to be a deterrent to poachers and timber mafias. Good on-site training is a vital component to prevent poachers and timber mafias from invading our forests easily. And if there are any delays in this process, temporary deployment of armed police will be essential as a preventive measure.

3. State governments must encourage good scientific research across all our tiger habitats. Sadly, so far this process has been discouraged and ignored. Many independent field researchers have been hounded and harassed. This must change. Field researchers are like doctors who assess a problem and then recommend a cure. Their advice must be heeded and their work supported. In a new National Park Service, the relationship between the park manager and wildlife scientist will determine the health of the area.

4. Last but not least are the local people. There must be training courses that create village protection forces and local intelligence-gathering cells. The youth in surrounding villages must be imparted the best training in forest management, be it water and soil conservation or scientific monitoring of wild animals. There is much to be done and local people can play a vital part. They need to be diverted away from exploitation and towards protection.

REFORMING THE INDIAN FOREST SERVICE

With forests vanishing and tigers dying, it is quite clear that the Indian Forest Service with its strength of 4,000 IFS officers, 8,000 state service officers, and nearly 175,000 men is in a total mess and urgently requires overhauling. Having suffered total neglect at the hands of political and bureaucratic leadership for the last seventeen years, the forest machinery, when most needed to turn out in full strength to deal with the crisis, is in a state of decay. Neglect is the best way to demoralize a team and the resultant weakening of all the forest protection mechanisms has allowed the timber and poaching mafias to take full advantage of the mess.

Can you imagine that one of the nation's premier national services has had no recruitment for seventeen years, there is a 30 per cent vacancy in posts, which means that 40,000 men are not on duty, and there is little or no training being imparted to anyone. The average age of the forest staff in the field is now 50 plus! The CBI report from Sariska states that 75 per cent of the forest staff were not fit for on-foot patrolling. That was a major factor in the success of poachers. Even so at least fifty of this aged forest staff die or are seriously injured in the call of duty each year by poachers' bullets or woodcutters' axes. It is tragic how this nation's leadership has neglected this sector.

The Prime Minister must set out the priorities for saving tigers in time-bound programmes for implementation. All the recommendations are with him and action on them cannot be delayed since our forests are on the perilous brink. If swift and decisive action is not taken scores of rich reserves will perish primarily from neglect and a lack of political will, and then will history ever forgive us?

We have had a huge debate on the Tribal Bill. Greater debate and consultation have been demanded so that a new draft can be made. It has come in for severe criticism in its present form. We must work on a new draft that protects the rights of tribals and strengthens the protection of both the forest and all its wild inhabitants. In fact the Bill should be called 'The Forest, Forest Dweller and Wildlife Bill' (Recognition of the Rights of all the above) since none of the three can live in isolation from the others and the Tribal Bill in its present form will only lead to greater strife between human beings and the forest. And let us be very clear—tribals and forests have no cosy relationship left. The recent 'State of the Forest Report' published by the MoF.F reveals that in the 187 tribal districts in India that house 60 per cent of India's forests there has been a loss of 10,000 sq. km of dense forest cover between 2001–3. Just in Madhya Pradesh that has 18 tribal districts, 12.6 per cent of dense forest in these districts was lost in these two years. Such are the realities!

As to saving wild tigers, the time for meetings, committees, and lip service is past and it is time for swift action. If the Chief Minister of Rajasthan can deploy more than 300 men to the two tiger reserves of Rajasthan in twenty-four hours, what are the other Chief Ministers waiting for? Surely they don't want any Sariskas in their states? Surely it is better to take instant preventive action. The Prime Minister must send an immediate directive to all Chief Ministers on this issue—we have no time to lose. The nation must learn a lesson from Sariska, then at least its tigers won't have died in vain. Every state government must engage with the problem before it overwhelms us. The central government must reform Project Tiger and give it 'teeth'.

The Prime Minister's Visit

Rajiv Gandhi visited Ranthambhore National Park in 1986 and Sariska Tiger Reserve the year after. No Prime Minister of India has been to a National Park in the country ever since. The only other visit from a Head of State has been a six-hour trip by President Clinton. Such is the sorry state of affairs. The sudden crisis in 2005 triggered a National Park visit from a Prime Minister after nineteen years. Prime Minister Manmohan Singh chose Ranthambhore National Park to spend twenty-four hours in.

When the Prime Minister decided to go to Ranthambhore on 23 May 2005, the Chief Minister of Rajasthan asked me to make a presentation on the state of affairs in Ranthambhore, Sariska, and Bharatpur to the Prime Minister. But since the Prime Minister had invited neither me nor the Tiger Task Force I excused myself from going to Ranthambhore and instead made a presentation to the Chief Minister in Jaipur who carried it to Ranthambhore. I was a little shocked that the Prime Minister's office had not had the grace or intelligence to invite the Tiger Task Force which he himself had created after the debacle in Sariska to Ranthambore. Sometimes our administrators' actions defy logic.

The Prime Minister arrived at Ranthambore at noon on 23 May. Apart from spending time on his own he spent nearly two hours in discussions with forest officials from all over India. He also interacted with local villagers to gain an insight into the day-to-day man–animal conflict. The next morning he was in the Park by 6 am and within ten minutes was watching the tigress Machli (she had two six-month-old cubs who did not show themselves). After a two-hour round of the Park, he reached Jogi Mahal for breakfast. A hectic press conference followed. It was clear that his first-ever sighting of a wild tiger had been a very special experience for the Prime Minister—the smile on his face said it all.

It was clear that he was placing a heavy trust on the shoulders of the Tiger Task Force. The question is whether we will be able to steer a safe course for the tiger in the future. Will the Prime Minister be able to deal with the Chief Ministers of the states since the powers of decision-making lie with them? Will he be able to chart a new course to strengthen the institutions that govern the tiger's habitat? These are vital questions that only time can answer. We can only hope that Ranthambhore's tigers have worked their magic and won a key player over to their cause.

Let us now take a close look at the functioning of one of the key tiger institutions in the country.

DIRECTOR PROJECT TIGER

Over the years, I have known many of the directors of Project Tigers. I have known the present incumbent, Rajesh Gopal, for more than ten years. He is a decent, honest person who for eight years had managed Kanha National Park before coming to Delhi in 2002 as Director, Project Tiger. For the first two years there was so much of a mess in the MoEF that he was overused to sort out problems unrelated to tigers. He confessed to me that Delhi was a nightmare for him and he couldn't even get the top brass of the MoEF to fix a date to convene the meeting of the Steering Committee of Project Tiger (SCPT) (which finally only happened after a two-and-a-half-year gap in April 2005 and then on the PM's instructions). The Director Project Tiger probably attended more 'other job'-related committee meetings in these years than tiger-related ones; but then this is how the MoEF works. Of course his confiding attitude towards me changed after December 2004 when the outcry over Sariska started. Since then I think he has slowly started hating me. He thought I was plotting against him to have him thrown out. But my attack was only against the institution of Project Tiger not against any individual. He was also really upset about my sister's article in *The Telegraph* where my sister has purportedly said, 'The Gods will strike the Director, Project Tiger down one day.' He intensely defended the government, when he might not himself believe everything he was defending. It was sad that a good man had got lost in the politics of the battle. Thinking that I was attacking him, he also had a go at me. I know that one of his colleagues gave out a paper to selected journalists accusing me of being a former 'poacher'! Well, the only one who really suffered was the tiger. In June 2005 Rajesh Gopal once again became more friendly towards me after we had a talk. But the system always tries to steamroll opposition. It forgets the real enemies—the Sansar

Chands—and starts a vicious propaganda campaign against those who dare to point out any problems. The WWF had clearly stated in March 2004, after a field survey, that Sariska had no tigers left. This was not liked by the authorities as also the fact that the tiger team was led by a former director of Project Tiger whom the present one did not see eye to eye with. The vicious campaign against the WWF that ensued made its work suffer and in fact made it very cautious about confronting the authorities. This is how the system crushes passion and idealism.

In a crisis, instead of engaging everyone in an effort to resolve it, the system divides to rule. Instead of fighting to save tigers it fought, through vicious and malicious campaigns, the very people trying to save them. Very clearly this is what occurred from February–June 2005 and a detailed record of it exists with many of us. Sadly it only changed when the MoEF was threatened by the passage of the Tribal Bill. They then needed individuals and NGOs to fight against the Bill!

Dr Karan Singh, now deputy leader of the ruling Congress Party in the Upper House, said in a television programme after Sariska, 'If such a crisis had taken place in Indira Gandhi's time she would have sacked the top brass of MoEF.' When questioned further he said that if he was Prime Minister he would have done it gently but that it was required since this was a terminal crisis for the tiger. Thank God, there is still some plain-speaking left in Indira Gandhi's Congress Party. However, nobody got sacked, and the subterfuge and politics dissipated all the energy that should have been focused to save tigers. To me, it was a great tragedy of intelligent leadership—the system had let the tiger down. I was no longer prepared to believe that we could save it from extinction. The Indira Gandhis and Karan Singhs were nowhere on the horizon. And however well-intentioned Dr Manmohan Singh was, his first and very special priority was the economy, and tigers were at the bottom of his list. But somewhere the tigress he saw in Ranthambhore on 24 May 2005 must have had an impact. His smile when he talked about her said it all, and even as I write this I know that on 25 June 2005 he held another meeting on the tiger where the CBI finally presented its report on Sariska which had been ready since April and it is also understood that he finally agreed to give the CBI a mandate to conduct a series of investigations across India on poaching and illegal trade.

One of the unhappy results for the MoEF is that they got 'told off' by the Prime Minister about the general state of affairs. How I wish it was compulsory for the Prime Ministers, Chief Ministers, Ministers to camp in a tent in a tiger forest for a few days or dive 20 m. under the sea to see the startling diversity of natural life; maybe then they would be more decisive defenders of the natural world. As things stand, the ignorance of top leadership is the biggest stumbling block for committed conservationists.

And it is this ignorance of the issues that is fully exploited by self-seeking bureaucrats. A case in point is the composition of the Tiger Task Force. How on earth did an informed and well-intentioned Prime Minister like Manmohan Singh agree to appoint three members out of a five-member task force on tigers who had no experience whatsoever with tigers? In one of my meetings with him he had asked me for a list of names since I had suggested this Tiger Task Force. I carefully wrote them out and gave it to him. But each one was rejected by the bureaucracy dealing with the issue.

And as I continue to write, whether it be coincidence or good fortune, on 29 June Delhi Police finally caught the kingpin of the illegal trade in tiger skins, bones, paws, and claws. Sansar Chand was caught in a temple after meticulous surveillance. Irrespective of everything else wild tigers can now get a breather from the pressures of gangs of poachers whose tentacles have spread to every nook and corner of north Indian forests. The CBI has the case and Sansar Chand is in jail. He has been thoroughly interrogated and I hope the networks will be smashed. This is the one ray of light on the horizon. Let us now look at the recent past and the terrible tragedy of Sariska.

THE MEDIA

I have never seen the kind of media blitz that has happened after Sariska (January 2005) and that is still continuing into August 2005. Never in the history of this country has there been so much on tigers in both the written media and the electronic media. I hope it creates more awareness and prods the system into action. In the second tiger crisis of the 1990s there was much media coverage but little action resulted and the system seemed immune to the criticism directed at it. This time it was different.

After a CNBC show, the host wrote an article in a newspaper which sparked an angry response by the MoEF, and a show on Doordarshan on the tiger also resulted in an angry response by the MoEF. Even before it was broadcast, two lines were cut and the MoEF applied strong pressure on Doordarshan. Without the intervention of the Secretary, Ministry of Information and Broadcasting, the show would probably never have been shown in its original form. In fact the Director, Project Tiger had found a way of being on the chat show twenty-four hours after the chat! Luckily they did not fudge it in the end, but tempers ran high for months. The *Indian Express* through one of its lead journalists ran at least six–seven excellent cover stories on Project Tiger reserves. A month later and before the PM's visit to Ranthambhore he suddenly ran one on the NGOs at Ranthambhore and the money they raise and spend, insinuating that much money was spent and little was done and he bandied my name with the Ranthambhore Foundation in a manner that was surprising. There were many factual mistakes and I never understood the logic of the piece since it said nothing either way. Sadly the journalist who I know did not even take time to meet me and talk about the 1990s in Ranthambhore before he wrote his piece. I wish he had done that. That is the only way forward if we want serious journalism in this sector. I think over six months, if you look at the national press, both English and Hindi, as well as the regional press, not less than 1,400 articles/news items have come out concerning tigers, and all because of Sariska. An amazing record but does it in the end amount to anything?

SCATTERED THOUGHT IN JUNE 2005

From April 2005 the crisis concerning the tiger was overpowering. I was happy to spend time writing this book. It keeps the history of the moment in its accurate form. At the same time as the book, I presented a film entitled *Tiger Zero* for Animal Planet on the crisis we were in. It was also a moment when Ruth Padel's remarkable book *Tigers in Red Weather* came out on the crisis that afflicted tigers across the world. I realized after reading this book and watching events unfold in India what a terminal crisis we were in.

The future of the tiger is BLEAK—I do not believe India can save her tigers and for all the reasons stated here. The months roll by and nothing happens. We do not act because as a nation we do not care. Decades of inaction have resulted in us reaching a point of no return. We fight each other rather than the identifiable enemy and there is much ignorance on the issue. I am quite clear that tribals and forest dwellers, armchair academics, and human rights activists are not going to save tigers. The latter two are only confusing the issue.

We may end up with just five or six safe areas for tigers and not the 100 we had:

1. Kanha—because it has a 1,000 sq. km core area with no people, surrounded by a 2,000 sq. km buffer to take all the shocks.
2. Kaziranga—because there no human beings dare enter unless they are armed poachers; the rhinos, elephants and wild buffalos would kill anyone.
3. Sundarbans—because it is very inaccessible and inhospitable and nearly a hundred cases of man-eating by tigers are reported in a year.
4. Corbett—much the same conditions prevail as in Kanha.
5. Nagarahole, Bandipur, Madhumalai, Wynad, etc.—this is a 5,000 sq. km stretch of excellent and well-protected forest.

Most of our other areas are in dire straits.

The Tiger Task Force will complete its report in July. I am really weary of it. The focus of at least three members is on people and not the endangered tiger. They believe that tiger and man can peaceably coexist. Everyone has forgotten Ranthambhore in its early days. When I first went there in 1975, it had sixteen villages and hardly a tiger was to be seen. The human disturbance was vast. The same was true of Kanha and several other areas. Village relocation has had a huge positive impact on tiger populations, as all those who have tracked tigers know. When Project Tiger started in 1973, Sariska had forty tigers and Ranthambhore fourteen. Ranthambhore got Project Tiger status and in the first year, twelve villages were relocated from the core area. In Sariska, on the other hand, the poachers used its strategic villages to shelter in and strike in its heart. They couldn't do so in Ranthambhore because there were no villages in the heart of the reserve. This is the only reason Ranthambhore has survived over the years.

This is the first premise of tiger conservation, but sadly the majority in the Task Force had no long-term experience of tigers even though an ecologist of repute was a member. The question that we had to tackle was how to reduce the negative impact of relocation. But for tigers to increase, villages had to be persuaded to move and as stated—in the best possible way available to us all. The Chair of the Task Force, a lady whom I greatly respect for the environmental battles she has fought, actually believes that people can live side by side with tigers and all parties can thrive! She had spent the last decade criticizing all those who had fought to create inviolate spaces for tigers. In fact, her writings are against the concept of wildlife for wildlife's sake. When she and my ecologist colleague went to Kanha, the jewel in Project Tiger's crown, as part of the Tiger Task Force, they had the amazing good fortune to see fourteen different tigers in two days—something most of us would give our right arms for. Their reaction was 'happy to see the tigers but unhappy that villages had to be relocated for this'. They were with a third member of the Task Force who had been responsible, in the early days, for making Kanha what it is. The director of Project Tiger who was escorting them was shocked by their reaction, and he told me of the many arguments that ensued. During Indira Gandhi's time, she created the atmosphere for good governance and the administration implemented her every word. It gave others the time to create places like Kanha and Ranthambhore which are more than world heritage sites. Today everything is in a sorry mess as bureaucrats enjoy the power to constitute committees that will fight among themselves and the Prime Ministers of the day are not decisive enough to trust their own judgements.

The human rights activists do not understand that tigers and tribals cannot coexist in modern times. If you take the forest offence records of the last five years across India, at least 3,000 tribals mainly from the Pardi, Bawaria, Mogiya, and Kalbelia tribes have been involved in wildlife crimes including tiger poaching.

They are closely connected to the illegal traders in skin and bone through endless middle men. This is the reality today.

If you want tigers to survive, you have to have undisturbed habitats, and forest villages will have to be relocated by giving the villagers the best deal that money can buy. Those who are then interested in serving the forest as protectors could be trained in different disciplines like basic protection, simple science, and soil and water conservation that could help in keeping our forests alive. It is sad that we cannot reach an agreement on this. We romanticize the tribal while happily living in the city. To me, this is akin to walking around with a pair of blinkers on, which is what the Tiger Task Force is doing. With the best intentions, we are administering the death blow to the tiger because we are putting humans first instead of tigers.

The nation is engaged in creating a new Tribal Bill—one of the most dangerous pieces of legislation ever, in my opinion, that could destroy all the forests and their inhabitants. The reasons are the same. Romanticize the tribal because of a belief that this is the civilized thing to do. The 'give the tribal rights over land—he will protect it' school of thinking is indulging in utter impracticality. Every bit of the land given will be gone overnight into someone else's pocket. All these much-bandied but little understood slogans of 'Let's change the exploitative colonial laws' or 'set right the wrong' or the endless tirades against 'wildlife elitists' and 'lobbies' emanate from a very respected bunch of armchair academics who are totally ignorant about the present state of both forests and wildlife. They believe that tribals and tigers can coexist comfortably. I would like them to try and manage a landscape of 500 sq. km with 3,000 people living inside with 10,000 livestock and with illegal timber cutters and armed poachers holding sway with their tribal contacts. Do you think even one tiger will survive? They should remember how H.S. Panwar created Kanha; F.S. Rathore, Ranthambhore; S. Deb Roy, Manas; and S.R. Chowdhry, Simlipal in the 1970s. In the 1990s came P.K. Chowdhry and Panna and G.V. Reddy and Ranthambhore. The armchair intellectuals should learn from these examples. It was not just about relocation of villages or guns and guards. It was a mixture of different strategies to suit the times. If you have to save tigers in 2005 you need guns and guards. The latter could be recruited from the tribals or locals. You need locals engaged in forest protection activities and tourism wherever possible. But, above all, you need to relocate people and give them the best deal possible.

We are at a point in history where winning battles is impossible. Everything is too polarized. We are damage controllers at best. There are so many problems and scams that time and manpower do not permit you to get to the bottom of it all and therefore strategy dictates action on the major ones alone. There are so many Supreme Court orders but with so few agencies to enforce them. The CEC is flooded with petitions and much more than we can handle. The big guns try and escape the law. Just look at the shocking Pataudi case.

The fashions of today are about sharing power and co-managing natural resources. Can this be done with the rampant corruption that has percolated every strata of our lives? Everything has a price. And some of the worst deals are struck in the forests. Do we have power-sharing with the police to deal with law and order or the army to manage our border areas? Why not?

Why is it so difficult to reach an agreement with all the parties that 50,000 sq. km of habitat must be inviolate for 2,000 plus tigers to live and breed in? This is what tigers need. Their biology demands undisturbed habitats to breed in. The tiger areas need to be sealed forever. This is not a matter for debate. Tigers need inviolate spaces away from the crazy world of so-called sensitive human beings.

On the first of July 2005 to clear my mind I wrote the following....

What do tigers need? That is the question.

Definitely not tribals or forest dwellers, or any human beings to interact with. And not livestock or crop fields or bullock carts either. And not miners or encroachers or even tourists. Or legislations like the Tribal Bill which would award forest land to hundreds of thousands of families. In fact such a Bill would kill tigers. Tigers do not breed in coexistence with human beings. They need inviolate spaces and so do the deer and the boar and the *gaur*. These are the prey of the tiger that eat grass and grow in population and then the tiger has enough of a prey base to increase its population. It is these essential basics that must be understood by human rights activists. It is then that tiger populations rise or are maintained at healthy levels.

If we track back to the 1970s, the early tiger reserves were full of villages be it in Ranthambhore or Kanha or any other area. We know that after many of the villages were relocated, ungulates flourished and tiger numbers also shot up. By the late 1980s the tiger population had risen to 4,000 from 1,800 in the early 1970s.

From 1975 to 2005 I have followed the story of Ranthambhore's tigers. I have witnessed the population rising from 12 to 14, when I first went there, to 50 in 1987. This is fact not fiction, and all due to village relocation. There are enough records that prove the same from Nagarahole in the south to Manas in the north-east. Human activity destroys tiger habitats and in 2005 the population dynamics are such that the tiger has no chance. As areas get more and more disturbed the tiger vanishes, as we have seen in Sariska. And there are many more Sariskas waiting to happen.

So what do we need to do?

We have 100–120,000 sq. km with some evidence of tigers. This could be reduced and probably will fall drastically because of neglect. It is still only 5 per cent of the forest area of India. We will decide that we want 50,000 sq. km or more of habitat for tigers. We already have 34,000 sq. km in our tiger reserves. This could look after 2,000 plus tigers if we are lucky. We must then make sure that all the villages inside are relocated by giving the people the best possible deals. This habitat must then be managed by hand-picked men from the IFS—and hand picked down to rangers, foresters, and forest guards. Something on these lines exists in Kanha and Kaziranga. The job at hand is to protect the tiger's turf like never before. In this mission, the fringe-area population can be engaged in protection, water and soil conservation, and other-forest related jobs. This is how local people will play a role in keeping tiger habitats inviolate. This will play a role in creating and increasing forest wealth. Income generation can take place from tourism if permitted. The locals need to participate with the management in the day-to-day decision-making process in order to keep the area disturbance free.

This is where the challenge lies.

Tiger biology tells us that there is no other way. Wildlife scientists across the world from Siberia to Sumatra, from India to Cambodia have all reached the same conclusion. This is a simple fact. It is not a matter for debate.

We have a vast tiger crisis. This is not the time for experimenting with tribal–tiger coexistence theories that make no practical sense for the tiger's survival. The mission at hand is the tiger's survival and not the forest dweller's rights.

We could create an environment where forests coexist with people but in non-tiger areas. It is non-tiger, non-wildlife areas that can be used to experiment with new models of coexistence between man and forest. Livelihood needs of the forest dwellers in the forests of India and from them cannot be fused with the needs of wildlife. These are two separate paths to be followed.

Rich tiger and wildlife areas have to be inviolate and human livelihood needs from forests can be met from non-wildlife forest areas and there are millions of hectares of them.

So in any strategy for saving wild tigers we have to discuss the tiger's future without confusing it with the livelihood issues of forest dwellers. There is no connection between the two. The tiger's livelihood is dependent on the absence of people. If you force people to live with tigers, man–animal conflicts increase tremendously, grazing livestock gets killed, man-eating is a possibility, tigers then get poisoned, and then it doesn't stop till the last tiger is wiped out. Today nearly 150 people are killed by tigers in India and 250 tigers are probably killed by people with about 10,000 livestock a year killed by tigers. Such are the levels of conflict, that co-existence between the two is a non-starter. We cannot forget Sariska. In the last five to seven years across India there have been at least 3,000 to 4,000 cases of poaching, illegal felling, and other forest offences by forest-dwelling communities and tribals. We have to try to stop this 'criminalization' of tribals.

Let us not forget that the Java, Bali, Caspian, and now even the South Chinese tiger in all likelihood have become extinct because of excessive human presence and interference in the tiger's habitat which resulted in sharp falls in the prey species that in the end triggered the tiger's extinction. These processes have been documented in great detail over the last century. We must learn from them so that we do not repeat the mistakes. Unthinking statements that tigers can coexist with people can kill tigers especially when these statements enter policy.

Let me conclude with a statement by Dr R.S. Chundawat, one of our top tiger scientists after his eight-year study on the tigers of Panna.[1]

The single most important finding to emerge from our work to date has been the importance of the watercourses and watering sites in this forest type as critical habitat for tigers. If small reserves such as Panna are to sustain their tiger populations then they must include as much of the water course as possible in a disturbance-free zone, so that tigers can hunt wild ungulates and rear their cubs undisturbed. What is urgently needed in Panna is the creation of at least two more disturbance free mini core areas in Balaiya Seha and the Ken river valley. This requires removing 4,000 people from the reserve; without this the future of the tiger population in Panna is very bleak.

This was written in 1999 and little was done to remove human disturbance. The park is in a mess and many of its tigers are dead. I hold little hope of recovery.

It is the end of July and the Tiger Task Force report is in and it is what I expected. I think that the three months I spent in the Tiger Task Force were the most frustrating that I have ever had on any committee. At least three of the members had no direct experience with tigers and even though we met and had consultations together there was little genuine discussion or gainful interchange of ideas and opinions—most of the consultations were driven by our chairperson's predetermined agenda of total and unconditional support to local people whatever their attitude towards the neighbouring forest and its denizens. Even when we went to Ranthambhore—a place that I have known and passionately loved for thirty years, I was not even consulted about

[1]R.S. Chundawat, in J. Seidensticker, S. Christie, and P. Jackson, eds, *Riding the Tiger: Tiger Conservation in Human-dominated Landscapes*, Cambridge, 1999.

where to go and whom to meet. And the chair seemed to bask in the media attention and encourage it, allowing journalists easy access. Even in Sariska a journalist was allowed to accompany us on a site visit to a village. The disconcerting thing was the clichéd understanding of issues in the Task Force itself. Even at Sariska the kind of questions asked of the villagers and forest staff were so much the stuff of armchair intellectuals for decades that I felt completely frustrated. Even on site visits I couldn't penetrate the armour of predetermined notions. Precious time was being spent in rhetoric and instead of being a short crisp report I was certain it would end up being encyclopaedic. A great chance to save the tiger was being lost.

And it became even worse in our last week of discussions on the final report. I realized that in the end there would be little agreement between me and my colleagues, the coexistence of people with tigers within national parks and sanctuaries being the issue. Utopian solutions were proffered and there was a complete inability or lack of desire to grasp the complexities at ground level. So when one managed to push for attractive relocation packages to create inviolate tracts, there would be checks in the form of someone demanding attractive packages also for those who would not relocate—as if people would relocate for the tiger when they knew they would be getting a new package of 'rights' to stay inside. I tried hard for a consensus but it was in vain. It ended with my sending a note of dissent to the chair which is (Annexure 1) on 27 July 2005 after which I had little communication with her and did not even get a copy of the final report till the day (5 August 2005) of its presentation to the Prime Minister and at 1 p.m. in the afternoon. So much for the right to information, forget the fact that I was a member of the Task Force. The Introduction that is signed by all four of my colleagues does not even mention my name or acknowledge me, and that when nearly twenty-five pages of this 200-page report are solely devoted to my plan to save tigers and my dissent note. The crowning audacity was to publish a letter in the report in response to my dissent which she had never done me the courtesy to send prior to the publication of the report. She ends the letter saying

You repeatedly allege the report has a 'people focus' and not a 'tiger focus'. I do not know how to respond to this, because then you clearly do not even begin to understand the challenge of tiger conservation in the country today, as we see it and have detailed in the report. Indeed, it is unfortunate you were consistently busy during the entire term of the Task Force, because of which your interaction with all of us was limited. If we had seen more of you, I am sure a better common understanding would have emerged.

What she forgot to tell the readers was that I had spent thirty years working with tigers and didn't need to accompany her to Periyar and Kanha for five days to gain an understanding of the issues of tiger conservation. She also forgot to mention others in the Task Force whose faces no one saw till the final week!

A paragraph in the main report states:

Over time, the interests of this small group of conservationists has also got embroiled in the tiger. The benefits they make from tourism, filming and conservation is not shared with the people or the parks. The problem is that this leads to even greater alienation of all against the tiger, which they believe is being protected for the sake of a few, against the interests of all.

I had objected to this during our discussions pointing out that she was casting aspersions on me. She claimed that it targeted not me but two of our other tiger conservationists. However, she finally agreed that it was irrelevant and deleted it. But when she got my dissent note she re-included it. Other paragraphs that were deleted also got re-included after my dissent! I wish her well, but I must point out that the report's key areas are a mass of contradictions, be it in terms of coexistence or the crime bureau.

Because the chair of the Task Force was so paranoid, when the newspapers leaked bits of the report, she is said to have exploded, blaming me for the leak. Little did she know that the leak came from people right around her. I think there existed a predetermined agenda that I was to be totally avoided and sidelined. I hope that as the years go by she grows and learns from this 'negative' experience. Her letter to me (published in the report) was full of innuendos about 'exclusivity' as of a 'club' of people (implying I was a part of it) controlling the National Parks. Did she not know that what she called the 'exclusive club' of the forests was the state forest departments, Project Tiger, and MoEF? The rest of us were powerless and irrelevant and had, in fact, failed to get any of our ideas implemented. The sourness of our interaction was very sad as I have great respect for her ability to battle for causes in her own field. This battle for the tiger is just not her forte or field of experience. To cap it all, the day the report was to be given to the Prime Minister, the mischief-making media completely erroneously quoted me as saying: 'People have to be thrown out of all tiger reserves.' I realized how immature our media was. On the whole, however, I believe my dissent note was vital and it is clear that because of it many subtle changes were made in the report that improved it.

The Tiger Task Force Report by foregrounding coexistence has negated the other positive elements of the report. A great opportunity has been lost. The report will in all probability gather dust in a shelf of the Ministry of Environment and Forests. Much more focused and practical was the report of Rajasthan's State Empowered Committee for Forest and Wildlife Management. The report went into the minutest detail of the functioning of the state's forest department and provided a whole set of 'do-able' recommendations. In a way a much more satisfying experience than the National Task Force. I keep my fingers crossed that this report does not also gather dust on a shelf. Sadly our institutions are so eroded and governance at such a brainless level that it is quite likely that important recommendations will never get implemented because the ability just does not exist.

I now know that India is living with her last tigers and there is little hope for the future.

Epilogue
Jeopardizing the Tiger—
Failure, Failure and More Failure

I think the moment has come for us to analyse some of the glaring flaws that exist both at the centre and state levels in our systems of monitoring the survival of the tiger. From 2004 to 2005 the report card shows total disaster. At least eighty tigers from just seven protected areas are gone—probably poached. If counts were done for the other seventy-five protected areas also, the toll would surely be appalling? We have lost all the tigers of Sariska Tiger Reserve; we lost at least twenty-one tigers in Ranthambhore Tiger Reserve, entire populations of tigers in Kela Devi Sanctuary, Sawai Man Singh Sanctuary in Rajasthan, and Palpur Kuno and Rani Durgawati Sanctuaries in Madhya Pradesh. Added to this are at least twenty tigers gone from the Panna Tiger Reserve. In the last few weeks there have been reports of the recovery of three freshly poached tiger skins from Periyar Tiger Reserve where a huge farcical exercise of rehabilitating poachers in the role of 'protectors' has been undertaken. Even as I write this another fresh tiger skin has been recovered from Assam, being carried, believe it on not, in a Police car! The area around the Sundarbans has seen the seizure of skins, there have been a couple of seizures in Orissa and U.P. and a haul of 5 tiger skins and 38 leopard skins on the borders of Nepal and Tibet. Poaching is rampant. And all this is going on in Project Tiger reserves. The sorry state of affairs in the area outside our premier parks can only be imagined. And we are not even talking of Manas, Indrawati, Nagarjunasagar, Palamau, Valmiki, Dampha, Namdapha, and Buxa, all tiger reserves that are plagued by a severe set of problems.

Let us look at a few examples in detail.

SARISKA

All Sariska's tigers were wiped out by October 2004 but it was only in early March, after the Prime Minister called in the CBI, that this fact was confirmed. The state government had two early warnings of this disaster. In late May the Field Director of the Park had written to the Chief Wildlife Warden (CWLW) of Rajasthan pointing out a problem in his census figures and asking for help:

On the basis of the available evidence and on ocular analysis of the pugmarks and movement of tigers the team reached a rough estimate that the number of tigers were between 16 and 18.... Since this estimate is quite different from that of last year's census and could lead to controversy.... Experts should be called to carry out examination of the evidence.

No help came. In August 2004 a signed letter to the Field Director warned him that massive poaching was going on. No one took notice of it till February 2005.

The central government also had warning of the catastrophe. In August 2004 the CWLW of Rajasthan sent his census data to the Project Tiger Directorate showing a drop of eight tigers, with his understanding of the reason for the decline: 'Due to bad weather most of the Pugmark Impression Pads were damaged and it obstructed effective trekking and collection of evidence.' The state had misled the centre about the reason for the decline but the tragedy is that the centre did not even have the ability to question how a census was done in 'bad weather'. Project Tiger and the Ministry of Environment and Forests (MoEF) took no action based on the letter. Even in November 2004 a WII team [an arm of the MoEF], after a field visit to Sariska, indicated that there was no evidence of tigers but still there was no action. The whole episode smacks of unwillingness to face facts. What is tragic in this example is that it took till late February 2005 for the MoEF to believe that a crisis existed and till then it spent its energies on proving that there was no crisis, saying that the tigers had migrated and would return. The system was completely on the defensive and in denial rather than responsive mode. It is only after the CBI report that the defensive posturing and bluster have been replaced by a belated attempt to close the stable door after the horse has bolted. The CBI clearly stated:

- The tiger estimation over the years, has been grossly exaggerated.
- Since July, 2002, at least 2–3 organized networks of poachers were killing tigers as well as leopards at periodic intervals.
- Through an organized network of middlemen, most of the skins are suspected to be reaching city-based buyers including notorious wildlife smuggler Sansar Chand of Delhi.
- The existing human resources of the Tiger Reserve were inadequate and ill-equipped to prevent poaching because of lack of training, age profile, and total collapse of the intelligence machinery.
- Enforcement and prosecution did not receive due priority of the Tiger Reserve staff over the years.
- Negligence of the Project Tiger staff in preventing extinction of tiger in the Reserve is evident and overwhelming. However, collusion, if any, needs further probe.

• Unless corrective remedial actions are initiated on an urgent basis, the existing leopard population of the Reserve faces serious threat and possible extinction.

RANTHAMBHORE

Today it is an indisputable fact that in Ranthambhore twenty-one tigers are missing. The first alarm was sounded by a local NGO in the monsoon of 2004 when a letter informed the state government that eighteen tigers could be missing from the National Park. After the Sariska catastrophe an MoEF team made up of the Additional Director General (DG) Wildlife, MoEF, and the Director, Project Tiger, finally visited Ranthambhore Tiger Reserve on 24 February 2005 and wrote in their inspection report:

The alleged disappearance of 18 tigers, from RTR is misleading and not true. There is a daily monitoring system in place wherein details of tigers using different parts of the habitat within the reserve are recorded....

The Project Tiger Directorate receives updating periodically from tiger reserves on important events/ happenings as well as mortality of wild animals due to poaching/ natural deaths complimented by factual information gathered during frequent visits of MoEF officials. Therefore, there is no collapse of any warning system.

The alleged decline of tiger counts across the country is only speculation at this stage by NGOs and media.

Even before this report was written there was no sign of tigers in the Kela Devi Sanctuary—they were extinct but the central government had no clue!

The report even attacks the local NGO that wrote the letter about missing tigers and states that it has a bad reputation because of land that it has acquired. Luckily the Chief Minister created an Empowered Committee that immediately declared an emergency in Ranthambhore—a red alert was sounded and more than 200 extra men moved in. Looking back, it is this action that saved the tigers of Ranthambhore. When the Prime Minister visited Ranthambore on 23 May 2005 he was fortunate to see a tiger—he probably wouldn't have if the Chief Minister hadn't sent a Special Protection Force to protect the tigers of Ranthambhore.

When the Empowered Committee conducted a census in May 2005 using the best available methodologies, the result was shocking—twenty-one tigers were gone! Ranthambhore National Park had only twenty-six tigers left and now this was also the figure for all of Rajasthan.

Let us look at some of the other data generated from the period. The WII examined all the plaster of Paris casts taken by the forest staff and this is what they said:

We photographed 341 pugmark casts of which 269 (78 per cent) were only from the left hind foot. Since there was a variation in the quality of these pugmark casts therefore, we classified them into good (n=51), moderate (n=90) and poor (n=128). Recorded good pugmarks were only from 28 against 72 compartments reported to have tiger pugmarks. Good pugmark (n=51) photographs amenable only for measurements were used. We measured 21 variables (linear and area) selected based on earlier published studies (Grigione *et al.* 1999; Sharma 2001 and Lewsion *et al.* 2001) on the calibrated image using SigmaScan Pro-4™ software. Preliminary analysis based on Hierarchical Cluster Analysis of the measurements indicates the presence of at least 12 different individual tigers in 51 casts. Further analysis of data are in progress to correctly classify these 51 pugmark casts based on use of other Multivariate Statistics.

Thirty-two years after Project Tiger, 290 plaster of Paris casts had to be rejected. And in a place that has the best soil straits for pugmarks. What is the reality across India? Furthermore, it was clear that only Ranthambhore National Park had tigers and prey; 800 sq. km of Kela Devi Sanctuary and Sawai Mansingh Sanctuary had no tigers—it had instead 55,000 goats, 10,000 buffaloes, 500 cows, camels, and very few wild herbivora. This is what happens to the tiger's landscape if disturbed by villages and livestock. The tiger vanishes. Tigers and people cannot coexist.

But even after such good data was collected in Ranthambhore using scientific techniques propagated and endorsed by the MoEF, the Secretary, MoEF, said in an interview to *The Times of India* of 19 July, the day after the data was released: 'We will only go by the all-India census, to be conducted in November– March with a refined, revised methodology. It will be reviewed by national and international experts from the stage of primary data collection. We'll stand by those figures whether less or more.'

Ranthambhore provides an example of a total systems failure in terms of the Project Tiger Directorate, the MoEF, and an initially unresponsive state government.

PANNA

From 2003 both the state and central governments have had plenty of warnings about the sorry state of affairs in Panna Tiger Reserve.

1. From early 2003 a renowned scientist working in Panna for eight years sent a desperate spate of letters about the mismanagement of the area and the decline of tigers to the government. His letters dated 12 January 2003, 11 March 2004, 23 February 2004 and 14 January 2005 are especially revealing.

2. The CEC constituted by the Supreme Court of India stated in its report on Panna dated 24 May 2004:

   (a) During discussions held with the Director of the Park, it transpired that the sighting and the evidences indicating presence of tigers such as pug marks, scats etc. has declined sharply both in Madla and Hinauta ranges this year in spite of which a comparison of the census figures of tigers during December 2002 and 2003 show loss of only two tigers. Tigers which were regularly seen in Judi Nullah (perennial water source with thick cover) in peak summers are now seldom seen in this area. The officials also informed that a large number of snares used by the poachers to trap and kill wild animals have been seized. The question is will the tiger population be able to recover, or is the damage permanent?

   (b) It is obvious that the day to day supervision on the part of the Deputy Director has been extremely poor which has led to near total breakdown of the protection and management of the park. Therefore, the State Government needs to go into this matter in detail and take immediate and effective corrective measures.

   (c) The Committee is dismayed and disappointed at what was visible to us in our site visit that the national park has been mismanaged. The general impression formed by the Committee after site inspection and discussion held with the officers is that the senior supervision in the Park has been woefully lacking.

3. More letters were sent by the aforementioned scientist to the Field Director, the Principal Chief Conservator of Forests, the Chief Wildlife Warden, and even the Principal Forest Secretary and Chief Secretary. Another letter went to the Forest Minister. But again the warnings were ignored.

4. The CEC's second report of 18 February 2005 stated:

    Panna is showing signs of Sariska. This note is like an early warning signal. It is necessary to put it right fast before it is too late otherwise the tiger will never recover here.

5. On 28 March 2005, the CEC wrote to the Chief Secretary of Madhya Pradesh stating:

Considering the gravity of the matter, it is imperative that protection measures on a war footing be taken particularly against poaching, grazing and illicit felling to ensure that Panna tiger population does not follow Sariska's example where the situation has become totally irretrievable. An action taken report may please be filed before the CEC at the earliest.

All of this also fell on deaf ears. In fact the state government treated the early warning of the CEC in a frivolous manner. So did the MoEF. When the same senior scientist who had been doing research in Panna put together a detailed 100-page report with scientific data on the mismanagement of the area, instead of responding to control the crisis, the system went into denial to control the criticism. The Director, Project Tiger in a letter to the *Indian Express* in March 2005 stated:

The researcher, like many others who have done breast-beating in the media over tiger, also appears to have a hidden agenda. It is learnt he has set up an NGO near the tiger reserve recently to further his cause, which perhaps warrants an anti-system posture to gain credibility.

It is truly amazing how governments have come to hate NGOs or even individuals outside the 'system'. The government abuses NGOs of 'making money' on the tiger's back but conveniently forgets all the hundreds of crores they waste on 'eco development projects' and other bilateral schemes. In fact in 2005, they are trying to control NGO funding by forcing NGOs to get prior permission from the Ministry for their grants. We have a Prime Minister wanting to live in the twenty-first century and a government living in the middle ages.

The Principal Secretary, Forests, in charge of Madhya Pradesh also talked of 'disgruntled researchers' and an 'alarmist attitude'. He wrote a shocking letter to the CEC on 5 April 2005:

We note with concern, however, that the CEC's report contains some unsubstantiated remarks and individual observation, which have been the basis of a spate of recent adverse reports in the media. To compare Panna with Sariska is unwarranted and unduly alarmist. The sentiment is, unfortunately, almost directly quoted from the report of a disgruntled researcher who bears a personal grudge against the Park Management. This researcher is also reported to be a close associate of one of the members of the CEC.

The CEC's observations, based on a 2-day visit to the Park that 'the sighting of tigers continues to be difficult' and that the 'tiger population in 2005 appears to have crashed in the Park probably due to poaching' are not backed by evidence and do not seem appropriate for a senior level committee appointed by the Supreme Court. While the Park like many other Parks in the country faces a number of problems and pressures, to indict the Park management without a full and impartial assessment of facts and data is a disservice to the cause of conservation and highly demoralizing for the staff which already works under great constraints.

It was shocking how the entire central and state governmental machinery went into top gear to disprove that any problem existed; a special census was conducted in Panna to prove exactly the same figures as before. It is important to note here that the census in Panna, unlike Ranthambhore, was conducted using a flawed old methodology rather than camera traps or the digital picture of pugmarks. Therefore the results had no meaning but to support the Park Director's view.

The State Forest Minister was quoted in *The Hindu*, dated 11 April 2005, as saying, 'The entire controversy about Panna and its declining tiger population had been generated by a disgruntled researcher.' The Chief Wildlife Warden was quoted in *Nav Bharat* (Hindi), on 9 April 2005, as saying, 'As far as the situation in Panna Tiger Reserve is concerned, the situation is quite satisfactory and there is no doubt regarding the tiger numbers.' On being questioned on the issue of missing tigers he responded that 'it has been blown out of proportion by one individual and his claims are baseless'.

Then on 29 July 2005 a poacher and his accomplice were caught in the district where the Panna Tiger Reserve is situated. They confessed to killing five tigers in Panna itself and thirty leopards in the area. It is the tip of the iceberg; they have connections across Madhya Pradesh and to the kingpins of the illegal trade in Delhi. Most of Panna's tigers could be gone. The poacher had killed a tiger in Panna even after the CEC's first warning. The denials of both centre and state were now fully demolished. In fact the people who denied the problem should hang their heads in shame and be held accountable for the loss. They are as culpable as the poachers themselves.

In all three cases, the response was the same—denial rather than crisis management. That denial led to many more tiger deaths. The Prime Minister and this country ended up being totally misled by such reports. The MoEF in the last six months has been shouting from the rooftops that it is a 'scientific ministry'. The Secretary of MoEF even went to the extent of stating in a letter to the *Hindustan Times* on 7 April 2005 that, 'these revealed that it is scientifically incorrect to conclude from the acknowledged problem at Sariska that there is large-scale decline of tigers in the country. Two, that it is also incorrect to say that generally, the tiger reserves are poorly managed.' My suggestion to MoEF is to please try and find even one fresh pugmark in Namdapha, Dampha, or Buxa tiger reserves and please see what the awful realities are in Nagurjunasagar, Indrawati, Palaman, Valmiki, and of course Manas tiger Reserves. There are no two ways about it. We have a horror situation on our hands. Just the analysis of the forest cover lost between 2001–3 shows 24,000 sq. km gone of dense forest in the tiger states of India.

Before any fanciful reports and recommendations to save tigers see the light of day it is imperative to make the system transparent, responsive, accountable, and answerable for its misdeeds. Three tiger reserves are in deep trouble because the authorities legally responsible to manage them did not respond, believe, or act promptly. The Tiger Task Force Report does not even take the Project Tiger Directorate to task for this!

What would have happened to Ranthambhore's tigers if the Chief Minister of Rajasthan had not created an empowered committee, or in Panna had it not been the arrest and confessions of a poacher? It may be too late to save the latter even now. I feel quite disheartened and have little hope of anything changing. The tiger is on the verge of extinction. I wouldn't be surprised to find if proper estimates were done that India in this last year lost more than 400 tigers. As most of my colleagues would agree, 'we all know that there are only 1,500–2,000 tigers left in India—we even know approximately where they are. Why play games about estimation and counting by a 'scientific ministry' which will be able to give its conclusions on the missing tigers, based on scientific study and methodology only by 2006. By then we may have lost another 400 tigers. The need of the hour is protection and more protection alone—without this there is no hope. First keep the tigers alive, then think of science and other management initiatives.

I have had a worry since 2004 that poaching pressures on India's tigers had accelerated. This has now been confirmed after a sting operation done in China in August 2005. (Please see Annexure). Since 2003 it is clear that truckloads of tiger, leopard and other skins have been smuggled into Nepal and across to Tibet where they are tailored into the most outrageous and cruel costumes for special festivals. At least 70 tiger skins, 750 leopard skins and thousands of other skins are now recorded as having gone this way. God knows the total figure as India's National animal—the tiger—ends up on the most horrific Tibetan costumes. Right now we must control the situation by immediately sending armed commandos to protect the periphery of our parks, seal our border crossings with Nepal etc. against this illegal trade and then our PM must take on this issue with China on a priority basis.

If he does not in the next two months before the turn of the year then the the fate of the Indian Tiger will be sealed in its 'coffin' forever. We can do nothing else in this emergency but protect in the very best of ways possible with trained forces or even the territorial army.... God help us if we don't. In the light of these revelations from Tibet I fear that there are less then 1,500 tigers left in India.

Annexure 1

A. Letter from the Prime Minister to the Chief Minister of Rajasthan

PRIME MINISTER

New Delhi
March 1, 2005

Dear Smt. Vasundhara Raje ji,

The recent reported disappearance of tigers from Sariska is a matter of great distress and concern. You may appreciate that immediate action needs to be instituted both by the Centre and the State Government to protect our wildlife, especially the tiger, and their habitats, and prevent any further deterioration in the situation. Perhaps it would not be an exaggeration to say that since the launching of Project Tiger, the current situation presents the biggest crisis in the management of our wildlife. Rajasthan has been particularly well-endowed in this regard and you will agree with me that your Government would need to take all possible steps to preserve this rich heritage for the people of the State, the country and the international community.

While I am taking up the matter with the Ministry of Environment and Forests, I would like to suggest, for your urgent consideration, the immediate steps that could be taken by the State Government. These suggestions are based on the reports and observations of experts and information that has reached me from other sources:

- Instituting a high level independent inquiry with outside experts to identify the cause[s] and fix responsibility for the disappearance of tigers from Sariska.
- The immediate stoppage of plying of all diesel vehicles within the Parks of Rajasthan.
- The filling up of all vacant posts in the Parks within the next 3 months.
- The preparation of a time schedule for the development of fuel, fodder and other necessities of villagers in the areas outside the Parks. [I am informed that a plan already exists and needs to be vigorously implemented].
- Tightening controls for stopping cattle grazing inside the Parks and developing alternative grazing areas.
- Working out arrangements with the Ganesha Temple authorities in Sariska to control and regulate the number of pilgrims and complete stoppage of cooking inside the Park.
- Carrying out raids in the vicinity of townships near the Parks to control sale and purchase of bush meat and identify the suppliers. This needs to be done on a campaign basis over a period of time.

- Construction of an alternative route for the canal that cuts through the Sariska park within the next year.

I would also request you to consider introducing a system of post-mortem and enquiry for every death of a tiger in a National Park or Reserve and independent audit once a year of every National Park and Reserve by a group of outside experts.

Looking forward to hearing from you about the steps taken/ being taken by your Government on these suggestions.

With warm regards,

Yours sincerely,

[Manmohan Singh]

Smt. Vasundhara Raje Scindia
Chief Minister
Government of Rajasthan
Jaipur

This instruction from the Prime Minister's office was received by the Ministry of Environment and Forests two days before the National Board of Wildlife's meeting on the 17th of March 2005. Till this letter was sent my agenda item had not been placed for discussion. As soon as the letter was received everything was rapidly made part of the agenda. This is how the system malfunctions.

B. Letter from the Prime Minister's Office to the Ministry of Environment & Forests

Prime Minister's Office   South Block
                                                  New Delhi

Please find enclosed a letter dated 07.03.2005 from Shri Valmik Thapar addressed to the Prime Minister regarding the agenda items for National Board for Wildlife meeting.

2. Prime Minister directed that the agenda items suggested by Shri Valmik Thapar may be included in the agenda of the second meeting of the National Board for Wildlife scheduled to be held on 17 March 2005.

(K.V. Pratap)
Deputy Secretary
Tel. No. 2301 7442

C. Note of Dissent by Valmik Thapar, Member on the Draft Report of the Task Force for Reviewing the Management of Tiger Reserves

I. The long-term survival of tigers will depend on the single most important factor, namely inviolate protected areas. A certain minimum area has to be managed exclusively in its natural form for the tiger. The area may be $^1/_2$ per cent, 1 per cent, or 2 per cent, or more of the geographical area of this country depending on the political mandate to do so. Let the principle of this be applied in the interest of the tiger. After all it is these areas which provide the water, food, and ecological security of the country. On the other hand the entire report is based on a totally different premise, namely that: 'there are two essential strategies here:

   1. The habitat must be shared between the people and the tigers, so that both can coexist, as they must. The poverty of one, otherwise, will be the destruction of the other.'

   (Page 4, Chapter 2, 'A Paradigm Change—Making Conservation Work')

II. The concept paper on 'A Paradigm Change—Making Conservation work' and the chapter on coexistence of people raise serious issues that impact the entire report. Let us not forget that the mandate of the task force was to suggest measures to save the tiger from vanishing off the face of India. It was a response to an ongoing tiger crisis. Unfortunately, in its eagerness to find 'long-term solutions' for all problems afflicting the country, the Task Force appears to have lost this mission focus; it has gone adrift trying to find solutions to the problems of inequity and social injustice that afflict India. In the process, the problem of the tiger's survival has been relegated to the background and lost sight of.

III. It is imperative to note that all the potential tiger habitats in the protected areas of India, add up to only 100,000 sq. km and populations where reproduction is taking place now occupy less than 20,000 sq. km. Thus a relatively small fraction of India's huge rural poor population is exposed to tigers. The premise that there are vast areas of India where tigers and people must be forced to coexist through some innovative scheme of increased use of underutilized forest resources and involving the local people does not make any sense to tiger conservation, especially when the human and cattle populations are constantly rising. The fact is each tiger must eat fifty cow-sized animals a year to survive, and if you put it amidst cows and people, the conflict will be eternal and perennial. Tigers continue to lose out as they did in Sariska (and over 95 per cent of their former range in India). The premise of continued coexistence over vast landscapes where tigers thrive ecologically and people thrive economically is an impractical dream, with which I totally disagree. Such dreams cannot save the tiger in the real world. On the contrary such a scenario will be a 'no win' situation for everyone and result in further declines and the eventual extinction of tiger populations. Alternatives where tigers have priority in identified protected reserves and people have priority outside them have to be explored fast and implemented expeditiously. There is no other way.

Blaming strict nature reserves and conservation laws which accord tigers priority over humans for all the poverty and inequity-driven ills that plague our vast country is pointless polemics: These ills are consequences of the failure of development, economics and politics of the country and society as a whole and cannot be simplistically blamed on conservationists.

IV. In Chapter 5.8 'The Co-Existence Agenda', it is stated that:

Exacerbating tensions with protection

If this was not bad enough, recent events have made things even more unbearable for the people who live in these reserves.

In February 2000, the Amicus Curiae (in the omnibus forest case ongoing in the Supreme Court), had filed an application seeking... The court in its order dated 14.2.2000 ordered that 'in the meantime, we restrain the respondents from ordering the removal of dead, diseased, dying or wind-fallen trees, drift wood and grasses etc. from the national park or game sanctuary or forest.'

This order has led to a number of directions:...

But matters (and confusion) did not end there.

On October 20, 2003, the Ministry of Environment and Forests wrote to all chief secretaries a letter detailing the guidelines for diversion of forest land for non-forest purposes under the Forest Conservation Act 1980....

But even this was not enough.

On July 2, 2004, the Central Empowered Committee (CEC) set up by the Supreme Court to assist it in the forest matters, wrote to all state governments....

Impact on conservation

The combined result of these directions, orders and clarifications has been that all hell has broken loose in the protected areas....

The report gives an impression that the Hon'ble Supreme Court's orders dated 14 February 2000, 3 April 2000, 10 May 2001, and February 2002, the application moved by the Amicus Curiae pursuant of which some of the above orders have been passed, guidelines issued by the MoEF, and clarifications dated 2 July 2004 issued by the CEC for implementation of the Hon'ble Supreme Court's order are unwarranted, misplaced, and that these have been issued without application of mind. This view is totally unacceptable. I firmly believe that the Hon'ble Supreme Court's orders have been most invaluable in furthering the cause of conservation and the protection of wildlife habitat. The large-scale destruction of the tiger habitat due to massive mining, tree felling, supply of bamboo to paper mills, diversion of protected area habitat for ill-conceived projects, etc. has been controlled significantly, something which would not have been possible but for the intervention by the Hon'ble Supreme Court.

V. The concept paper simply ignores what sound science tells us about tiger conservation. It fails to note the deteriorating protection of the tiger reserve, and the need to put in place alternative, effective mechanisms to protect the core breeding populations of tigers in these protected areas. 'A Paradigm for Change' should have included a blueprint for complete revision in the process of protection and enforcement coupled with reform. Though this is suggested in other chapters its absence in the concept paper is perplexing. In the chapter on coexistence with people the recommendation to relocate people will come into direct conflict with the recommendations for coexistence of people with tigers. The suggested measures because of the inherent contradictions will only cause further degradation of tiger habitat and the tiger will be the end sufferer. After all, why would anyone want to leave a protected area when the coexistence package is so attractive? We know only too well that there are criminal elements out there ready to kill tigers and plunder their home under the cover of livelihood-related uses given a chance. The report of the CBI about Sariska has confirmed this. Let us not overlook the fact that our mandate is about securing the future of the tiger and this can only be done within the framework of our laws. Let there be no doubt about our mandate.

VI. Even after many rounds of discussions, the final chapters have changes that were never discussed. For instance:

(i) The decision taken by the Task Force was that the Hon'ble Prime Minister alone should Chair the Steering Committee of Project Tiger, not 'of the National Board of Wildlife' as suggested in the chapter 'The Way Ahead'.

(ii) It was agreed that the Wildlife Crime Bureau should be headed by a senior officer in the super time scale. Now added to this is 'the person should report to the Additional Director General of Forests'. Will this make any sense? All it will do is to prevent his independent functioning in such a sensitive investigative job. This is a typical bureaucratic approach to make the post ineffective (Chapter 'Domestic Enforcement' 3.3(a)).

(iii) Regarding the State Empowered Committee of Rajasthan, I had clearly mentioned that the extension of the term of the Committee was to do with the census the Committee was carrying out. The Committee had taken a series of actions from its inception. Now the said paragraph states, '…but has now extended its term by another three months which has delayed the urgent action needed' (page 7 of Chapter 2 'The Sariska Shock'). This is factually incorrect and misleading.

(iv) There was a boxed section in Chapter 3.5 'The Science Agenda' on how senior researchers and scientists have been hounded and harassed by officials in the Parks. This has now been deleted.

VII. I am also quite shocked how the report has glossed over the role of the MoEF including the Project Tiger Directorate in recent years. In the report I submitted in the first meeting itself on 29 April 2005, I had clearly brought out the role of the Project Tiger in the debacle that took place in Sariska and the extinction of tigers in Keladevi Sanctuary. I then pointed out that there was need to inquire into and fix responsibility for the debacle. The vital issues raised in the above report find no mention in the final report with no apparent reason for the omission. Since then more than twenty-one tigers have been found to be missing in Ranthambhore Tiger Reserve. This is a very serious issue. Again very little of this finds place in the report (Annexure D).

I had earlier sent to you (i) a draft report (now final) identifying specific problems of tiger conservation and giving specific solutions (Annexure A); (ii) an action plan for coexistence of people (Annexure B); and (iii) objection to the 'Research and Study' chapter (Annexure C). I have also objected to the recommendation of creating a sub-cadre in wildlife and have instead proposed the alternative of creating a panel of suitable officers (Para 1 (I to v) of Part II of my report [Annexure A]). I have also urged that a Central Forest and Wildlife Protection Force may be set up (Para 2 (vi) of Part II) of my report [Annexure A]).

Copies of the above are enclosed as Annexures A to C to this Note of Dissent. These together with Annexure D form part of my Dissent Note.

Lastly, I am constrained to observe that sadly much of the report has become focused on how to improve the life of people inside protected areas rather than protecting their tigers. This people focus should have been the job of another task force. The focus on the tiger has become blurred since the priorities have shifted. This is tragic and if some of the recommendations are endorsed in policy they could have dangerous repercussions for the tiger.

Dated: 27.07.2005

Valmik Thapar
Member
Task Force for Reviewing the
Management of Tiger Reserves

An Action Plan for the Long Term Survival of Tigers

INTRODUCTION

1. The Sariska tiger crisis happened because (a) the Tiger Reserve was completely mismanaged thereby leaving the field open for poachers; (b) the actual number of tigers was much less than that reflected in the earlier census figures because the census was not participatory, transparent, and scientific—the total count pugmark census methodology used since the 1970s has been proved inaccurate; and (c) excessive human and livestock disturbance right across the area.

2. The Sariska tiger crisis is symptomatic of most of India. In 2004–5 local extinctions have taken place not only in Sariska Sanctuary but also in Kela Devi Sanctuary in Rajasthan. These two sanctuaries between them lost twenty-four tigers. There was also a sharp decline of twenty-one tigers in

Ranthambhore Tiger Reserve. All the seven tigers in the Palpurkuno Sanctuary and the six tigers in Rani Durgawati Sanctuary in Madhya Pradesh have been wiped out and are now locally extinct. The decline in the Namdapha and Dampha Tiger Reserves in the north-east coupled with the losses in places like Palamau Tiger Reserve, Valmiki Tiger Reserve, Dudhwa Tiger Reserve, Indrawati Tiger Reserve, Panna Tiger Reserve, and Nagarjuna Sagar Tiger Reserve make for a grim national scenario. The states have obviously not given the required priority to the issue of conservation and protection of tigers notwithstanding the existence of many reports, recommendations, and the Wildlife Action Plan that are drawn up from time to time after involving experts at national level. The non-implementation of the National Wildlife Action Plan (2002–16) particularly stands out starkly in this regard.

3. The tremendous pressure on forests and the unsustainable levels of biomass removals by local people as well as by the forest department and rampant grazing have adversely affected the National Parks/sanctuaries/reserve forests. The State of the Forest Report, 2003, clearly reveals that forests in India having more than 70 per cent density cover only 51,285 sq. km (1.56 per cent of this country's geographic area). Further, an area of 26,245 sq. km (0.75 per cent of the country's geographic area) of dense forests having more than 40 per cent density has been lost in just two years. Out of this, 26,245 sq. km a total of 23,140 sq. km is in potentially rich tiger habitats and includes, among others, states like Assam, Jharkhand, Karnataka, Madhya Pradesh, Maharashtra, Uttar Pradesh, and Uttaranchal. The trends revealed in this latest report are exceedingly grave and disturbing and, if not reversed, could have serious

consequences for the tiger's forests. The country would have 300,000 sq. km of potential tiger habitat. Less than 10 per cent contains breeding population.

4. The unregulated biotic pressure has resulted in a conflict of interests between the local population and the forest management with the real threat of large-scale destruction of wildlife habitat looming on the horizon. Encroachments, delayed settlement of rights of the people, and the diversion of forests for ill-conceived projects have compounded the problems. In this background the populist approach of liberally regularizing encroachments and granting of pattas in forest areas and management interventions in the form of dry bamboo extraction, underplanting, etc. will mean further fragmentation inviting irreversible ecological disaster. Ultimately the tiger itself will be on the brink of extinction.

5. Tiger populations breed well and grow rapidly in population in habitats without incompatible human uses. They cannot coexist with people particularly in a situation where both human impact and livestock grazing are continuously on the increase. In the Ranthambhore Tiger Reserve the tiger has gone locally extinct in Keladevi Sanctuary and Sawai Mansingh Sanctuary in the year 2005. The reason for this is the presence of 52,510 goats, 10,178 buffaloes, 4,928 cows, and even 37 camels. Not to talk of forty villages and their ever-increasing human population. One wonders whether this is a sanctuary to protect forest and wildlife or cattle? The long-term survival of tigers will therefore depend on how secure and inviolate the protected areas in which they live are.

6. In this scenario an attempt has been made to highlight the problems (Part I) under six heads as below:

    i) Forest Personnel;

    ii) Infrastructure;

    iii) Biotic Pressure on the Wildlife Habitat;

    iv) Policy and Enforcement Issues;

    v) Research, Science, and Monitoring; and

    vi) Funds-related Issues

7. Similarly, an attempt has also been made to provide possible solutions to the problems listed in the preceding paras within the existing legal and administrative framework in the country. The solutions suggested (Part II) have been indicated under the following heads:

    i) Manage the Protected Area with Competent Officials so that Problems are Resolved;

    ii) Sensitize the Centre and State Administrations to the Needs of the Tiger;

    iii) Prevent Destruction of the Tiger's Habitat;

    iv) Strengthen Research and Training across Tiger Habitats;

    v) Provide Timely Funds to All Specially Designated Tiger Areas;

    vi) Legal Support; and

    vii) International Cooperation.

8. The Plan of Action drawn up identifies the problems and provides solutions without attempting to be all-embracing. The problems have to be tackled on a war footing to ensure that the solutions are faithfully implemented in the field in a time-bound manner. The need of the hour is implementation.

9. Issues related to personnel matters need to be given very high priority because the officials who manage the tiger's habitat and the local people have to be committed and dedicated and trained to be effective. This also raises issues about how to create a system to ensure that the best person is on the job and how to make him fully effective in that job. Particularly

given that state governments really make the final decisions in all personnel posting in reserves.

10. Similarly, how do you involve the forest management and the local inhabitants to minimize human disturbance? Ultimately both the forest management and the local people have to develop a sense of pride and satisfaction in what they are doing if protection and conservation of forests and wildlife are to be sustainable in the long term. Today the area in which tigers live undisturbed is grossly inadequate and therefore the long-term survival of the tiger hangs in the balance.

11. There has to be close coordination and dovetailing of the activities initiated by the National Level Committee headed by the Prime Minister, the State Level Committees headed by the Chief Ministers, and the National Advisory Committee on Research so that they all move and act in tandem and become receptive mechanisms for change.

12. It is with all these factors in mind that this plan of action has been outlined in a simple and straightforward way without too much detail which, wherever required, has been left to the appropriate expert administrative and research committees. This Plan of Action has been so structured so as to ensure that the existing delicate balance of responsibility and power between the centre and the states is not disturbed.

PART I
THE PROBLEMS

I. Forest Personnel

i) Lack of professionally trained, committed, competent and physically fit Field Directors and other officials.

  ii) The Forest Department's mindset is that of an owner and not a custodian.

 iii) There is no system of selective appointments to the sensitive posts at various levels in the protected areas (PAs)/ Tiger Reserves (instead many are treated as punishment postings).

 iv) Vacant posts numbering nearly 5,000 in PAs/Tiger Reserves.

  v) The average age of forest guards is above 50 years.

 vi) No effective system of specialized training (induction stage, in service, etc.).

 vii) Transfer policy—no fixed tenure. Irrational transfers on extraneous considerations.

viii) Lack of incentives including special pay, housing, etc.

 ix) Insufficient promotion avenues—forest guards remain stagnant for years.

  x) Poor service conditions for front-line staff in terms of provisions for ration, special pay, family accommodation, working hours, schooling, medical facilities, compensatory leave, and life and other insurance policies.

 xi) Physical fitness programme—No training or drill centres on site.

 xii) Lack of effective disciplinary action system against the delinquent officials. Punishment should be swift and act as a deterrent.

xiii) Lack of priority for deployment of armed police in times of crisis/to sensitive areas.

II. Infrastructure

  i) Forest officials are not empowered to use firearms for protection of government property/forest produce/wildlife except in Karnataka/Tamil Nadu.

ii) The officials are equipped with inadequate as well as outdated firearms and, wherever available, no proper training programme/facilities exist.

iii) Lack of uniform, shoes, patrolling kit for staff.

iv) No/inadequate wireless hand-sets for communication.

v) Inadequate mobility (motorcycles, jeeps, trucks, boats, etc.).

vi) Inadequate forest *chowkies*/posts, anti poaching camps, patrol camps, and staff quarters.

vii) Poor service and maintenance of vehicles, wireless, chowkies/checkposts, buildings, equipments, etc.

III. Biotic Pressure on the Wildlife Habitat

i) Settlement of acquisition rights under Wild Life (Protection) Act, 1972 pending for decades in PAs.

ii) No effective steps taken to prevent and remove encroachments.

iii) Very poor progress of relocation of villages located inside the National Park/sanctuary.

iv) Inadequate compensation for the loss of life and property including crops, resulting in anger and deliberate damage both to wildlife and habitat.

v) Habitat fragmentation due to ill-conceived projects/schemes which have an adverse impact on PAs.

vi) Absence of adequate wildlife corridors connecting one PA/ Tiger Reserve with another.

vii) Conflict of PA with local community (within as well as in peripheral villages).

viii) Rampant legal/illegal mining continues.

ix) Unregulated and poor tourism management.

x) Excessive/illegal grazing and removal of fuelwood, minor forest produce, etc. continues at unsustainable levels.

xi) Roads (state and other roads) with heavy traffic passing through PAs.

xii) Poor management of tigers outside PAs/tiger reserves.

IV. Policy and Enforcement Issues

i) Lack of will in the higher political and administrative echelons at both centre and state levels (committees hardly meet, decisions kept pending, decisions when taken remain unimplemented, posts not filled, dual charge, powers of transfer/posting misused, etc.).

ii) Ineffectiveness of the MoEF in terms of convening meetings of committees, decision-taking, follow-up action on decisions taken, appointments etc. Recommendations of endless expert committees have been gathering dust in the MoEF for years, e.g. Subramanayam Committee.

iii) Lack of a grasp of human and ecological concerns in wildlife conservation resulting in poor policy.

iv) National Wildlife Action Plan (2002–16) exists only on paper. Completely ignored and remains unimplemented.

v) Lack of professionally trained wildlife officials leading to poor enforcement of forest and wildlife laws which is a critical component in the protection work.

vi) Lack of coordination between centre and states in the implementation of policies, laws, guidelines, and directives.

vii) Lack of coordination among the various agencies/departments.

viii) National Wildlife Crime Bureau is yet to be set up even though the decision to create it was taken eight years ago.

ix) Ineffective intelligence collection and networking at local state, national, and international levels, and absent or ineffective in most states.

V. *Research, Science, and Monitoring*

i) No wildlife management manual—the PA manager has no guidelines to refer to and no clear prescription to follow which leads to ad hoc decision-making.

ii) Absence/poor quality of Management Plans for PAs. Wherever they exist the prescriptions are poorly implemented due to lack of funds or expertise.

iii) Poor scientific input in management and monitoring of PAs.

iv) Unscientific estimation of tiger population—grossly inflated because of defective methodology; also lacks transparency.

v) Size of the breeding tiger population depends on good protection/adequate prey base, minimum disturbance, and adequate water availability.

vi) Independent scientific researchers discouraged, even harassed.

vii) Poor management of the area (habitat, animals, people tourism, etc.). Should include independent ecological audit and monitoring.

VI. *Funds-related Issues*

i) Grossly inadequate allocation—(State Plans, Central Plan).

ii) Diversion of central assistance—in absence of proper funding mechanism.

iii) Earmarking of funds necessary so that they are not diverted for non-forestry/non-wildlife activities.

iv) Delay in disbursement and utilization of funds—late release of funds results in them either being misutilized or remaining unutilized because it is not possible to use them before the financial year ends on 31 March of that particular year.

v) Inadequate delegation of financial powers—purchases, etc.

vi) No funds for intelligence gathering.

PART II

SOLUTIONS

I. Manage the Protected Area with Competent Officials so that Problems are Resolved

i) Prepare a panel of officials who have evinced keen interest in wildlife—at the level of Field Director (Conservator of Forests/ Deputy Conservator of Forest level), ACF, and RFO. Make a small beginning—say with 10 Field Directors, 25 ACFs, 50–100 RFOs and then increase the numbers.

ii) The panel to be drawn up by the MoEF in consultation with independent experts and state governments. The detailed procedure and standards for this purpose to be laid down by the National Committee headed by the Prime Minister (refer para II (i)).

iii) The empanelled officers may be considered for posting in any of the premier PAs within their home cadre and in other states (on state to state deputation basis).

iv) In addition to forest officers, the panel may include non-government experts and willing officers from other services on deputation. Lateral induction may also be resorted to.

v) Extensive training on a continuous basis to empanelled officials.

vi) Security of tenure to be ensured—officials to be shifted before completion of tenure only in exceptional cases with reasons to be recorded and communicated along with transfer orders.

vii) Like some of the specialized government agencies, the tenure may be extendable in deserving cases—no cap need be fixed.

viii) Eligibility for in situ promotion to ensure continuity.

ix) Special pay and facilities for officials posted in the field.

x) Mechanism for swiftly fixing accountability and responsibility against lax/corrupt/defaulting officials.

II. Sensitize the Centre and State Administrations to the Needs of the Tiger

i) A National Tiger Management Committee, at the central level, chaired by the Prime Minister with members from the Ministries of Environment and Forests, Home, Finance, Tribal Welfare and Rural Development, and the Planning Commission as well as independent experts should be constituted to provide policy input and inject innovative reforms in the system. The said Committee, wherever required, may intervene to provide the requisite political and administrative inputs and support at the central/state level. The central committee will regularly interact with the state committees chaired by the chief ministers.

ii) A High-powered committee in each state under the Chairmanship of the Chief Minister with the Forest Minister, Chief Secretary, Secretaries looking after Departments of Forests, Home, Finance, and Planning. Principal Chief Conservator of Forests, and Chief Wildlife Warden as members to be constituted immediately for taking decisions for filling up vacant posts, imparting training to the front-line staff, providing incentives to the officials, improving service conditions and facilities, and the deploying of armed police in sensitive areas in times of crisis. This committee will also deal with other administrative issues such as authorizing the use of firearms, providing uniforms, patrolling equipment, wireless networks and vehicles, and the allocation and release of adequate funds for wildlife conservation with adequate delegation of financial powers, etc.

iii) To accord priority to and focus on conservation and protection issues, a separate department for Forests and Wildlife should immediately be carved out within the MoEF. It may be mentioned that during the meeting of the National Board of Wildlife held on 17 March 2005 chaired by the Prime Minister, there was a general consensus on a separate Department for Forests and Wildlife.

iv) Immediate implementation of the National Wildlife Action Plan (2002–16). Funds to be earmarked for the implementation of this Plan.

v) The Wildlife Crime Bureau should immediately be made effective, preferably before 1 September 2005, and even after it is set up, the CBI should continue to play a lead role.

vi) A Central Forest and Wildlife Protection Force should be constituted by drawing officials on deputation from the Police, CRPF, CISF, ITBP, etc. This fully equipped and trained force can be deployed at short notice to any trouble spot.

vii) The officials posted in PAs should not be used for election or any other non-protection work. Similarly the vehicles belonging to PAs should not be diverted for any work relating to election or other duties.

viii) Projects like eco-development should not be handled by the Forest Department whose sole focus must be protection.

ix) The environmental impact of all commercial and developmental projects proposed in and around the tiger's habitat needs to be thoroughly scrutinized by experts before the projects are cleared.

x) The impact of externally aided projects in the field of wildlife conservation and protection has by and large been negative and therefore should be discouraged.

III. Prevent Destruction of the Tiger's Habitat

i) Settlement/acquisition of rights in the PAs under the provisions of the Wild Life (Protection) Act, 1972 should be undertaken on priority basis.

ii) A time-bound programme for the relocation of villages from within the protected areas should be prepared and implemented at the earliest. The rehabilitation plan should ensure that the compensation package is liberal and attractive so that it leads to a better quality of life. As far as possible the relocation process should be outsourced with the Forest Department playing only a catalytic role.

iii) Since the above matter is of critical importance, the State Committees chaired by the Chief Ministers should regularly review the all-round progress. Funds for this purpose may be made available by the MoEF, Ministry of Tribal Affairs, Ministry of Rural Development, and the state governments. Other sources like the Compensatory Afforestation Fund may also be tapped.

iv) Prevention and eviction of encroachments should be emphasized.

v) The villagers in and around the PAs should be effectively involved in conservation and protection of the area. Some of the suggested measures are:

a) Creation of village patrols where local villagers are trained and given monthly remuneration, and like home guards can be effectively deployed. A specially designed course may be drawn up for their training.

b) Use of local villagers for water and soil conservation, fire protection, as tourist guides and interpreters, and in any other PA based activity. Suitable training courses for these activities may be drawn up.

c) Creation of a network of local people in intelligence gathering against timber mafia and poachers.

d) Build up close rapport with forest staff and local anti-poaching patrols (to use their traditional knowledge of the area) to track poachers.

e) Impart training for their involvement in scientific research (special courses that are site-specific to the ongoing research can be conducted).

f) The revenue from tourism collected by the Park authorities may be used for the establishment of a Village Trust Fund for engaging the local population in the protection of the PA—to be administered by the village elders. Some of this revenue could also go towards staff welfare.

g) The local population may play an effective role in conservation and protection of the area by establishing Management Boards/Committees for the PA consisting of representatives of the villages, Park officials, and locally based conservation NGOs and scientists. This Management Board/Committee may meet every three months in order to encourage a transparent and participatory approach towards management and thereafter will regularly send its recommendations to the State Level Committee.

h) Rehabilitation of hunting tribes, traditional poachers living in and around PAs should be done on a priority basis (as was done in Periyar). One way of rehabilitating them is by involving them in anti-poaching work which gives rich dividends. They could also be resettled away from forest areas and then given alternatives for their livelihood. This would need to be closely monitored.

vi) Specific prescriptions for tiger protection should be incorporated in the Working Plans in respect of identified tiger-rich habitats in forests outside the protected areas.

vii) Priority needs to be accorded for identification and protection of wildlife corridors for the movement of tigers/ wildlife from one PA/habitat to another.

viii) Imposing a cess on hotels and tour operators who depend on the PA for their business. The cess will be determined by the State Committees chaired by the Chief Ministers. The cess can be used for the welfare of the local population such as schooling, and medicine.

ix) Efforts should be made to provide alternate routes to the existing roads/National/State Highways passing through the PAs which are playing havoc with the tiger and wildlife.

x) Mining (new leases as well as renewal cases), hotels and resorts, and other activities which have a negative impact on the habitat and wildlife should not be permitted within the safety zone (say 1 km from the boundary).

xi) Protected Areas affected by insurgency/naxalites and which have good forests and tiger habitats require special attention through special measures. Both Central and State Committees will deal with this issue.

xii) Under no circumstances should mining, agriculture, regularization of encroachment, and other activities which lead to fragmentation/destruction of the habitat be permitted.

Many of the above activities can be prohibited/regulated under the existing provisions of the Wild Life (Protection) Act, 1972 and also by issuing of notifications under the Environment (Protection) Act by the MoEF.

IV. Strengthen Research and Training across Tiger Habitats

   i) A Wildlife Management Manual/Code should be prepared in a time-bound manner by the MoEF with the assistance of the Wildlife Institute of India. It should be ensured that every PA is managed as per the prescriptions of the Management Plan for that particular PA. The Manual would be akin to a handbook that provides detailed information for the better management of the PA.

   ii) An important component of management will be a detailed prescription for tourism, managing it and ensuring both respect for the tiger and the visitor.

   iii) A National Level Research Advisory Committee with independent experts and institutional members may be constituted (this should be an autonomous body free of government shackles so that it renders independent and objective advice fearlessly) to give inputs/frame guidelines from time to time regarding:

      a) tiger census methodology (to be decided after a complete review by all scientists associated with this especially because of the serious limitations of the total counts in the pugmark methodology);

      b) research, monitoring, and ecological audit; and

      c) issue of transparent guidelines for Research Projects including redressal of grievances expeditiously.

   iv) Revamp the course and curriculum at the IGNFA which imparts training to IFS probationers and also organize special refresher courses for serving IFS officers.

   v) A full-fledged Centre for Wildlife Studies consisting of (a) forest officials and other experts on deputation to the Indira Gandhi National Forest Academy; (b) visiting faculty consisting of reputed national-level experts; and (c) experts from the Wildlife Institute of India, etc. should be set up in the Indira Gandhi National Academy of Administration.

vi) The Centre for Wildlife Studies in coordination with the MoEF should be made responsible for the preparation of the curriculum and imparting of training for the IFS probationers, conducting refresher courses, and specialized studies/research., etc.

vii) This Centre may also be used for providing specialized refresher courses/training programme for other officials (from the Forest Department as well as other Departments).

viii) A detailed annual presentation can be made to the NBWL/ Prime Minister's Committee by the National Advisory Board of Research in order to apprise him each year regarding the prevailing state of affairs.

V. Provide Timely Funds to All Specifically Designated Tiger Areas

The central assistance, instead of being routed through the normal state government machinery, should be released directly to the field staff on the existing pattern of release of funds by the MoEF through the Forest Development Agency (FDA). This will not only ensure timely release and utilization of funds but responsibility and accountability can also be easily fixed for non-utilization and misuse of funds. A system of concurrent financial audit as well as ecological audit should be put in place

VI. Legal Support

i) Legal cells headed by experienced legal officers should be set up in each state for imparting training to officers/staff in investigative skills, collection of evidence, preparation of charge sheets/complaints, etc.

ii) The Legal Cell will vigorously and closely pursue and monitor serious cases of poaching, etc. They shall in such cases appoint special counsels/senior lawyers so that cases are taken to their logical end without delay.

iii) Regional forensic laboratories to be established and recognized under the provisions of Code of Criminal Procedure. The opinion/reports of these laboratories to be accepted as evidence in the Courts.

iv) Provide prompt and effective legal support to officers/staff facing harassment on account of false retaliatory cases filed against them.

v) Should also expedite cases (departmental or criminal) against officials by pursuing them vigorously.

VII. *International Cooperation*

In some areas, India's tiger habitats are contiguous across national boundaries with Nepal, Bhutan, Bangladesh, and Mynamar. These transboundary issues need to be taken up at bilateral level as also at SAARC meetings so that a joint/special task force could be set up for better protection and management of these areas. This will greatly help the present population of tigers that move to and fro across international borders.

Recommendations of the Task Force Regarding Coexistence of People in the Protected Areas— Draft Prepared by Valmik Thapar

BASIC CONSERVATION STRATEGY

i) The areas falling within the National Parks should be made inviolate. People living in these areas should be relocated and their rights acquired under the Wild Life Protection

Act (WLPA). If any village is found to be in an area not of strategic importance within the National Park the boundary of the Park should be altered to exclude such villages. The excluded village may be included in the adjoining sanctuary, if any. Needless to say that the rehabilitation package should be the best available and attractive.

ii) Relocation from the sanctuary should be restricted to the minimum, taking into account the conservation value of the area, i.e. the relocation should be restricted to the areas which are absolutely vital for the protection of tigers and are to be treated as 'core area' for tiger conservation.

iii) A detailed time-bound plan for relocation of villages identified should be prepared and funds required should be made available at the earliest.

iv) It should be made clear that the existing provisions of the WLPA allow the right holders to carry out their legitimate activities such as agriculture, grazing, etc.

v) Pursuant to the Hon'ble Supreme Court's order dated 14 February 2000 in IA No. 548, no harvesting/removal of forest produce including minor forest produce is permissible from national parks/sanctuaries.

vi) It may be clarified that the WLPA allows making of alternate arrangements for making available fuel, fodder, and other forest produce to the existing right holders (Section 18-A(2)). Section 29 of the WLPA provides that any forest produce required from the sanctuaries should be distributed for meeting the personal bona fide needs of the people living in and around the sanctuaries (and not for any commercial purpose).

vii) In view of the above legal provisions, the MoEF may move the Hon'ble Supreme Court for modification of its order dated 14 February 2000 to enable the legal right holders to enjoy the benefits in the sanctuary and in the areas where final notifications have not been issued. The CEC has filed its report dated 4 November 2004, which is under consideration of the Hon'ble Supreme Court. The MoEF may intervene in the said IA and modification of the said order.

viii) A number of sanctuaries have been notified which include non-strategic areas of very low conservation value with many villages. A time-bound exercise of rationalizing the boundaries of such sanctuaries should be undertaken by the MoEF in consultation with the states. This process will result in the exclusion of many areas. This will be of great help in mitigating the sufferings of a large number of people.

ix) Even in non-strategic areas of the sanctuaries, if the villagers volunteer to shift out, such shifting should be facilitated.

x) The villages from the sanctuaries may be allowed to be shifted into reserve forest/protected forest/unclassed forest without payment of compensatory afforestation, NPV, etc. For this purpose a simplified procedure for granting approval under the FC Act should be formulated.

xi) For the villages which remain inside the sanctuary, innovative interventions within the framework of the law and the Supreme Court's order should be introduced to ensure that the bona fide livelihood needs of the local people are taken care of. These may include :

a) preference in employment in various government departments;

b) engagement in water and soil conservation and other forest management measures;

c) involvement in village protection force;

d) passing on part of cess collected from nearby hotels;

e) employment in private sector hotels and in other developmental projects around the park;

f) tourist guides, trackers, intelligence gatherers, etc.

The above list is indicative and not exhaustive. The management plan should include a detailed prescription for involving the local population in the park management, mitigating man–animal conflict with a view to improve their quality of life.

The existing provisions of the Wild Life (Protection) Act, 1972 provide for meeting all the concerns and requirements of the local people. The only issue is its effective implementation, therefore, there is no need for any review/revision of the Act.

The MoEF's directions are in consonance and in compliance with the Hon'ble Supreme Court's orders and therefore cannot/ should not be withdrawn. It may be mentioned that the Hon'ble Supreme Court in Pradip Krishen v/s UOI (AIR 1996 SC 2040) has specifically directed completion of settlement proceedings expeditiously.

Objection by Mr Valmik Thapar, Member Tiger Task Force on Research and Science to be Incorporated in the Report

Mr Valmik Thapar, Member of the Task Force, has submitted the following note of dissent in relation to the recommendations on approaches to be adopted for monitoring tiger populations in the future.

The past history of Project Tiger is strewn with failures to reform the monitoring system due to lack of attention to detail and ignoring of inputs from scientists seriously engaged with tiger conservation issues.

Since then the proposed scheme has been thoroughly examined and critiqued by leading carnivore ecologists who have specialized in population survey methodologies for decades at the specific request of the Task Force. These inputs have come from Dr Ullhas Karanth, Dr Raghu Chundawath, Dr M.D. Madhusudan, Dr A.J.T. Johnsingh, Dr S.P. Goel, Dr Yoganand (the last three are from the Wildlife Institute of India). All these analyses, have endorsed the broad idea of Project Tiger taking up countrywide distribution surveys of tigers under a new sampling-based paradigm (instead of total count censuses). But they all have pointed out several flaws in the proposed scheme. Their critique covers the issue of the very design of the surveys in proposed stages, practical problems in implementing many of the survey methods in field conditions, problems of analysis as well as with the demonstrated example from Satpura–Maikal Pilot Project which actually has not implemented the occupancy estimation approach. Given this, Valmik Thapar strongly believes that a technical panel of experts proposed by the Task Force should examine all these aspects of the proposed methodology before it is implemented in order to resolve the problems that are admitted to exist with this protocol. This should be done within a time frame of just 3 months. Such a process will ensure the removal of any flaws and errors which may be present and prevent costly expenditures from taking place before the method has been vetted. This safeguard will be vital to this new step we are taking.

Therefore Valmik Thapar disagrees with the view that the protocol regarding tiger estimation should be implemented immediately and even before the technical panel has a chance to examine and improve it.

Special Note

From: Valmik Thapar
Member—Tiger Task Force (TTF)

To: The Chairman and all other Members,
for the meeting of the Task Force on 29 April 2005.

Date: 28 April 2005

The Tiger Task Force (TTF) was born of a crisis that resulted in the extinction of the tigers in Sariska and Kela Devi Sanctuaries.

The Prime Minister described the state of affairs as the worst crisis of wildlife since the inception of Project Tiger.

OBJECTIVE

The objective of this note is to spell out short-term and long-term measures that will help save wild tigers. I presume that is the objective of the TTF.

Short-term Measures

1. Deployment of additional Home Guards and Armed Police in different tiger reserves across India which are facing serious problems. This is an essential preventive measure pre-monsoon 2005.
   a) Manas Tiger Reserve, Assam
   b) Namdapha Tiger Reserve, Arunachal Pradesh
   c) Simlipal Tiger Reserve, Orissa
   d) Valmiki Tiger Reserve, Bihar
   e) Palamau Tiger Reserve, Jharkhand
   f) Nagarjuna Tiger Reserve, Andhra Pradesh
   g) Indravati Tiger Reserve, Chhattisgarh
   h) Panna Tiger Reserve, Madhya Pradesh
   i) Pench Tiger Reserve, Madhya Pradesh
   j) Tadoba Tiger Reserve, Maharashtra
   k) Dudhwa Tiger Reserve, Uttar Pradesh
2. Ranthambhore and Sariska Tiger Reserves are not on this list as the Government of Rajasthan has already taken the essential steps of deploying more than 300 home guards and armed Police on the periphery as a precaution against armed intruders. All regular raids are being conducted against possible poachers and unwanted elements. A full infrastructure of vehicles has also been provided for patrolling

(details of this can be made available from the state as an example of what can be done as preventive steps for other states to follow).

DISSEMINATE ALL INFORMATION. This is vital as a case study so that everyone realizes what happened and can learn a lesson from it to prevent repeats. This case study should be sent across India as an example of what can happen.

What Happened?

Let's not forget that as far as Sariska is concerned the Director of the Reserve provided an early warning in his census report on 25 April 2004. It remained unheeded by the Chief Wildlife Warden of Rajasthan and he only communicated it or part of it on 17 August 2004 to the Directorate of Project Tiger who did not react till February 2005 after each tiger had been wiped out.

On 25 April 2004 the Field Director of Sariska reported to the Chief Wildlife Warden of Rajasthan that:

on the basis of the available evidence and on ocular analysis of the pugmarks and movement of tigers the team reached a rough estimate that the number of tigers were between 16 and 18.... Since this estimate is quite different from that of last year's census and could lead to controversy...experts should be called to carry out examination of the evidence.

However, the Chief Wildlife Warden ignored this letter and on 17 August 2004 sent a letter to the Director, Project Tiger, stating that the Sariska Tiger Reserve had sixteen–eighteen tigers. An asterisk note adds that 'due to bad weather most of the Pugmark Impression Pads were damaged and it obstructed effective trekking and collection of evidence.'

Why did Project Tiger in Delhi not reject the census and order a new one?

3. It is also understood that a Tiger Assessment Report was submitted by the Wildlife Institute of India after a ten-day site visit by two senior biologists and eight Ph.D. students. They also found no evidence of tigers and shockingly found a wild boar stumbling around dragging a tiger trap on its leg. This was March.

4. It is understood that the CBI report on Sariska talks of:
   a) Grossly inflated census figures over 10 years related to the maximum sustainable population—80 per cent margin of error.
   b) 75 per cent of the staff is untrained and unsuitable for extensive on-foot responsibilities.
   c) More than 3,000 hectares of the tiger reserve is encroached.
   d) Complete lack of monitoring and astonishment regarding the fact that NO intelligence was gathered on poachers— glaring failure of intelligence by forest staff.
   e) No effort to effectively patrol or maintain communication with villagers.

We must examine this example—it must be reflective of several areas in India. If these factors are true for other areas, there is little chance of saving tigers. Also examine why the CBI was able to find out all this in two days and Project Tiger 'not at all'. This is the only way to understand the root of the problems that afflict our tiger reserves. We need to send the Sariska case history to all our Project Tiger reserves and other protected areas so that such a debacle is never repeated.

If the CBI can examine predator-prey density ratios,

statistics, and census analysis what stopped Project Tiger from doing this in earlier years?

5. We also need to study the Kela Devi example where in 600 odd sq. km of this sanctuary (a part of Ranthambhore Tiger Reserve) in February 2005 there were written records stating that for months there had been no sign of any tigers. In fact in February this was communicated to the Field Director of Ranthambhore Tiger Reserve.

Yet when the Additional DG (Wildlife) and the Director, Project Tiger went to Ranthambhore Tiger Reserve for a site visit immediately after Sariska (23 February 2005) they wrote in their site visit report:

The alleged disappearance of 18 tigers from Ranthambhore Tiger Reserve is misleading and not true. There is a daily monitoring system in place wherein details of tigers utilizing different parts of the habitat within the reserve are recorded.

The idea of daily monitoring of tigers without radio collars is an absurdity. While on 23 February 2005 the Director, Project Tiger, made these comments on a site visit to Ranthambhore Tiger Reserve, the Deputy Director, Project Tiger, Sawai Madhopur (buffer) had on 3 February 2005 (twenty days earlier) sent a letter to the Field Director saying that in a large component of Ranthambhore Tiger Reserve—which is Kela Devi Sanctuary—there was no evidence of tigers, pugmarks or faecal matter. On 16 March 2005 he again sent a letter to the Field Director stating that after intensive patrolling he could not find anything and finally the Field Director sent a letter to the Chief Wildlife Warden on 31 March 2005 saying that the tigers in Kela Devi were down from six to zero, that is a local extinction had taken place.

The Project Tiger Directorate receives updating periodically from tiger reserves on important events/happenings, as well as mortality of wild animals due to poaching/natural deaths, complemented by factual information gathered during frequent field visits of MoEF officials. Therefore, there is no collapse of any warning system.

The alleged decline of tiger counts across the country is only a speculation at this stage by NGOs and media.

Is this why the Deputy Director's letters of 3 February and 16 March, 2005 were not acted on? Or is it because there was no knowledge of them? Both are terrible examples of monitoring or early warning mechanisms!

It is obvious that from both the examples of Sariska and Ranthambhore that one part of Project tiger (the field) did not know what the other part of Project Tiger (Delhi) was doing. There is obviously no daily monitoring, let alone communication of it to Project Tiger, Delhi. Project Tiger (Delhi) appears to live in the dark about most matters.

Analyse both these examples. They must be symptomatic of reserves across India. We need to find ways to prevent a recurrence.

6. We must also look at the role of activist NGOs both in Sariska and Kela Devi. In Sariska, Rajendra Singh's Tarun Bharat Sangh was deeply involved with wildlife matters. They had in the late 1990s held a Bagh Bachavo Yatra and have stated that they had sent some warning of the crisis of 2004 to the forest department. In Kela Devi another NGO had played a role in preventing livestock from outer areas from coming in and it was a much-quoted example of people's participation in wildlife protection. Arun Jindal from the Society for Sustainable Development based in Karauli had for years been supporting a process of participation. So had Rajendra Singh.

Let us learn from their failure—since the tiger has disappeared from both areas.

7. Co-opting as a special invitee the head of the investigation in Sariska, Shri B.K. Sharma from the CBI, and asking him to make a presentation both on Sariska and other areas in terms of poaching and illegal trade.

8. Provide a mandate to the CBI to continue investigations into poaching, illegal trade, etc. all over India and this will be an immediate deterrent to the accelerating activities of poachers. This will have to be recommended by the Prime Minister.

9. Immediate educational awareness campaigns in the media regarding threats of poaching, illegal woodcutting by timber mafias and encroachment on forest land by commercial groups including mining mafias.

10. All relevant reports, CBI, WII, Project Tiger assessments and evaluations, earlier reports, i.e. Wildlife Crime Bureau, Subramanyam Committee, affidavits of the MoEF to the Supreme Court, Supreme Court orders to be provided for the reference of the Committee immediately. The CBI report will be essential reading for every Park Director across India.

11. Activate all State Wildlife Advisory Boards to convene meetings since these institutions need to be alerted to the gravity of the problem and thereby take necessary steps to diffuse the problems. These boards are also like early warning systems that can help detect other problems.

12. Immediate implementation of the *new* Wildlife Crime Prevention and Control Bureau as endorsed by the National Board of Wildlife in its 17 March 2005 meeting. This is an immediate necessity to prevent the illegal trade in tiger derivatives and minimize the activities of poachers.

Extracts from

Report (Uncorrected) of the Department-Related Parliamentary Standing Committee on Science & Technology, Environment & Forests

(139ᵗʰ & 146ᵗʰ Reports)

Presented to the Rajya Sabha on 25 April 2005 (Laid on the Table of the Lok Sabha on 25 April 2005)

The Committee expresses its serious concern over the sudden disappearance of the Tigers from Sariska Tiger Reserve. The Committee feels that the negligence of Forest staff coupled with large-scale poaching has cost the country dear. Conditions in most of the national parks are more or less same, posing a clear danger to protected animal species. Poaching is not a new phenomenon but the poachers are now more advanced with latest weapons and very powerful communication network, making the lackadaisically managed tiger reserves easy picking. In contrast, forest guards are usually equipped with a wooden stick and most of the times without any means of communication. Taking note of this alarming situation, the Committee is of considered opinion that a Special Task Force at the central or state level with the involvement of paramilitary forces must be constituted to combat the menace of poaching of wildlife.

Moreover, the Ministry should also involve the villagers living in and around National Parks/Tiger reserves to prevent the poaching as they are aware of the tentative movements of the poachers but because of poachers' threats or any other compulsion, they refrain from coming out openly to help the Forest Department to catch the poachers. The Committee strongly recommends that all vacant positions should be filled immediately and at no time any tiger reserve in the country should be left with the junior officers.

The Committee notes the reply of the Ministry and is strongly of the opinion that Ministry's efforts have in no way improved the state of 'Project Tiger' and management of tiger parks in the country as sadly reflected in the increased incidence of poaching of tigers and disappearance of a section of wild cats from strategic areas in the country. The Ministry needs to undertake complete review of its programmes and plug the loopholes, where necessary to implement them effectively.

The Committee feels that the Ministry has not taken much action in pursuance of its recommendation for protecting and developing wildlife parks. The Ministry has informed only about tigers and their habitats. Nothing has been mentioned about other animals like elephant, lion, rhino, etc. Even achievements of the programmes under 'Project Tiger' have come under scrutiny as evident from recent news reports that tigers have disappeared from the Sariska and Ranthambhore Tiger Reserves. The Committee feels that for proper development and protection of the wildlife parks, emphasis should be given on anti-poaching camps, mobile squads, capacity building of frontline staff in intelligence gathering, detection and successful prosecution of cases and providing necessary infrastructure to them.

The Committee is of the view that quoting statutory provisions is not the proper action expected from the Ministry. What is more important is proper and holistic implementation/enforcement of these provisions. These provisions/guidelines themselves cannot act as a deterrent. With the support of these provisions, Ministry should evolve a mechanism to implement its plans/steps emphatically.

The Committee observes that despite various schemes of the Ministry, effective patrolling of wildlife is almost missing as is evident from rampant poaching. In the recent past, the Committee during its study visits to some Tiger Reserves/Wildlife Sanctuaries was anguished to see the forest rangers equipped with a wooden stick and roaming on feet [sic] whereas poachers, in contrast, are believed to be equipped with latest communication network, modern weapons and vehicles. In view thereof, any financial assistance for the wildlife protection which was made has not been successfully utilized in the past. The Committee reiterates that interested NGOs should be encouraged to provide latest transport and communication facilities to the staff responsible for the protection of wildlife parks. The Committee is also of the opinion that a 'Special Task Force' must be constituted to combat the menace of poaching of wildlife.

The Committee feels that by merely including endangered species of animals in Schedule I of the Wildlife (Protection) Act, 1972, may not be enough. The Ministry should also take some stringent measures along with enforcing the provisions of the Act for their survival. The Committee would have appreciated if the Ministry had come forward with a comprehensive plan of action for preserving the aforesaid species.

Long-term Measures

1. Discussions on creating a dedicated Ministry for Forests and Wildlife by bifurcating the present Ministry of Environment and Forests.
2. Creating a dedicated and specially trained National Park Service meant to govern and administer 100 of the best protected areas in India. This service must allow inter-state transfers.
3. Opening fresh recruitment for all forest staff on a priority basis just like the Police and Army, and filling up of all vacancies.
4. Extra allocation of finances by the Planning Commission for the forests and wildlife sector especially in the area of protection. A meeting will be essential with the Deputy Chairman of the Planning Commission.

5. A meeting between the Prime Minister and all Chief Ministers regarding the crisis of the tiger and other wildlife; Members of Parliament to be present; slide presentations to be made. We must realize that saving the tiger and forest is a state subject and therefore Chief Ministers will have to be inspired to act.

6. Encouraging the role of scientific research and its recommendations in the management of our wilderness.

7. Encouraging the protection of our wilderness areas by local communities/tribals/forest dwellers who can be fully trained in special schools for this purpose and for other requirements of forests and wildlife management, i.e. eco-tourism etc. Even if 10 people each are trained in one Park and the programme started in 20 Parks within 6 months we will have 200 people engaged in protection. And this figure can be tripled over the years.

8. Creating a Manual or Code of Conduct and Procedure for all protected area managers that becomes their 'Bible' to follow in the field and includes systems for early warning and detection of problems etc.

9. A review of the entire structure of Project Tiger with a view to overhaul it and the creation of a Project Tiger Division in the MoEF that is streamlined, efficient, and effective, especially in a crisis situation. Better communication from the field to Project Tiger (Delhi) so that Kela Devis and Sariskas don't happen again.

10. Financial allocations and disbursement of money—how to create a rapid flow and prevent non-utilization of funds, etc.

11. Corridor connectivity from one tiger area to another is also vital for the prevention of habitat fragmentation and vital existing corridors must be identified for protection.

WHY DO TIGERS DIE AT THE HANDS
OF POACHERS OR OTHERS?

a) as revenge against livestock kills;
b) by accident as poachers try for ungulates;
c) by intent and for commerce be it skin or bones;
d) orchestrated by mining mafias or those who want protected areas denotified and habitats destroyed.

The above note warns that if the climate of Sariska or Ranthambhore prevails then there could be a wipe out of tigers across India. To prevent their death by poachers or others we need early implementation of both short-term and long-term measures. This is the only way forward.

Valmik Thapar

Annexure 2

The Tiger and Tibet
by Belinda Wright

It has now become clear that Tibet and other nearby regions of China are the biggest markets for tiger, leopard, and otter skins smuggled from India. In the markets of Lhasa, the capital of the Tibet Autonomous Region, tiger, leopard, and otter skins can be seen openly for sale sown onto Tibetan costumes called *chubas*. Fresh tiger and leopard skins can also be found for sale in Lhasa, and a large number of leopard and snow leopard skins are being openly sold on the streets of Linxia. The skin chubas are worn by Tibetan people, mainly from Kham, at their festivals in Tibet and adjoining Sichuan.

These are the findings of a survey which was carried out in August 2005 by a UK-based NGO, the Environmental Investigation Agency (EIA), and the Wildlife Protection Society of India (WPSI). It confirms earlier reports—notably in October 2003 when China's Anti-Smuggling Bureau seized a truck in the Tibet Autonomous Region containing 31 tiger, 581 leopard, and 778 otter skins from India. In an earlier survey in May 2004, the EIA found whole fresh leopard skins for sale in Lhasa.

In August, we found that the open sale and use of fresh tiger, leopard, and otter skins is now even more widespread. All the dealers that we talked to said the skins had come from India, and most of the Tibetans wearing them said that they had purchased the skins in the past 18 months. It appears that funds to purchase the expensive skins come from the recently increasing sale of a local caterpillar fungus (*yasa gompe*) which is used in oriental medicine, and of a rare mushroom—both highly valued in Japan and elsewhere. The skin chubas are only worn twice a year, at local horse festivals—where we witnessed dancers, horse riders, visitors, and even organisers and officials, wearing skins— and at the Tibetan New Year.

One young man wearing a skin was Pentsok, a 21-year old, who had just returned home to the town of Litang in Sichuan Province from studies in India. He told us that, when he arrived home, his father gave him a tiger skin that he had bought for Rmb100,000 (approx. US$12,500 or Rs 5,37,500). He said that he didn't really like the skin but, since it was a gift from his father, he would wear it for festivals and new year—and no, he had not really thought about where the tiger came from or where it was killed.

In Lhasa, we found an alarming increase in the number of shops that were openly selling tiger and leopard skin chubas, compared to the 2004 survey. Out of 46 shops selling skins in the main Barkhor circuit, 10 stocked a total of 24 tiger skin chubas, and 20 had 54 leopard skin chubas. The other shops sold otter skins and chubas, and fox skins and hats. Prices for a tiger skin chuba varied from Rmb 28,000 to 120,000 (approx. US$3,500–US$15,000 or Rs 1,50,500–Rs 6,45,000), while the price for a leopard skin chuba varied from Rmb 12,000 to 40,000 (approx. US$1,500–US$5,000, or Rs 64,500 to Rs 2,15,000).

We were also shown three fresh tiger skins priced at from Rmb 50,000 to 100,000 (approx. US$6,250 to US$12,500 or Rs 2,69,000 to Rs 5,38,000) and seven fresh leopard skins by dealers in Lhasa, all of which were said to be from India. It appears that the shop keepers buy their skins from middlemen and 'wholesalers'.

In Linxia, we saw a staggering number of leopard, snow leopard, otter, fox, wolf, and domestic cat skins being openly sold in Bai Ta Je street. In the 70 shops we surveyed, we found over 30 snow leopard skins (from both China and India) and over 100 fresh leopard skins—with many more skins rolled up in the backs of the shops ready for supplementary cleaning and tanning.

We were told by the sellers and wearers that the Tibetan chuba is exempt from the law, even if it is adorned with an entire tiger skin. In Linxia, traders told us that in the Hui Autonomous Prefecture of Gansu Province, there is a 'special policy' that allows them openly to sell skins. Many people also claimed that skins on chubas are 'traditional', although when questioned further they admitted that neither their fathers nor grandfathers had worn skin chubas.

The information collected by the EIA/WPSI team, including smuggling methods that we were told about from dealers, has been passed on to the Chinese authorities. The survey confirms without doubt that there is large-scale poaching of tigers and leopards in India whose skins are smuggled to Tibet. This grave issue must be immediately addressed by all concerned governments and conservationists if the tiger and the leopard are to have any future in the wild.

Annexure 3

A. Letter from the Prime Minister of India and
   Reply by Valmik Thapar

24th August 2005

Dr Manmohan Singh
Prime Minister of India
7 Race Course Road
New Delhi

Dear Prime Minister,

Thank you for your letter of the 11th August and I am happy
that you value my comments in my dissent note of the TIGER
TASK FORCE REPORT. I hope this reflects itself in the
proposed policies concerning tiger conservation.

• More important than all that I write to you in a state of distress.
  By later February 2005 after it was confirmed that the tigers
  of Sariska were poached to extinction, the Ministry of
  Environment and Forests (MoEF) maintained and still does,

सत्यमेव जयते

प्रधान मंत्री

Prime Minister

New Delhi
August 11, 2005

Dear Shri Thapar,

Thank you for your letter of August 5, 2005 regarding your notes to the Tiger Task Force Report. I appreciate your valuable comments and contributions in the matter.

With regards,

Yours sincerely,

(Manmohan Singh)

Shri Valmik Thapar
19, Kautilya Marg
Chanakyapuri
New Delhi – 110 021

that this was an isolated example. This unfortunate fact even gets reflected in the Tiger Task Force report. I have always held that Sariska is symptomatic of the crisis that afflicts the tiger all over India. By denying the crisis, tigers are poached at a faster rate since deterrents to discourage poaching are not in place.

• Sadly because of little field action the last six months have seen a rapid acceleration of the illegal and therefore poaching—tigers and leopards have been slaughtered and their skins and body parts have ended up in Lhasa and China. This is still going on at an accelerated pace. Markets in Lhasa and China are flooded with tiger and leopard skins and many of them are being tailored for ceremonial festivals—Imagine people dancing clothed in the skins of Indian Tigers.

• My job, Prime Minister, is to alert you before it is too late. I believe that *Sariska*-like situations exist in
  1. Buxa Tiger Reserve—West Bengal
  2. Namdapha Tiger Reserve—Arunachal Pradesh
  3. Dampha Tiger Reserve—Mizoram
  4. Indrawati Tiger Reserve—Chhattisgarh
  5. Panna Tiger Reserve—Madhya Pradesh

I further believe that in some the tiger has vanished completely and in others a few strays may exist (all non-viable numbers). In order to verify this you need to order immediate field surveys by teams from Wildlife Institute of India (WII) to determine the presence or absence of tigers in the above five locations and the immediate use by these teams of camera traps to verify the reality. The entire process should be coordinated and supervised by India's senior most wildlife field biologist Dr A.J.T. Johnsingh before he retires in October from the WII (please do not entertain any excuses about bad weather or post-monsoon season. There is no time to lose). If this is not done the five Project Tiger Reserves will become the biggest national and international embarrassment that we have ever faced since the launch of Project Tiger.

- I had made three suggestions to you more than six months ago.

    (1) To give the CBI a mandate to undertake investigations into the poaching and illegal trade in tigers right across India.

    (2) To convene a meeting of Chief Ministers on this issue in order to illustrate the gravity of the matter and ask them to take urgent steps.

    (3) To make the system answerable and accountable to the loss of tigers.

    I believe today that these above points are more important than ever. None of these interventions can wait till 2006.

- Prime Minister, I have been interacting with you since 2004 regarding tigers even though many of my remedial measures have been dismissed by the MoEF and other individuals that advise decision-making. As far as I am concerned I am shocked that after a lifetime's service to tiger conservation (30 years) the government of the day refuses to heed my warnings. I have stood firm in my resolve regarding the gravity of the situation. I am not prone to melodrama or exaggeration. At this moment we desperately need the best of guns and guards to keep wild tigers alive. By endless denials of the problem and inaction of the last decade the tiger has been placed in its coffin. It appears to be in a terminal crisis. I believe nothing short of a miracle can take it out of this situation. That 'miracle' is now in your hands to create.

Please let me know if I can assist you in any way.

With best wishes,

Valmik Thapar

B. Letter from the Chief Minister of Rajasthan to the Prime Minister

CHIEF MINISTER OF RAJASTHAN

Jaipur
Dated: 19.09.2005

As we are all aware, the wilderness areas of the country are being subjected to unprecedented pressures and the threats to wildlife and wildlife habitats are assuming dangerous proportions.

The Government of Rajasthan had constituted a high level fact finding committee to look into the malaise facing Protected Areas, with specific reference to Sariska Tiger Reserve, Ranthambhore National Park, and Keoladeo Ghana National Park in Rajasthan. This committee, headed by Shri V.P. Singh, Hon'ble Member of Parliament had Shri Bharat Singh, Hon'ble MLA, Digod, Rajasthan, Shri Valmik Thapar, Member, Rajasthan State Wildlife Advisory Board, Dr V.B. Mathur, Faculty of Wildlife Sciences, Wildlife Institute of India and Ms Belinda Wright, Executive Director, Wildlife Protection Society of India, as its members.

In August 2005, Ms Belinda Wright visited certain parts of China, including Tibet. She, in the course of her visit, came across shocking evidence of open trade in a number of wildlife articles, including Tiger and Leopard skins. In the course of her interaction with locals, she discovered that skins were mostly of Indian origin and smuggled across our northern borders. I am enclosing a copy of her note, which is one of the annexures of the report of the high level committee, who submitted their report on 6th September 2005.

In October 2003, the Chinese authorities reportedly had seized 31 Tiger skins, 581 Leopard skins and 778 Otter skins of Indian origin in the Tibet Autonomous Region. In August this year, Ms Wright came across innumerable instances where Tiger and Leopard skins have been used in traditional attire, available for sale openly. Not only so, entire Tiger skins are also being sold.

The sheer numbers of wildlife products in the markets of Tibet are testimony to the fact that they could not be from any one state or Protected Area of India. Evidently, rampant poaching has been taking place for some time, all over the country. Thus, to single out any one State for this nationwide problem would be unfair. The revelation as brought out by the high level committee in its report, also raises questions as to the functioning of central enforcement authorities like the Regional Offices of Wildlife Preservation, Customs, Indo-Tibetan Border Police, Border Security Force etc. It is obvious that such large scale illicit trade cannot take place unless a section of the central enforcement authorities being totally indifferent or colluding with poachers and unscrupulous traders. Only an in-depth investigation can bring the actual facts before the country.

It is clear that if illicit trade of these proportions is not checked immediately, the future of wildlife in the country is doomed. It is imperative that state and central enforcement authorities work together in curbing these illegal activities. At the same time, it is important to sensitize the international community to the threat being posed to our environment due to such illegal trade.

I would like to request you Sir, to take all necessary steps so that both central and state authorities work together effectively and at the same time, take all such necessary diplomatic steps as are warranted and at the same time, sensitize the international community, especially China on this vital issue.

With regards,

Yours sincerely,

(Vasundhara Raje)

Dr Manmohan Singh
Prime Minister of India
New Delhi.

C. Letter from Valmik Thapar to the Prime Minister

23ʳᵈ September, 2005

Dr Manmohan Singh
Prime Minister of India
7 Race Course Road
New Delhi

Dear Prime Minister,

You would have seen from the spreads in the newspaper today the answer to the question as to 'Where has the Indian Tiger gone'. (Enclosed for reference.) It is quite clear to conservationists and tiger experts in India and across the world that from 2003–2005 HUNDREDS OF DEAD INDIAN TIGERS have gone to TIBET and to make traditional costumes for dancers. The footage and visuals are available and a presentation can be made to you if required. While this disaster struck the tiger in the last two years the Ministry of Environment and Forests (MoEF) continued in its mode of denial, unable to accept the gravity of the crisis. Instead of acting to protect the field they sheltered in pointing fingers at individuals and NGOs and suggested that the extinction of the tiger in Sariska was an isolated example. Just this fact or 'defensive response' has concealed the truth.

Because of this we are in a terminal crisis and now only a miracle can save the Indian Tiger.

May I immediately suggest the following:

1. Immediately commence operations of the 5 YEAR pending Wildlife Crime Bureau.
2. Provide CBI a total mandate to investigate the horrors of wildlife crime and what is going on around our borders.

3. Immediately deploy in order to assist the forest staff trained and armed forces on the outside periphery of our 20 best tiger areas (easily identified).
4. Instruct all our border forces especially along Nepal–Bhutan to seal and patrol all smuggling points with a new zeal. A special operation must be worked out.
5. Call for immediate talks with both China and Nepal at the highest level to prevent this disastrous illegal trade.

Prime Minister, what I have stated is the need of the day. Please do not take it lightly. It cannot be delayed any more. The crisis is so far gone that only immediate action can stem the rot. The Tibetan Tiger Trail has proven that the tiger and people can not co-exist except or unless co-existence means draping a tiger skin on your shoulder. Nothing else is important but to fully gear up our field protection machinery—it is essential that guns and guards take position.

With best wishes,

Valmik Thapar

D. Sonia Gandhi's Letter to the Environmental Investigation Agency

The most rapid response to the exposé of the horrors of tiger and leopard skins in Tibet came from Sonia Gandhi as Chairperson of the National Advisory Council on September 16th, 2005.

In a letter to the Environmental Investigation Agency she stated:

I have received your letter of 5th September, 2005 and seen the shocking and painful photographs you have enclosed. I fully share your concern about the trade in animal skins. With a view to controlling poaching of wildlife and trade in animal skins, the Government of India had recently set up a Task Force. Based on the recommendations of this Task Force, the Government is planning to institute a number of steps including the setting up of a Wildlife Crime Control Bureau. The Government is also working with the Chinese authorities to set up a system to share intelligence regarding the cross-border trade in animal skins. We all need to work together on this issue of prime importance. I am assured that the present Government will do all that is possible to control this menace.

E. Letter from Joint Secretary to Prime Minister, to Valmik Thapar

27th September 2005

Dear Shri Thapar,

1. I am desired to inform you that the Prime Minister would like to discuss some select provisions relating to the Scheduled Tribes (Recognition of Forest Rights) Bill, 2004 on Friday, 30th September 2005 at 11.00 am at South Block with a group of experts.

2. Given your immense experience in this area, we shall be grateful if you could kindly make it convenient to attend the meeting.

With regards,

Yours

(R. Gopalakrishnan)

Shri Valmik Thapar
Ranthambhore Foundation
19, Kautilya Marg
Chanakya Puri
New Delhi.

* * *

On the 27th of September 2005 I received a telephone call from Prime Minister's Office and this was followed by the letter given above.

Our system works in funny ways. This Tribal Bill has been drafted and re-drafted since February 2005. It has even been on a website and it has nearly got to Parliament. Now at the fag end the Prime Minister decides to have a brainstorming with experts. This is what should have been happened one year ago.

For two hours the Prime Minister heard the views of eight experts on tribal rights, human rights and wildlife rights. He then had to go to another meeting. It was seven in the evening, he turned to us all and said: '*Keep talking through the night. I will ask my office to serve you dinner and I will join you at 10 p.m. but I want a consensus.*' As soon as he left, the Ministry of Environment and Forests and Ministry of Tribal Affairs started arguing with each other regarding the draft of the Bill. I suggested to the Minister-in-Charge of the Prime Minister's Office that it would be more constructive to continue the discussion after both the Ministries are reconciled to one approved draft. This suggestion was accepted and they were given one month to agree to one draft. All of us would meet again in early November; but can you imagine how the country works. A Bill which is nearly ready for Parliament is being reviewed and rediscussed yet again. The Prime Minister is very keen that the Bill must be fair to both forest dwellers and the rich wildlife of India. An impossible mission! But we will try yet again in November when I think all the Protected Areas will be deleted from the purview of this Bill. That will be the compromise.

In the last few years I have been communicating with Smt. Sonia Gandhi regularly in order to keep her updated with the prevailing state of affairs. Her recent letter is enclosed with my response. We are now into October 2005 and the tragedy is that little has happened in the field.

The Prime Minister's Office has fixed the 28th October 2005 for a full day of discussions on the Tribal Bill (letter details enclosed). My fingers are crossed in the hope that we can save our National Parks and sanctuaries from the impacts of tribal rights. We should all pray for a miracle—at least there is a thinking on 'inviolate spaces for wildlife'.

F. Letter from Sonia Gandhi to Valmik Thapar, and reply by Valmik Thapar

No.1316/CP/NAC/05

SONIA GANDHI
CHAIRPERSON
NATIONAL ADVISORY COUNCIL

सत्यमेव जयते

2, MOTI LAL NEHRU PLACE
NEW DELHI - 110 011
PHONES : 011-2301 8669
011-2301 8654
FAX : 011-2301 8646

October 10, 2005

Dear Valmik,

I have received your letter dated 30th September, 2005 alongwith the enclosures. The situation in Sariska and other reports regarding depletion and poaching in wild-life sanctuaries is a matter of extreme concern. I am told that this and other issues were discussed in the meeting held recently by the Prime Minister on the Tribal Rights Bill. I hope that the genuine concerns of all stakeholders will be fully taken on board in arriving at a final decision in the matter.

I have read the note which you have given to the Prime Minister on the Tribal Rights Bill.

With good wishes,

Yours sincerely,

Shri Valmik Thapar,
19, Kautilya Marg,
Chanakyapuri,
New Delhi – 110 021.

18th October 2005

Smt. Sonia Gandhi
President, Congress Party
10, Janpath
New Delhi

Dear Mrs Gandhi,

Thank you for your letter dated October 10th.

(1) There are a lot of issues being discussed but little field action results—The Ministry of Environment and Forests continues to deny the extent of the problem—tigers therefore DIE—probably 1,000 in the last 3 years.

(2) I am afraid that many of the 'leftists' and tribal activists will thwart the Prime Minister's efforts and good intentions to find a just solution to both the rights of wildlife and the tribals. I am enclosing a *sociological* note that I have written on the Tribal Bill which should be of interest to the National Advisory Council (NAC).

I believe strongly that on both the issue of wildlife and forest protection, and the Tribal Bill, there is a total lack of in depth understanding and this has created great confusion. Decision-making is at its lowest ebb—be it at the centre or in the states. The natural treasures of this country are therefore suffering enormously. There must be a way where the NAC interests with the Chief Ministers of the States or the Prime Minister calls a meeting of the Chief Ministers so that collectively we can put our house in order. Without this exercise things will deteriorate to a point of no return.

I believe your intervention is essential in this rather 'hopeless situation'. The last tigers of India are struggling to survive and they require all our help.

Best wishes,

Valmik Thapar

G. Letter from Joint Secretary to Prime Minister, to Valmik Thapar

17 October 2005

Dear Valmik

1. As you are aware, the Ministry of Tribal Affairs had been mandated to formulate a 'Scheduled Tribes (Recognition of Forest Rights) Bill'.

2. The Ministry had accordingly prepared a draft 'The Scheduled Tribes (Recognition of Forest Rights) Bill, 2005' in consultation with Ministries which after due vetting by the Ministry of Law & Justice was also posted on the website of Ministry of Tribal Affairs (*www.tribal.nic.in*) to enable public debate.

3. Some important suggestions have come up in the Bill especially on negotiating the complex issue of ensuring protection to wildlife and sanctuaries and the need to get this in harmony with peoples' rights to land, even if no specific commonly agreed technical grounds, they are to be resettled. A practical option that is respectful of both rights of the people to the land in their possession as well as the need to create inviolate spaces for wildlife needs to be evolved and incorporated into the Act. A preliminary consultation was held on this and it was felt that a larger body of experts could discuss and reconcile this.

With regards,

Your sincerely,

(R. Gopalakrishnan)

Annexure 4

The Tribal Bill: Going Beyond Tigers...

The present draft of the Tribal Bill will not only destroy forests but also wipe out tigers in all scheduled tribal areas of India. But today I am not getting into this issue—I am going to look more closely at forest tribes and their fate in relation to this Bill.

The demarcation between forest tribes and caste society has been a feature of Indian civilization since times immemorial. Forest tribes were regarded as different both physically and in their life pattern—and generally beyond the pale of civilization. When labour was required from them, they were converted into low castes. Forest-dwellers were hunter-gatherers and shifting cultivators in the main. Contact with peasant society led to some of them turning into cultivators.

The conversion of forest tribes to castes was most frequently twofold. One was when a forested area was conquered by an adjoining kingdom. The forest would be cut and the land cleared for cultivation; this increased the revenue for the kingdom. The land would be cultivated by peasants brought in and settled by the state. Sometimes the forest-dwellers would be converted into peasant castes, and thus became landless labour.

Such changes destroyed the essential characteristics of a tribal society, as doubtless they were intended to. The major demarcation between tribal and caste society is that the unit of tribal society is the clan and not the patriarchal family, and even more important than the essential nature of the clan is that it is egalitarian. Unlike caste society, inequality is not a requirement. There are no hierarchies based on pollution, occupation, religious sects and the such. One is born into a clan and this becomes a life-long identity.

The greatest tragedy is that we are supposed to have a left of centre government supported by the Communists and left parties, who are regarded as some of our best 'thinking minds', but sadly the application of these minds to issues like the tribal bill is abysmal. Communist philosophy believes in social equality—in egalitarianism. This Bill, that they support, will destroy the very concepts on which their ideology is based.

The most significant contribution of tribal culture to Indian civilization is the deeply embedded conviction that social equality is the bedrock of society. This is an aspect that is seldom mentioned because it frontally contradicts the factor from which caste society draws its strength, namely social hierarchy. *Jatis* are arranged hierarchically and the hierarchy affects all social actions, but not forest tribes, which do not find a place in this hierarchy.

The proposed Bill will ensure that the commitment to social equality that was essential to the tribal way of life will be terminated. Giving land to a nuclear family of tribal origin, isolated from clan links, is not a return to tribal rights and values nor does it assuage injustices suffered by forest tribes. A nuclear family owning land today together with the current overtones of patriarchy is as alien to a forest tribe as is caste society. It merely encourages the rapid creation of more and more lower castes to be further exploited by those to whom exploitation is a way of life.

The Bill will become yet another mechanism for de-tribalizing the tribe and converting the erstwhile forest dwellers to the status of low castes. This old feudal approach is being again resurrected through the Bill. And its supporters think it is about rectifying the injustices of the past and protecting human rights—shocking is all I can say. Do the proponents of this Bill even know that for 60 per cent of India average landholding is less than 1 hectare for a nuclear family? Just think of the conflicts that will take place when $2^1/_2$ hectares are given!

The question that is being intensely raised is the need to undo the injustice that tribal society has been subjected to in the past. The manner selected for this is to settle tribal nuclear families in forests. They will get nothing and this Bill will become the engine for the land and timber mafias to plunder our natural resources.

This is not to suggest that we treat tribal culture as frozen and make tribal society into a museum but in our endorsement of democracy and social equality we should incorporate these elements wherever they are available in our cultural heritage and be proud of them and not attempt to stamp them out. There are many ways in which the injustices to tribal people can and need to be set right. Giving land is not the best way to do justice to the problems that confront the tribals. So much social legislation these days begins with the refrain that we are undoing the injustices of history. These cannot be undone as they have happened. It is a thing of the past. In fact the present effort will make matters worse since the repercussion of a new and dangerous legislation will be felt by the entire nation.

Why are reservations not extended to all Dalits since they all suffer from being discriminated against? Why is land being given only to families of forest tribes, why not to all poor families irrespective of caste and tribe who have been forced off their land, and so on? Do we have to ghettoize communities in an effort to improve their conditions, with the fearful prospect that the ghettoes will remain?

So what will this Bill do?

(1) This Bill will destroy the egalitarian nature of tribal communities both in terms of how they share land and the resources from land.

(2) The near feudal impact of this Bill would create more landless labour, lower castes and unparalleled class and caste wars much worse than what happened with the Mandal Commission.

(3) In the resulting chaos the land and timber mafias will wipe out forests in scheduled tribal areas. The future of the tribal populations may be dire.

Those powering the Bill must reflect on the damage that can be wrought by the Bill to both forest and tribals is enormous. For a society where one-third lives in wretched poverty, giving land here and there to some, or making concessions towards reservations in education and employment to some, remains a temporary, ad-hoc and uncertain solution. It makes no sense. We require to move away from temporary mollifications like the Tribal Bill to more permanent solutions in ensuring at least the basic human requirements for all our communities.

Manmohan Singh is doing the right thing—he is into a brainstorming session with a view to do justice to both tribals and the forests of India. Surely we must have the patience to examine a new draft bill finalized by Ministry of Environment and Forests (MoEF) without trying to negate it even before it is seen? Surely this must make common sense to all the parties and surely it is in the national interest. There should also be exhaustive discussions about its provisions to ensure that the proposed law is brought within the bounds of constitutionality.

Let's be patient. Let the Prime Minister do his job in his usual well-intentioned way without interference from political parties or activist quarters. Let us all wait for the outcome.

In the meeting on the 28th of October at the Prime Minister's office, the Secretary in the Ministry of Environment and Forests launched a scathing attack on the Bill calling it an 'invitation to chaos' and ended his presentation by stating that the Bill, if passed in its present form, would 'haunt future generations'. At least 9 participants out of 16 had reservations regarding the draft of the Bill, especially about the fact that it differentiated between tribals and other forest dwellers, which could lead to a serious conflict between the different groups. The end result of the meeting was to take on board the valid suggestions of the participants and the MoEF, and to produce a revised draft which would address the concerns raised. Once again, my fingers are crossed in the hope that the dangers of this Bill for the forests of India are removed once and for all.

Just before this book went to press, I heard the horrifying story of how the Rajasthan police had busted a gang of poachers, and their interrogations revealed that in the last few years, they had struck deep into the heart of Ranthambhore National Park, killing at least a minimum of ten tigers, two leopards, bears, and many other animals. This gang was also operative in parts of Madhya Pradesh, in places like Shivpuri and Panna. The great tragedy is that what we suspected all along has come true. But only now will the government stop its endless denials. Does it really matter if we have a Crime Bureau or a Prime Minister in the chair dealing with Project Tiger? I fear it is too late.

Valmik Thapar

Bibliography

SELECTED REFERENCES OF BOOKS BETWEEN 1827–1965

Allan, Hugh. *The Lonely Tiger*. London: Faber and Faber, 1960.

Archer, Milfred. *Tippoo's Tiger*. London: Victoria and Albert Museum, 1959.

Baikov, N.A. *The Manchurian Tiger: Big Game Hunting in Manchuria*. London: Hutchinson and Co., 1925/1936.

Baker S. *Wild beasts and Their Ways*. London: Macmillan and Co., 1891.

Baldwin J.H. *The Large and Small Game of Bengal and the North-Western Provinces of India*. Kegan Paul, Trench, and Co.,1883.

Barras, J. *New Shikari at Out Indian Stations*. London, 1885.*

———. *Indian and Tiger Hunting*. London, 1885.*

Baze, William, Beatson, A. *Tiger, Tiger*. London: Elek Books, 1957.

Bennet, E.T. *The Tower Menagerie*. London: Robert Jennings, 1829.

Berg B.M. *Tiger und Mensch*. Berlin: Halltorp, 1934.

Best J.W. *Forest Life in India*. London: John Murray, 1935.

———. *Tiger Days*. London: John Murray, 1931.

Braddon E. *Thirty years of Shikar*. London: William Blackwood and Sons, 1895.

Bradley M.H. *Trailing the Tiger*. D. Appleton and Co.,1929.*

Brooke, V. *Big Game in India*. 1894.*

Brown, J.M. *Shikar Sketches: With notes on Indian Field Sports*. 1887.*

Bruke, W.S. *The Indian Field Shikar Book*. London, 1920.*

Burton, E.F. *Reminiscences of Field Sport in India*. 1885.*

Burton, R.G. *The Book of the Tiger*. London: Hutchinson, 1933.

———. *Sport and Wildlife in the Deccan*. London: Seeley Service and Co. Ltd., 1928.

———. *The Tiger Hunters*. London: Hutchinson and Co., 1936.

Caldwell, H.R. *Blue tiger*. London: Duckworth, 1925.

Campbel, W. *The Old Forest Ranger*. London: How and Parsons, 1842.

Champion, F.W. *In Sunlight and Shadow*. London: Chatto and Windus, 1925.

_____. *With a Camera in Tiger Land*. London: Chatto and Windus, 1927/1933.

Corbett, J. *Man Eaters of Kumaon*. Oxford: Oxford University Press, 1944.

Cumingham A.H. *Indian Shikar Notes*. 1920.*

Davies, D. *Tiger Slayer by Order*. London: Chapman and Hall, Ltd., 1916.

Digby, D. *Tigers*. London: Gold and Witchdoctors, 1928.

Eardley-Wilmot, S. *The life of a Tiger*. London: Ames, 1911.

_____. *Forest Life and Sport in India*. London: Edward Arnold, 1910.

EHA. *Naturalist on the Prowl*. Calcutta: Thacker Spink and Co., 1897.

Ellison, Bernard. *The Prince of Wales in India*. London: Heinemann, 1925.

Evans, G.P. *Big-Game Shooting in Upper Burma*. London: Longmans, Green and Co., 1912.

Fayer J. *Thirteen years among the wild beasts of India*. London, 1882.*

_____. *The Royal Tiger of Bengal: His life and Death*. London: J.A Churchill, 1875.

Felix, *Recollections of a Bison and Tiger Hunter*. London, 1906.*

Fife-Cookson, Col. J.C. *Tiger Shooting in the Doon and Ulwar*. London: Chapman and Hall, Ltd., 1887.

Fletcher, F.W.F. *Sport on the Nilgiris and in Wynaad*. London: Macmillan and Co. Ltd., 1911.

Forbes, James. *Oriental Memoirs*, 3 Vols. London: R. Bentley, 1834–5.

Forsyth, J. *The Highlands of Central India*. London: Chapman and Hall, 1919.

Gay, J.D. *The Prince of Wales in India*. Toronto: Belford Brothers Publ., 1877.

Gee, E.P. *The Wildlife of India*. London: Collins, 1964.

Glasfurd, A.I.R. *Musings of an Old Shikari*. London: John Lane the Bodley Head Ltd., 1928.

Gordon-Cumming, R. *Wild Men and Wild Beasts.* London, 1872.*

Gouldsbury, C.E. *Tiger Land.* London, 1913.*

_____. *Tiger Slayer by Order.* New York: G.Bell and Sons, 1915.

Hamilton, D. R.H. Porter. *Records of Sport in Southern India.* London, 1892.*

Hanley, P.D. *Tiger Trails in Assam.* London: Robert Hale Ltd., 1960.

Hewett, J.P. *Jungle Trails in Northern India.* London: Methuen and Co. Ltd., 1938.

Hicks, F.C. *Forty Years among the Wild Animals of India, from Mysore to the Himalayas.* Allahabad: Pioneer Press, 1910.

Hingston, R.W.G. *The Tiger Kills.* London: Ames.*

Jadho, K.R.B.S. *A Guide to Tiger Shooting.* London.*

Jepson, Stanley (ed.). *Big Game Encounters.* London: Stanley Jepson, 1936.

Johnson, D. *Sketches of Indian Field Sports.* London: Robert Jennings, 1827.

Locke, A. *The Tigers of Trengganu.* London: Museum Press Ltd., 1954.

Mockler-Ferryman, A.F. *The Life Story of a Tiger.* London, 1910.*

Mundy, Captain A. *Pen and pencil Sketches being the Journal of a tour of India.* London: John Murray, 1933.

Musselwhite, A. *Behind the Lens in Tiger Land.* London, 1933.*

Panwar, H.S. *Kanha National Park.* London: Cassell and Co. Ltd., 1964.

Perry, Richard. *The World of the Tiger.* London: Cassell, 1964.

Pocock R.I. *A Lion Tiger Hybrid. The Felid,* February, 1929.*

Reid, M. *The Tiger Hunter.* New York: G.W. Dillingham Co., 1897.

Rice, W. *Tiger-Shooting in India.* London: Smith, Elder and Co., 1857.

_____. *Indian Game (from Quail to Tiger).* London: W.H. Allen and Co., 1884.

Rousselet, L. *The King of the Tigers.* London: S. Low, Marston, Searle, & Rivington Ltd., 1888.

Sanderson, G.P. *Thirteen Years among the Wild Beasts of India.**

Shakespear, H. Major. *Field Sport of India: 1800–1947.* London: Smith Elder and Co., 1862.

Singh, K. *One man and a thousand tigers.* New York: Dodd, Mead. 9,206, pp. 1959.

Singh, K. *The Tiger of Rajasthan*. London: Robert Hale Ltd., 1959.

Smythies, E.A. *Big Game Shooting in Nepal*. Calcutta: Thacker, Spink and Co., 1942.

Smythies, O. *Tiger Lady*. London, 1953.*

Stacton, David. *A Ride on a Tiger*. London: Museum Press Ltd., 1954.

Stebbing, E.P. *Jungle By-ways in India*. London: John Lane and Bodley Head, 1911.

_____. *The Diary of a Sportsman Naturalist*. London: John Lane, 1920.

Stewart, A.E. *Tiger and other Game*. London: Longmans Green and Co., 1878.

Sutton, R.L. *Tiger Trails in Southern Asia*. St. Louis: C.V. Mosby Co., 1926.

Taylor, M.L. *The Tiger's Claw*. London, 1956.

Todd, W.H. *Tiger! Tiger!* London: Heath Cranton Ltd., 1927.

Trench, Philip. *Tiger Hunting: A Day's Sport in the East*. London: Hodgson and Graves, 1836.

Wardrop, A.E. Major. *Days and Nights of Indian Big Game*. London: Macmillan and Co. Ltd., 1923.

SELECTED REFERENCES OF BOOKS PUBLISHED AFTER 1965 WHEN CONSERVATION STRATEGIES FOR THE TIGER FIRST START

Alvi, M.A. and Rahman, A. *Jahangir—The Naturalist*. Delhi: Indian National Science Academy, 1968.

Amore, C. *Ways to Track a Tiger*. USA: Wildlife Worlds, 2003.

Barnes, Simon. *Tiger*. London: Boxtree, 1994.

Bedi, Rajesh and Ramesh Bedi. *Indian Wildlife*. New Delhi: Brijbasi, 1984.

Bergmann Sucksdorff, A. *Tiger in Sight*. London: A. Deutsch, 1970.

Boomgaard, P. *Frontiers of Fear*. London: Yale University Press, 2001.

Boyes, Jonathan. *Tiger Men and Tofu Dolls: Tribal Spirits in Northern Thailand*. Thailand: Silkworm Books, 1997.

Breeden, Stanley and Belinda Wright. *Through the Tiger's Eyes*: *Chronicle of India's Vanishing Wildlife*. USA: Ten Speed Press, 1997.

Brunskill C. *Tiger Forest—A Visual Study of Ranthambhore National Park*. London: Troubador, 2003.

Chakrabarti, Kalyan. *Man-eating Tigers*. Calcutta: Darbari Prokshan, 1992.

Choudhury, S.R. Khairi. *The Beloved Tigress*. Dehradun: Natraj, 1999.

Choudhary L.K., and S.A. Khan. *Bandhavgarh Fort of the Tiger*. Sandhya Prakash Bhavan, 2003.*

Chundawat, R.S. and Neel Gogate. *Saving Wild Tigers in a Sub-Optimal Dry Forest Habitat*. Unpublished. 2001.

Courtney, N. *The Tiger—Symbol of Freedom*. London: Quartet Books, 1980.

Cubitt, Gerald and Guy Mountford. *Wild India*. London: Collins, 1985.

Daniel, J.C. *The Tiger in India: A Natural History*. India: Natraj, 2003.

Davis, Duff-Hart. *Honorary Tiger*. Delhi: Lotus, Roli, 2005.

Denzau, Getrude and Helmut. *Königstiger*. Steinfurt: Teclenborg Verlag, 1996.

Elliot, J.G. *Field Sport of India: 1800–1947*. London: Gentry Books Ltd., 1973.

Ellis, Richard. *Tiger Bone, Rhino Horn*. USA: Island Press, 2005.

Fend, Werner. *Die Tiger von Abutshmar*. Vienna: Verlag Fritz Molden, 1972.

Forest, Denys. *The Tiger of Mysore: Life and Death of Tipu Sultan*. London: Chatto and Windus, 1970.

Ghorpade, M.Y. *Sunlight and Shadows*. London: Gollanck, 1983.

Green, I. *Wild Tigers of Bandhavgarh—Encounters in a Fragile Forest*. Tiger Books. 2002.*

Gurang, K.K. *Heart of the Jungle—The Wildlife of Chitwan, Nepal*. London: Andre Deutsch, 1983.

Harris, H.A. *Sports in Ancient Greece and Rome*. London: Thames and Hudson, 1972.

Hodges-Hill, Edward. *Man Eater—Tales of Lion and Tiger Encounters*. London: Cockbird Press, 1992.

Horton, Barbara Curtis. *Tiger Bridge*. USA: John Daniel, 1993. USA

Hornaday, W.T. *Two Years in the Jungle*. London: Kegan Paul Trench and Co., 1985.

Hornocker, M. *Track of the Tiger*. Sierra Club Books, 1997.*

Israel, S. and Toby Sinclair. *Indian Wildlife*. Singapore: Apa Publications, 1987.

Ives, Richard. *Of Tigers and Men*. New York: Doubleday, 1995.

Jackson, Peter. *Endangered Species—Tiger*. London: Apple Press, 1990.

Jahn and Verlag E, Dieter Zingel. *Tigerland on Kipling's Traces in the Heart of India*. Germany: Dieter Zingel, 1996.

Jung, S. *Tryst with Tigers*. London: Robert Hale Ltd., 1967.

Lindblad, Jan. *Tigrata—Vart storsta aventyr*. Belgium: 1982.

Lipton, Mini. *The Tiger Rugs of Tibet*. London: Hayward Gallery, 1998.

Manfredi, Paola. *In Danger*. New Delhi: Ranthambhore Foundation, 1997.

Martin Booth. *Carpet Sahib: A Life of Jim Corbett*. London: Constable and Co., 1986.

Mathiessen, Peter. *Tigers in the Snow*. London: Harvill, 2000.

McDougal, Charles. *The Face of the Tiger*. London: Revington Books, 1977.

Mcneely, A. Jeffrey and P.S. Watchtel. *The Soul of the Tiger*. New York: Doubleday, 1988.

Meacham, Cory. *How the Tiger Lost its Stripes*. New York: Harcourt Bace, 1997.

Mills, Stephen. *Tiger*. London: BBC Books, 2004.

Montgomary. S.Y. *Spell of the Tiger*.Boston: Houghton Mifflin, 1995.

Mountfort, Guy. *Saving the Tiger*. London: Michael Joseph Ltd., 1981.

———. *Back From the Brink*. London: Hutchinson, 1978.

———. *Tigers*. London, 1973. *

Naidu, M. Kamal. *Trail of the Tiger*. Dehradun: Natraj, 1998.

Niyogi, Tushar K. *Tiger Cult of the Tiger Sunderbans*. Calcutta: Anthropological Survey of India, 1996.*

Padel, Ruth. *Tigers in Red Weather*. London: Little Brown, 2005.

Peisse, Michael. *Tiger for Breakfast: The Story of Borris of Kathmandu*. India: Allied Publishers Pvt. Ltd., 1972.

Perry Richard. *The Worlds of the Tiger*. London: Cassells, 1974.

Prater. S. *The Book of Indian Animals*. Bombay: BNHS, 1988.

Rabinowitz, Alan. *Wildlife Abuse*: Chasing the Dragon's Tail. 1991.*

Rangarajan, M. *India's Wildlife History*. New Delhi: Permanent Black, 2001.

Ranjitsinh, M.K. *Beyond the Tiger, Portraits of South-Asian Wildlife*. New Delhi: Brijbasi, 1997.

Sankhala, K. *Tiger*. London: Collins, 1978.

_____. *Tiger Land*. New York: The Bobbs-Merrill Company Inc., 1975.

Schaller, G.B. *The Deer and the Tiger*. Chicago: Chicago University Press, 1967.

Seidensticker, John, Sarah Christie, and Peter Jackson (eds). *Riding the Tiger*. Cambridge: Cambridge University Press, 1999.

Shah, Anup and Manoj. *A Tiger's Tale*. Kingston-upon-Thames: Fountain Press, 1996.

Singh, Bhagat. *Wild Encounters*. India: Pelican Creations International, 1999.

Singh, Billy Arjan. '*The Lost Cause?*', *Tiger Haven*. London: Macmillan, 1973.

_____. *Tara, A Tigress*. London: Quartet Press, 1981.

_____. *Tiger! Tiger!* London: Jonathan Cape, 1984.

_____. *The Legend of the Man Eater*. New Delhi: Ravi Dayal, 1993.

_____. *Tiger Book*. Delhi: Lotus Roli, 1997.

_____. *A Tiger's Story*. Delhi: Harper Collins, 1999.

Singh, L.S. *Tara, the Cocktail Tigress: The Story of Genetic Pollution of the Indian Tigers*. Allahabad: Print World, 2000.

Sinha, V.R. *The Tiger is a Gentleman*. India: Wildlife, 1999.

Stracey, P.D. *Tigers*. London: Arthur Barker, 1968.

Sunquist, Fiona. *Tiger Moon*. Chicago: University of Chicago Press, 1998.

Sunquist, Mel. *Wild Cats of the World*. Chicago: University of Chicago Press, 2002.

Thapar, Valmik. *Saving Wild Tigers*. New Delhi: Oxford University Press, 2004.

———. *Tiger—The Ultimate Guide*. USA: Two Brothers Press, 2004.

———. *Battling for Survival*. New Delhi: Oxford University Press, 2003.

———. *The Cult of the Tiger*. New Delhi: Oxford University Press, 2002.

———. *Wild Tigers of Ranthambhore*. New Delhi: Vikas, 1983.

———. *With Tigers in the Wild*. New Delhi: Vikas Publishing, 1983.

———. *Tiger: Portrait of a Predator*. London: Collins, 1986.

———. *Tigers: The Secret Life*. London: Hamish Hamilton, 1989.

———. *The Secret Life of Tigers*. New Delhi: Oxford University Press, 1998.

———. *The Tiger's Destiny*. London: Kyle Cathie, 1992.

———. *The Land of the Tiger*. London: BBC Books, 1997.

———. *Tiger: Habitats, Life Cycle, Food Chains, and Threats*. London: Wayland Publishers, 1999.

Tilson and Seal (ed.). *Tigers of the World*. New Jersey: Noyes Publications, 1987.

Toovey. J. (ed.). *Tigers of the Raj*. Gloucester: Alan Sutton, 1987.

Turner, Alan. *The Big Cats and their fossil relatives*. New York: Columbia University Press, 1997.

Tyabji, Hashim. *Banbhavgarh National Park*. New Delhi: 1994.*

Verma, Prakash. S. *Flora and Fauna in Mughal Art*. Marg Publications, 1999.

Ward, Geoffrey C. *Tiger Wallahs*. New York: Harper Collins, 1993.

Ward, Geoffrey C. and Diane Raines Ward. *Tigers Wallahs: Saving the Greatest of the Great Cats*. New Delhi: Oxford University Press, 2000.

Zwaenepol, Jean-Pierre. *Tigers*. San Francisco: Chronicle Books, 1992.

LIST OF PAPERS IN BOOKS AND JOURNALS FROM 1892–1965

Ali, Salim. 'The Moghul Emperors of India as Naturalists and Sportsmen'. *Journal of the Bombay Natural History Society* 31 (4): 833–61.

Bannerman W.B. 'Capturing Tiger with Birdlime'. *Journal of the Bombay Natural History Society* 25: 753, 1917.

Biscoe, W.A. 'Tiger Killing a Panther'. *Journal of the Bombay Natural History Society* 9 (4): 490, 1895.

Boswell K. 'Scent Trails and Pooking in Tigers'. *Journal of the Bombay Natural History Society* 54 (2): 454–4, 1957.

———. 'Following up Wounded Tiger at Night'. *Journal of the Bombay Natural History Society* 54 (2): 454–5, 1957.

Burton, R.G. 'The Tiger's Method of Making a Kill'. *Journal of the Bombay Natural History Society* 49 (3): 538–41, 1934.

Burton, R. 'Death Cry of a Tiger'. *Journal of the Bombay Natural History Society* 48(1): 176–8, 1948.

———. 'Rabies in Tiger—Two proved instances'. *Journal of the Bombay Natural History Society* 49(3): 538–41, 1950.

———. 'A History of Shikar in India'. *Journal of the Bombay Natural History Society* 50 (4) 845–69, 1952.

Campbell, T. 'A Tiger Eating a Bear'. *Journal of the Bombay Natural History Society* 9 (1): 101, 1894.

Champion, F. 'Tiger Tracks'. *Journal of the Bombay Natural History Society* 33 (2): 284–7, 1884.

Champion, F.W. 'Preserving Wildlife in the United Provinces'. *Journal of the Bombay Natural History Society*, xxxvii.

Chaturvedi M.D. 'Future of the Tiger'. *Indian Forester.* 81 (2): 7334. Dehradun: 1955.

Christopher, S.A. 'Tiger-lore in Burma'. *Journal of the Bombay Natural History Society* 29: 276–7, 1937.

Corbett. G. 'A Tiger Attacking Elephants'. *Journal of the Bombay Natural History Society* 1 (7): 192, 1892.

Corbett, Jim. 'Wildlife in the Village'. Nainital: *Review of the Week*, 1932.

Fenton, L. 'Tigers hamstringing their prey before killing'. *Journal of the Bombay Natural History Society* (4): 756, 1905.

Fraser, S.M. 'Tiger netting in Mysore'. *Journal of the Bombay Natural History Society*, 1902.

Gilbert, R. 'Wounded tigers and how should they be killed'. *Journal of the Bombay Natural History Society* (1): 61–5, 1908.

Hearsey, L. 'Tiger Killing swamp deer or gond'. *Journal of the Bombay Natural History Society* 35 (4): 885–6, 1932.

Hubback, T.R. 'Three Months after Big Game in Pahang'. *Journal of the Bombay Natural History Society.**

Littledale, H. 'Bears being eaten by tigers'. *Journal of the Bombay Natural History Society* 4 (4): 3416, 1889.

Morris, R. 'A tigress with five cubs'. *Journal of the Bombay Natural History Society* 31 (3) 810–11. 1927.

Pocock, R.I. 'Tigers'. *Journal of the Bombay Natural History Society* 33: 505–541, 1929.

Richardson, W. 'Tiger Cubs'. *Journal of the Bombay Natural History Society* 5 (2): 191, 1890.

Toogood, C. 'Number of Cubs in a Tigress Litter'. *Journal of the Bombay Natural History Society* 349 (1): 158, 1936.

LIST OF PAPERS IN BOOKS AND JOURNALS AFTER 1965 WHEN THE PROCESS OF CONSERVATION REALLY STARTS TO IMPACT THE TIGER.

Choudhury S.R. 'Pragmatic practice in a tiger-tracer and grass-tracer'. New Delhi: Project Tiger, Government India. Department of Environment, in International Symposium on Tiger, pp. 358–65, 1979.

Desai, J.H. and A.K. Malhotra. 'The White Tiger'. New Delhi: Publications Division, Ministry of Information and Broadcasting, 1992.

Dinerstein, E., E. Wikramanayake, J. Robinson, U. Karanth, A. Rabinowitz, D. Olson, T. Mathew, P. Hedao, M. Connor, G. Hemley, and D. Bolze. 'A framework for identifying high priority areas and actions for the conservation of tigers in the wild'. Washington, DC: World Wildlife Fund & US and Wildlife Conservation Society, 1997.

Green, M.J.B. *IUCN Directory of South Asian Protected Areas.* Cambridge: IUCN, 1990.

Jackson, P. 'The Bengal Tiger—Man-eater or Large-Hearted Gentlemen?' TV Guide, 1985.

Karanth, K.U., and J.D. Nicholas. 'Estimation of tiger densities in India using photographic captures and recapture'. *Ecology* 79 (8): 2852–62,1998.

Karanth, K.U. 'Estimating tiger Panthera tigris populations from camera-trap data using capture-recapture models'. *Conservation Biology* 71: 333–38, 1995.

Karanth, K.U., and M.D. Madhusudan. 'Avoiding paper tigers and saving real tigers: Response to Saberwal'. *Conservation Biology* 11 (3): 818–20, 1997.

Karanth, K. 'Tigers in India: A critical review of field census' in *Tigers of the World—Biology, Biopolitics, Management and Conservation of an Endangered Species.* R. Tilson and U. Seal (eds), New Jersey: Noyes Publications, Park Ridge, pp. 118–132, 1987.

Kronholz, J. *'You can tell a tiger by its face stripes—but it isn't advised: Using paw-print ID system. India finds its Bengals are burning brighter now'. Wall Street Journal,* 6 August 1982.

Leyhausen, P. 'What is a Viable Tiger Population?' *Cat News* 4: 3–4, 1986.

Mills, S. 'The Tiger, The Dragon, and a Plan for the Rescue'. *BBC Wildlife* 12 (1): 50, 1994.

Rabinowitz, A. *The current status of tiger conservation —Where are we now?* Report on the year of the Tiger Conference, Dallas, Texas, USA, 1998.

Smith, J.L.D. 'The role of dispersal in structuring the Chitwan tiger population Behavior'. 124: 165–95, 1993.

Sunquist, M.E. 'Radio Tracking the Tiger' (originally titled 'Radio Tracking and its Applications to the Study and Conservation of Tigers). Paper presented at the International Symposium on Tiger Conservation, India. 1979.

_____. 'The Social Organization of Tigers (Panthera tigris) in Royal Chitwan National Park, Nepal'. *Zoology*: 336:1–98,1981.

SPECIAL

Report of The National Task Force on Tigers, Delhi: Ministry of Environment and Forests, 2005.
Report of The State Empowered Committee (Rajasthan) on Forest and Wildlife, Jaipur: Government of Rajasthan, 2005.

[NOTE: The items marked with an asterisk (*) have incomplete information]

Index